MW01127547

Ilse Koch on Trial

Ilse Koch on Trial

Making the "Bitch of Buchenwald"

Tomaz Jardim

HARVARD UNIVERSITY PRESS

CAMBRIDGE, MASSACHUSETTS

LONDON, ENGLAND

2023

Copyright © 2023 by the President and Fellows of Harvard College
All rights reserved
Printed in the United States of America

First printing

Publication of this book has been supported through the generous provisions of
the Maurice and Lula Bradley Smith Memorial Fund.

Library of Congress Cataloging-in-Publication Data
Names: Jardim, Tomaz, 1974– author.
Title: Ilse Koch on trial : making the "Bitch of Buchenwald" / Tomaz Jardim.
Description: Cambridge, Massachusetts : Harvard University Press, 2023. |
    Includes bibliographical references and index.
Identifiers: LCCN 2022025532 | ISBN 9780674249189 (cloth)
Subjects: LCSH: Koch, Ilse, 1906–1967. | Koch, Karl Otto, 1897–1945. |
    Buchenwald (Concentration camp)—Trials, litigation, etc. | War crime
    trials—Germany. | Dachau Trials, Dachau, Germany, 1945–1947. | War crime
    trials—Germany (West) | World War, 1939–1945—Atrocities. |
    War criminals—Germany—History—20th century. | Women war
    criminals—Germany—History—20th century. | Sex discrimination in
    criminal justice administration—Germany—History—20th century.
Classification: LCC D804.G3 J365 2023 | DDC 940.53/1853224—dc23/
    eng/20220714
LC record available at https://lccn.loc.gov/2022025532

Contents

Contents

Ilse Koch on Trial

Introduction

At some point during the night of September 1, 1967, Ilse Koch picked up a pencil in her cell at Aichach prison and wrote a brief note to her son Uwe: "There is no other way. Death for me is a release."[1] After nearly twenty-four years in prison, the woman infamously dubbed the "Bitch of Buchenwald" fashioned a noose from a bedsheet, fastened it to a heating pipe, and hanged herself. With this last act of defiance and despair, Koch protested her innocence as vociferously as she had done since her legal odyssey had begun more than two decades earlier. Yet while *Newsweek* described her suicide as the dismal end to "the best-hated woman in the world," Koch never relinquished the claim that she had been little more than a good mother with scant knowledge of the concentration camp on the fringes of which she had raised her children.[2] In truth, Koch's complicity was far greater than she admitted and far more complex than newspaper headlines allowed. This book sets out to explain how Ilse Koch—a woman who had no official position in the Nazi state and who was cleared of the most nefarious crimes attributed to her—became one of the best-known and most widely reviled Nazi figures in the postwar era, and a strikingly potent symbol of the barbarism of the Third Reich.

At the center of this story stand three judicial proceedings that brought Koch before an SS "Special Court" in Nazi Germany in 1944, then an American military commission court at Dachau in 1947, and finally the West German judiciary at Augsburg in 1950–1951. These trials and the rich archival record they generated are used here to reconstruct Koch's crimes and to explore how a single concentration camp perpetrator was perceived, represented, and judged in three dramatically different legal, political, and social contexts. This book asks how the application of three divergent bodies of law, by three very different courts composed of individuals with distinct political perspectives and allegiances, shaped the depiction of Koch's activities at Buchenwald. It reveals the critical role that gender played in why Koch was pursued with such vigor by postwar legal authorities, even as Nazi perpetrators responsible for crimes of far greater magnitude often escaped prosecution or received comparatively light sentences. The extensive press coverage of Koch's trials, rivaled only by reporting on the trials of Hitler's leading henchmen at Nuremberg, allows for an examination of popular perceptions of Nazi criminality in the postwar era and how judicial proceedings contributed to their formation.

In the wake of the liberation of the concentration camps, the world was made aware of the full extent of the horrors committed by the Nazis and their many sites of genocidal violence that dotted the map of Europe. But among the newspaper revelations of death marches, mass killings, and gas chambers, few accounts stoked the imagination and indignation of the global public more than reports that Buchenwald commandant Karl Koch's wife, Ilse, had ordered the murder of tattooed inmates in order to collect their skins for the production of lampshades. To a world struggling to grasp what had occurred in the concentration camps, these widely circulated but unsubstantiated stories epitomized Nazi savagery and made Ilse Koch a household name. Yet even as her rumored activities deeply permeated postwar consciousness, the popular fascination with Koch tended to hinder rather than promote popular comprehension of Nazi crimes and to obscure her role in their commission. Following a war with no shortage of villains, what was it about Ilse Koch and her alleged crimes that made her so potent an emblem of the evil of the Third Reich? To what extent did legal proceedings serve to advance this popular representation?

Understanding Koch's prominent place in the postwar imagination and the fervor with which her case was pursued requires interrogating how gender norms and expectations shaped perceptions of Koch's exercise of violence and her moral and criminal culpability. By and large, German women at the end of the war were viewed as passive actors or blameless victims untainted by the masculine political realm of the Nazi state and lacking the disposition necessary to commit violent crimes in its name. The fact that Allied authorities seldom prosecuted female perpetrators both reflected and reinforced this view.[3] Indeed, among the thousands of accused war criminals brought to trial in Allied courts, the number of female defendants was exceedingly small.[4] Yet German women had participated in the Third Reich's most infamous crimes: thousands of women had served as guards in concentration camps like Ravensbrück, Bergen-Belsen, and Auschwitz, and had taken part in the abuse and murder of inmates there; female nurses made up nearly a quarter of the staff of the Nazi "euthanasia" campaign that carried out the mass murder of the mentally and physically disabled; and half a million young women headed to the occupied territories in the East, both as SS wives and civilian employees, where a significant number contributed to the dispossession, brutalization, and murder of local populations.[5] As recent studies have emphasized, the women of the Third Reich were every bit as capable as their male counterparts of committing horrifying and often ideologically motivated acts of violence and murder.[6] Nonetheless, the lack of agency implied in prevailing notions of femininity encouraged many to perceive these women as innocent and to downplay or overlook their criminal responsibility.

What then accounts for Ilse Koch's zealous prosecution? As depicted by American and German jurists alike, the egregious crimes attributed to Koch were products of a deviant femininity, replete with perverse sexual impulses and a barbarism that placed her outside the community of "ordinary" women. According to Dachau trial chief prosecutor William Denson, Koch was "a creature from some other tortured world" who had overstepped the bounds of womanhood. She was, he insisted, nothing less than a "sadistic pervert of monumental proportions unmatched in history."[7] In court, prosecutors juxtaposed Koch's alleged cruelty with her roles as wife and mother and drew attention to her purported promiscuity and immodest, dissolute sexual tendencies. Insofar as Koch was portrayed as a sexual miscreant devoid of "natural" feminine sensibilities, her prosecution resembled those of some of the few other women tried for concentration camp crimes. Dorothea Binz, for example, was described in court as a "sadistic slut" before being sentenced to death for atrocities committed at Ravensbrück. The infamous Auschwitz and Bergen-Belsen guard Irma Grese, dubbed the "Beautiful Beast" during her trial, was the object of frequent speculation and insinuations regarding her sexuality.[8] These women committed brutal acts of violence, but their crimes were depicted as particularly abhorrent because they clashed with traditional norms of "womanly" behavior. Ilse Koch, like Grese and Binz, was therefore viewed as bearing a dual guilt, not only having committed serious statutory crimes, but also, through her exercise of violence and her licentious sexuality, having violated accepted gender norms.[9]

The intense public interest generated by the particularly infamous crimes attributed to Ilse Koch, in addition to their express sexualization in the courtroom, served to transform her into a lightning rod for the popular condemnation of Nazi crimes. Yet the atrocities she was alleged to have committed were not representative of the modern, bureaucratized form of terror that precipitated the death of millions under the Third Reich. Indeed, the fixation on Koch as a uniquely diabolical perpetrator who delighted in torture and objects made of tattooed human skins inadvertently helped to obscure the systematic, "everyday" violence of the concentration camp system and the Nazi state as a whole. As a result, Koch provided a safe target for the postwar German public to comfortably condemn without having to reflect more broadly on the criminality and violence implicit in the National Socialism that most had either supported or enabled. Further, Koch was cast as the antithesis of the German women later celebrated by West Germany's president Richard von Weizäcker for their "quiet strength" that saw Germany through its "darkest years" and "preserved the light of humanity from extinction."[10] Koch's condemnation as a "deviant" female served to preserve and reinforce the popular image of the "good" and "decent" German women who supposedly emerged from the Second World War as morally intact vessels of national rebirth.

Koch's postwar trials stood at the nexus of Cold War politics and social and cultural efforts to reckon with the Nazi past. In the United States and in East and West Germany, Koch's high-profile prosecutions represented opportunities for postwar governments to broadcast resoluteness in dealing forcefully with the remnants of Nazism. In 1947, the American military court that tried Koch handed down a life sentence; the unexpected and dramatic reduction of that sentence the following year was widely regarded in the United States as a humiliation that made the country appear soft on war criminals. The controversy that followed played out not only in the press but also in public protest, inspiring demonstrations on the streets of US cities and even a folk song by Woody Guthrie that bore Koch's name. The widespread outrage was sufficient to prompt US Senate hearings and to spur the intervention of President Harry Truman.

The political stakes of Ilse Koch's 1950–1951 West German trial were similarly high. When American jurists concluded that a desired retrial of Koch could not occur under US law, judicial authorities in the soon-to-be-independent East and West German states jockeyed for the chance to prosecute so infamous an offender. When officials in the Soviet zone of occupation demanded Koch's extradition and accused the West of coddling Nazis, the United States coordinated with the Bavarian Ministry of Justice to ensure her retrial in the city of Augsburg. The subsequent trial gave the newly independent West Germany an opportunity to illustrate its antifascist credentials and the integrity of its judiciary, both of which were touted as evidence of the country's successful democratization. Although the Augsburg court cleared Koch of the crimes for which she was infamous, it nonetheless arrived at the same sentence she had received before: life behind bars. The rejections of the numerous appeals for clemency Koch filed in the long years that followed revealed that the political and social value of her imprisonment would not lessen with time. Acknowledging Koch's enduring infamy, Bavaria's minister of justice, Hans Ehard, encapsulated the unbending official line taken toward her incarceration in his assessment of a 1965 clemency petition lodged on her behalf: "public opinion wouldn't have any understanding that such an exponent of National Socialism's violent rule . . . should be released by an act of mercy."[11]

Chapter 1 of this book examines Ilse Koch's early life and her uncommonly early attraction to National Socialism. Central to this story is Karl Koch, the ambitious and ideologically committed Nazi Ilse would marry, whose increasingly important role in the concentration camp system would lead the couple eventually to Buchenwald, the scene of Ilse Koch's crimes. Exploring the establishment and nature of the Buchenwald concentration camp, and the particular brutality and corruption that defined Karl Koch's tenure as its commandant, provides vital context for understanding the criminal allegations Ilse Koch would face. The focus here is on Ilse Koch's increasing moral and criminal complicity as she raised three children in the shadows of Buchenwald's barbed wire, and on the unique interplay of familial power, greed, and the ideological fanaticism and violence that the world of the Nazi concentration camps permitted.

Chapter 2 charts the spectacular downfall of Ilse and Karl Koch, and the curious 1943 SS investigation that culminated in their arrest. It explores the endemic corruption at Buchenwald that first caught the attention of Nazi authorities, and the nepotism among the SS elite that the Kochs initially relied upon to shield themselves from prosecution. SS investigators came to pursue Ilse largely as an accessory to and beneficiary of Karl's financial crimes, yet a dissection of the resulting indictment shows how it invokes notions of gender and sexuality to underscore her criminality and alleged deviancy. The subsequent SS trial of the Kochs for embezzlement, and for Karl's unauthorized murder of concentration camp inmates, is used to probe the inherent contradictions in the concepts of justice at the heart of the Nazi legal system.

Though Ilse Koch would fare better than her husband at the hands of Nazi judicial authorities, her rearrest by the US military following the Third Reich's collapse signaled the beginning of a far more perilous legal reckoning. Chapter 3 traces the origins and course of Ilse Koch's American military trial at Dachau. It reconstructs the circumstances of the American liberation of Buchenwald and the critical role of camp survivors in the subsequent war crimes investigation that led to Ilse Koch's detention. Establishing the origins of the most explosive allegations Koch faced helps to explain why she was chosen as one of thirty-one defendants to stand trial for crimes committed at Buchenwald. This chapter evaluates the nature and quality of the evidence against her, and how Koch's alleged crimes were presented and adjudicated in court. Also examined are her defense strategies. As a woman who had lacked official position in the Nazi state, Koch could not resort to the justification used by virtually all of her codefendants: that she had merely been following orders.

At the center of Chapter 4 is the commutation of the life sentence imposed on Koch by the US military court at Dachau, and the heated controversy surrounding this act of clemency. The chapter begins by considering why American judicial authorities judged Koch's sentence as "excessive" upon review, and what their reevaluation of Koch's case revealed about the shortcomings of the American military proceedings that had resulted in her conviction for war crimes. It explores the polemical reaction of the American press to the clemency granted Koch and its role in fueling public protests and a US Senate investigation into the conduct of her trial. It uses the subsequent Senate hearings to examine how Koch's alleged crimes were understood in the United States, why they were pursued so zealously, and how their explicit politicization shaped the course of Koch's ongoing legal odyssey.

Chapters 5 and 6 together tell the story of Koch's West German retrial. Chapter 5 starts by tracing the diplomatic machinations and Cold War political pressures that led Bavarian authorities to open a judicial investigation of Koch at the behest of the United States. It examines the circumstances of Koch's 1949 rearrest and the origins and implications of the fresh criminal charges brought by the newly independent German judiciary. Particular attention is paid to the role of the Buchenwald Committee, the predominantly communist association of former camp inmates that both assisted and at times hindered Koch's indictment. Chapter 6 provides a reconstruction of

Koch's subsequent trial at Augsburg and its popular reception in Germany. It explores how prosecutors sought to illuminate the "base motives" that allegedly drove Koch to act, and how Koch herself contested the criminal charges even as her mental health declined. It scrutinizes the particular emphasis that prosecutors and judges placed on Koch's alleged sexual deviance and failings "as a woman," and the gendered lens through which the court—and the German public at large—judged her criminal culpability. It accounts for the seeming contradiction that Koch's trial and reconviction should prove so popular among a public that otherwise largely backed amnesty for Nazi war criminals.

Chapter 7 examines the sixteen years Koch spent in prison following her reconviction by the Augsburg court. It considers the various petitions for clemency that Koch and her supporters submitted in the hopes of securing her release, and the political pressures that prompted Bavarian authorities to reject them out of hand. It draws upon Koch's extensive personal correspondence, interviews with her daughter, Gisela, and innumerable reports prepared by prison staff to elucidate her own views on her criminal guilt and moral culpability, and her outlook as she faced the prospect of dying behind bars. It reckons last with Koch's dramatic psychiatric decline, her subsequent institutionalization, and the circumstances surrounding her suicide.

The book draws to a close with a consideration of the legacy of Ilse Koch and her trials. The Epilogue asks what the popular reaction to Koch's death reveals about the German process of "coming to terms with the past," and how and why Koch came to be remembered as one of the "true culprits" of the Nazi dictatorship. It also explores Koch's curious place in the American postwar imagination, the implications of the highly sexualized images of the "Bitch of Buchenwald" that permeated American popular culture, and what these reveal about popular perceptions of Nazi crimes.

The story of Ilse Koch's judicial reckoning, with all its twists and turns, serves to illuminate the broader political, social, and cultural forces that would transform a relatively inconsequential woman into one of the most enduring symbols of Nazi terror. To contemplate Ilse Koch and her crimes is to confront not only the violence and fanaticism of the Third Reich, but the very processes that shape our common understanding of the past.

1 Ilse Koch and the World of the Concentration Camps

Understanding how Ilse Koch emerged at the end of the Second World War as one of the most infamous and loathed Nazi figures starts with contemplating her earliest encounters with National Socialism and exposure to the concentration camp system. The documentary record of Koch's life prior to her 1937 arrival at Buchenwald is exceedingly spare and, aside from a few key details, relates almost entirely to the activities of her commandant husband, Karl. It would be Karl Koch, an ambitious and corrupt SS officer integral to the establishment of the Third Reich's apparatus of terror, who would draw Ilse into the world of the concentration camps and embroil her in crimes for which both would have to answer.

Ilse Koch was born Margarete Ilse Köhler in the city of Dresden in 1906. Alongside her two brothers, Koch was raised by her parents, Max and Anna Köhler (née Kubisch), in a Protestant, lower-middle-class household that provided the foundation for a stable and apparently unremarkable childhood. According to the scant record of Koch's early life, her primary and lower secondary school education in the compulsory German *Volksschule* system was followed not by attendance at the more academic *Gymnasium*, or high school, but by a stint in a trade school where she learned secretarial skills.[1] Yet while Koch's schooling

Fig. 1.1 Ilse Köhler, age four. Courtesy Gisela Koch.

and subsequent employment as a secretary in various Dresden firms suggest an early life rather ordinary in its detail, she marked herself apart from the majority of her female contemporaries when she joined the Nazi Party at the age of twenty-five.[2] While the party's membership had grown by leaps and bounds in the midst of the Depression and the political deadlock that gripped Germany in the years immediately prior to Hitler's seizure of power in 1933, few women joined it during this period.[3] Assigned party number 1130836 in May 1932, Koch swore an oath "to serve the party with all my strength."[4]

Though Koch would later deny and then refuse comment on her party membership, many young Germans of her generation saw the Nazi movement as dynamic, disciplined, and driven by a revolutionary zeal they hoped could erase the deep social, political, and economic fractures that had riven German society during the interwar years. From the fragmentary record that remains, it is clear that Ilse also was drawn to the movement through her social engagement with members of the local SS detachment in Dresden. Ilse's romantic relationships within this circle suggest she was attracted to these uniformed, ideologically committed, and often ambitious young men. It was perhaps Ilse's ideological commitment as much as her athletic build, green eyes, and reddish-blond hair that in 1934 drew the attention of the ruthless SS man with whom she would soon start a relationship, and whose professional trajectory in the Nazi state would eventually pull Ilse into the inner sanctum of the concentration camp system.

The Rise of Karl Koch

Nearly ten years Ilse's senior, Karl Otto Koch was a slim and stern man with a round face and combed-back, receding, greyish hair.[5] Born in Darmstadt in 1897, his parents were unmarried—ironically, given his father's position as a registrar in the local marriage license bureau—but soon resolved the problem of his illegitimacy with a wedding a few months later.[6] Karl's father died, however, when Karl was just eight, leaving him to be raised by his mother. His education, geared like Ilse's toward the learning of a trade, led him to take up an apprenticeship as a bookkeeper and then a job in the accounting office of a local munitions factory. As his sense of patriotic enthusiasm grew, his decision in March 1916 to volunteer for service in the German army would soon send him to the trenches of the Western Front. Karl's rather colorless war diary does not present his service as the sort of life-altering experience that shaped the political outlook of so many of his contemporaries, but he was wounded twice, taken prisoner by the British, and awarded the Iron Cross, Second Class.[7]

Once released from British captivity in October 1919, Karl Koch initially stayed clear of the various radical associations and political movements that arose in the wake of Germany's catastrophic defeat and proved popular with so many young veterans. He appears to have changed jobs frequently, first finding work in the 1920s at a number of firms and banks, and then as an insurance salesman. According to later Nazi investigation records, however, Karl also suffered long periods of unemployment, and at times resorted to petty thievery and small-time embezzlement.[8] His 1924 marriage to Käte Müller, a union which produced a psychiatrically troubled son named Manfred, was in shambles by decade's end and resulted in divorce "through the sole fault" of the husband.[9] Like many of his contemporaries in this period, Karl apparently became radicalized in his political views as his fortunes waned and the Depression took its toll on the German economy. As financial crisis gripped his nation, Karl joined the Nazi Party in March 1931, and shortly thereafter the SS, channeling his bitterness and desperation into a movement that promised to restore prosperity and pride to Germany while rooting out its perceived enemies.

Despite the fact that, in 1932, Karl was briefly ejected from the party, for reasons that are no longer clear, his subsequent rise through the National Socialist ranks was impressive.[10] He first acted as treasurer of the party in Darmstadt while continuing to sell insurance on the side. In February 1933, he was sent to Kassel to establish an office of the Hilfspolizei, a short-lived auxiliary police force created by Hitler to combat political opponents following his rise to power. It appears that Karl's success with this commission drew him into the police apparatus of the Nazi state, leading to his appointment to the staff of SS Brigadier General Theodor Eicke, chief of the Concentration Camp Inspectorate, in October 1934. Koch's personnel report from that year makes it clear that he was regarded by his superiors as both competent and ideologically committed. His "National Socialist worldview" was described as "correct and firm"; his character as "hard and vigorous" and also "goal-oriented" and "reliable and decent"; his mental state as "very intelligent, confident and correct"; and his relationship to subordinates as "strict but just."[11] Koch's ascension also owed much to his ability to make friends in high places, including with SS chief Heinrich Himmler—a friendship that would later prove vital.

When Ilse met Karl in Dresden in May 1934, therefore, she encountered a man whose star within the movement clearly was on the rise. Having already achieved the rank of SS-Lieutenant, Karl was entrusted with increasingly important leadership roles in the growing number of concentration camps (designated KZ, for *konzentrationslager*) created by the Nazis primarily for the purposes of destroying their political opponents and soon their "racial enemies." Over the course of the following two years, Ilse and Karl were on the move and frequently apart. Karl was appointed commandant of KZ Sachsenburg, then troop leader at KZ Esterwegen, then protective custody chief at KZ Lichtenburg, then commandant of KZ Columbia Haus, and then commandant back at Esterwegen—all by the spring of 1936.[12] His growing reputation as an efficient and dedicated administrator led to his promotion, on September 1, 1936, to commandant of Sachsenhausen, one of the largest concentration camps in Germany.[13] Under

Fig. 1.2 Ilse and Karl Koch vacationing on the island of Norderney, off the North Sea coast of Germany, 1936. Ilse Koch Personal Album 1, Records of the Office of the Judge Advocate General (Army), Record Group 153, National Archives and Records Administration.

Karl's leadership, the camp site, located thirty-five kilometers north of Berlin at Oranienburg, was cleared of trees and the first barracks and administrative buildings were erected to allow for the incarceration of some ten thousand prisoners.[14] The camp layout was triangular, with barracks built in lines radiating from a roll-call yard just inside the main gate. The high stone wall and electric fences that ringed the camp were punctuated by imposing guard towers and patrolled by an armed SS troop. Sachsenhausen would eventually see some 200,000 prisoners pass through its gates, 35,000 to 40,000 of

Fig. 1.3   Ilse and Karl Koch at Esterwagen, 1936. Ilse Koch's Personal Album 1, Records of the Office of the Judge Advocate General (Army), Record Group 153, National Archives and Records Administration.

whom would die there, whether by backbreaking forced labor, hunger, disease, or execution.[15]

At Sachsenhausen, Ilse and Karl's relationship came into full bloom, prompting Karl to apply to the SS Race and Settlement Main Office for permission to marry. In 1931, Himmler had issued the Engagement and Marriage Order by which any member of the SS was required to prove the racial purity of his betrothed before vows could be exchanged. "The SS," the decree stated, "is a band of German men of strictly Nordic descent. . . . The future of our people rests upon the preservation of the race through selection and the healthy inheritance of good blood. . . . The desired aim is to create a hereditarily healthy clan of a strictly Nordic German sort. The marriage certificate will be awarded or denied solely on the basis of racial health and heredity." Ilse, therefore, set about providing the genealogical evidence of Aryan ancestry back to 1750 required of all wives to guarantee this biological "up-breeding" of the SS.[16] Ilse's forbearers, as she documented, were of pure German stock—a Protestant family of tradesmen largely from the regions of Thuringia, Saxony, and Lower Saxony.[17]

On May 25, 1937, Ilse and Karl were married at Oranienburg City Hall, followed by a torchlit midnight ritual in the oak grove at Sachsenhausen. The cultish quality of the SS ceremony, in which Ilse appears to have been the only female participant, does not seem to have intimidated the new bride, who looks both serious and filled with wonderment in the existing photos. Ilse, who wore a long, flowered, dark dress with a cape over her shoulders and carried a bouquet of roses in her arms, does, however, strike a marked contrast with her new husband, who dressed in full SS regalia, complete with white gloves and ceremonial saber. Once the SS officiant had spoken of the value of marriage for National Socialism and had pronounced the two husband and wife, the couple exited between two rows of more than fifty SS men standing at attention in black uniforms.[18] It would seem that behind closed doors the newlyweds had a genuine love for each other; in family photos they are often holding each other close.[19] Affectionately, Ilse called her husband "Karli" and he nicknamed her "Pimpf," borrowing the word used to describe the youngest, prepubescent, members of the Hitler Youth.[20]

The meager documentary record of Ilse's day-to-day activities during Karl's tenure at Sachsenhausen allows only for broad generalizations about her time there. Despite claims to the contrary made in a number of studies, it is certain that she never had an official position at the camp or acted as a common guard.[21] Such activities would have been deemed below Ilse's elite station as the commandant's wife. Nonetheless, although Koch would deny that she ever entered the Sachsenhausen camp compound, a number of survivors would later testify that she participated in their abuse. They recalled how Koch would watch inmates work from her window, shout reproaches at any who dared cast glances in her direction, and instruct guards to administer beatings.[22] Whether or not she visited the Sachsenhausen enclosure, however, Ilse's primary obligation, as Himmler's Marriage Order made clear, was to produce the "pure-blooded" children that her background allowed. It appears that the couple jumped the gun while waiting for official SS sanction, as Ilse gave birth to their first child, a son named Artwin, on January 17, 1938, only seven months after their marriage.[23]

Ilse's position and place following her marriage to Karl help to illustrate the seemingly contradictory roles for women that the Nazi state permitted. In voting for Hitler in 1933, Ilse, like many women of her generation, paradoxically supported a movement that promised to curtail the role of women in the public sphere and to undo the great political strides that German women had made during the Weimar years. The women of the Third Reich were to concern themselves primarily with the three Ks, *Kinder, Küche, Kirche*—children, the kitchen, and the church. Yet it would be wrong to see Nazi women solely as victims of a misogynist state.[24] As their husbands engaged daily in the perpetration of state-sanctioned brutality, SS wives like Ilse helped to provide emotional support and maintained a level of familial order that lent the appearance of decency to the Nazi system of terror.[25] Ilse's path also helps to illustrate that, beyond providing domestic normalcy in genocidal contexts, many SS wives used their positions to gain a degree of autonomy outside the household while benefiting from their husbands' influence.[26] For Ilse, this possibility arose in July 1937, when Karl relinquished his post at Sachsenhausen to establish and take command of a new concentration camp—a massive complex to be called Buchenwald.

Buchenwald

The preceding four years had provided Karl with considerable expertise in the establishment and governance of concentration camps, making him an obvious choice for the Buchenwald commission. Himmler, who as SS chief had managed to wrest total authority over the concentration camps from other organs of the Nazi state, was intent on expanding the reach of the concentration camp system to deal with the opponents of the Reich while at the same time building up SS economic enterprises through the use of the inmate slave labor the camps provided. In particular, Himmler intended to use SS industry to supply materials for Hitler's monumental building program, which sought to reconstruct some cities entirely, such as Linz and Berlin, and fill others with epic architectural landmarks.[27] The location of Buchenwald, atop the high, picturesque hill called Ettersberg on the outskirts of the city of Weimar, was no random choice. The SS recognized that the site was near population centers in the provinces of Saxony and Thuringia that could supply prison labor, and that its soil was rich in the sort of clay required for brickmaking—the work that Buchenwald's arriving prisoners would soon be forced to perform.[28] Karl's mandate was to create a camp that at once provided the slave labor required by SS industry and fulfilled the state's need to punish and terrorize its opponents. As part of the program the Nazis sometimes referred to as *Vernichtung durch Arbeit*—extermination through work—Buchenwald would develop into a key site.[29]

Finding little more than a heavy oak forest on Ettersberg when he arrived, Karl had much to organize and oversee. His first task was to clear a patch of woodland and construct the barracks and administrative buildings that form the core of the camp. Never short of labor with a pool of prisoner-slaves at his disposal, Karl put the camp's first inmates to work clearing trees, building roads, and erecting the camp's central structures—all without the help of heavy machinery or sufficient rations of food or water. The loss of life that resulted under such working conditions was massive.[30] Yet the camp, designed initially to hold as many as ten thousand prisoners, continued to expand. The prisoner compound soon consisted of thirty-three wooden barracks, fifteen two-story buildings, a roll-call square, numerous workshops, an infirmary, a disinfection building, a kitchen, a laundry, storerooms, a canteen, and various other structures. The murderous slave labor, malnutrition, disease, and terror the prisoner population was exposed to also led to the building of a crematorium in 1940 to deal with the growing number of corpses requiring daily disposal.[31] The prisoner enclosure itself was ringed by twenty-two guard towers and an electrified barbed-wire fence, three kilometers long and three meters high, that was patrolled with the aid of German shepherd dogs.[32] Outside the fences stood an additional series of buildings, including the barracks for the members of the SS-Totenkopfstandarte 3 "Thürigen" (Death's Head Regiment) that guarded the camp, the commandant's headquarters, the political department that coordinated with the Gestapo in Berlin, various administrative buildings, a canteen, a garage, various workshops, and a housing settlement for senior officers.[33] Over time, Buchenwald would grow to cover 470 acres, and eventually would spawn more than one hundred sub-camps under its administrative authority. By war's end, these collectively held nearly fifty thousand additional prisoners.[34]

The establishment of Buchenwald coincided with the dramatic expansion of categories of German citizens subject to arrest and internment in concentration camps. When Karl served at camps such as Esterwegen and Columbia Haus, the inmates were predominantly left-wing political opponents swept up by a wave of emergency laws created by the new Nazi state to crack down on communists, who had conveniently been blamed for the arson attack that partially destroyed the German parliament building, the Reichstag, in February 1933.[35] After 1936, however, the SS significantly widened the net, promulgating a series of laws and decrees that targeted not only the Nazis' political opponents, but habitual criminals, homosexual men, Jehovah's Witnesses, and "asocials"—an elastic category that included the homeless and so-called "work shy" as well as the Sinti and Roma ("gypsies").[36] By broadening its definitions of groups deemed to be threats to German state and society, and thereby increasing the number of inmates, the SS at once justified the expansion of the camp system it governed and grew the pool of slave labor at its disposal.

Transports of prisoners to Buchenwald began July 15, 1937, with the arrival of 149 inmate craftsmen from Sachsenhausen concentration camp.[37] By year's end, nearly three thousand had been admitted, and by the end of 1938, more than twenty thousand.[38] Karl ensured that prisoner life at Buchenwald was hell. New arrivals, many having already spent hours or days languishing in crowded railway cars, were either marched the eight kilometers from the city of Weimar to the camp with their arms raised above their heads, or squeezed into trucks for the journey. Upon arrival, they were greeted by camp SS with blows from fists and whips and forced to stand for hours with their hands crossed behind their heads—a position referred to sarcastically as the "Saxon salute"—before being registered one by one in the political department. Prisoners then entered the prisoner compound through an iron gate crowned with the mocking and sardonic phrase *Jedem das Seine*—to each his own. To further break the morale of the new arrivals, guards forced the prisoners again to stand for hours in the Saxon salute position, with their faces to the cell block wall, and then to submit to a "disinfection" process of undressing, total shaving, showering, and inspection. Once allotted a striped uniform and pair of shoes, prisoners were assigned to a crowded barrack (or "block"), and to one of the many bunks that were stacked in threes or fours and covered with thin straw mattresses.

Karl ensured that the daily routine at Buchenwald was punishing for the growing prisoner population. Waking at dawn, prisoners received a piece of bread and a pint of thin soup or ersatz coffee for breakfast, and then stood to be counted in the roll-call square in a process that lasted at least an hour no matter the weather. Work then began, with some prisoners marching five abreast through the camp gate to slave in stone quarries, the brick works, and later in armaments production, and others proceeding to work stations inside the camp, in the kitchen, the hospital, the lumberyard, the latrines, the laundry, and various other workshops and offices. Prisoners spent their workdays in constant fear, as punishments were meted out ruthlessly and often arbitrarily by the SS and the *kapos*—prisoner-functionaries who took on supervisory roles in the camp in exchange for minor privileges. Jews in particular, whose numbers in the camp grew after the November 1938 nationwide pogrom known as *Kristallnacht,* were singled out for the most brutal treatment and often received the most murderous work assignments. At day's end, the entire exhausted prisoner population returned to the roll-call yard to be counted at dusk, and once dismissed, to eat a meager ration, and to sleep. This program of slave labor led to mass mortality as prisoners weakened through starvation, disease, and overwork. Executions of prisoners also occurred at the camp, often following interrogations in the political department, as did various mass-killing operations aimed predominantly at Jews and later at prisoners of war, largely from the Soviet Union. Horrific medical experiments claimed the lives of hundreds more prisoners, as SS doctors injected inmates with contagious diseases such as typhus and cholera in search of vaccines or attempted to "cure" homosexual prisoners through hormone treatments and "artificial glands."[39] Of the 238,980 prisoners who eventually passed through Buchenwald's gates, some 56,000 died there.[40]

When Karl Koch arrived at Buchenwald in July 1937, the SS settlement and housing for its senior officers had yet to be constructed. Ilse, who was four months pregnant, therefore took up residency until November in the Kaiserin Augusta Hotel in Weimar, where Karl would visit her most evenings.[41] Karl continued his professional ascent, with his growing reputation leading to promotions through the SS ranks to lieutenant colonel, and shortly after, to colonel. Karl's tenure at Buchenwald would be marked by unbridled brutality, deep corruption, and growing arrogance—traits that sowed terror among the inmate population and earned him deep contempt from many of his own men. He saw his power at Buchenwald as virtually absolute, but it was this very tendency toward graft and ruthless violence, and inclination to act independently of orders from Berlin, that would eventually bring his downfall.

"Under Koch," one Buchenwald survivor remembered, "a regime of true arbitrariness prevailed."[42] Fear of violence at the hands of the SS and kapos was universal among inmates. Karl's frequent insistence that prisoners were not working hard enough prompted guards to administer beatings for even the smallest of disciplinary infractions. Prisoners could be punished for merely warming their hands in their pockets, losing buttons on their uniforms, or spending what was deemed to be too much time in the latrines.[43] Karl also took direct action to instill terror in the camp, often without the permission of his SS superiors. In one particularly brutal incident, Karl resolved to take revenge for the unsuccessful bomb plot hatched against Hitler on November 8, 1939, at the Bürgerbräukeller in Munich. The day after the failed assassination attempt, Karl requested that all Jewish prisoners, who in his mind were tied to the incident by their sheer ethnicity, remain behind at roll call when the rest of the inmates were dismissed. Seemingly at random, he instructed his troop to select eighteen to twenty prominent Jewish men and march them to the camp quarry. There, each was shot dead from behind by SS guards, many of them still drunk from the previous night's anniversary celebration of Hitler's 1923 Beer Hall Putsch. This unauthorized mass execution raised eyebrows in Berlin and resulted in an internal investigation—which yielded no disciplinary measures following Koch's insistence that the men had been "shot while trying to escape."[44] With his power unchecked, Karl made a habit of unilaterally ordering executions, often of new inmates who committed disciplinary infractions shortly after arriving at Buchenwald or otherwise caught his eye. He apparently had one prisoner shot simply because he recognized the man from another concentration camp he had previously supervised. "Now this bird won't follow me anymore," Koch reportedly joked.[45]

Commandant Koch reserved his most savage punishments, however, for those who tried to escape. Prisoners daring enough to attempt escape were returned to the camp and executed, often in the presence of the entire camp population so their deaths would serve as a warning. Eugen Kogon, a Catholic anti-Nazi resister who survived six years in Buchenwald and became its chief historian, recounted a particularly barbaric incident involving a "Gypsy" (Roma) prisoner apprehended after attempting to break out. On the orders of the commandant, he was placed inside a wooden box with a single open side covered with chicken wire, and put on display for the whole camp to see. Too small to permit a man to stand, the box had nails hammered through its boards that stabbed at the prisoner whenever he attempted to move. For three nights his public agony continued, before he was killed with a lethal injection. So great was his suffering, Kogon recalled, that "his dreadful screams . . . lost any semblance of humanity."[46]

Karl Koch's brutality at Buchenwald was matched by his brazen corruption and, in particular, his proclivity to divert into his own coffers both the valuables and cash of arriving prisoners and the resources delivered by the state, earmarked for the maintenance of the camp and its population. But while his SS superiors in Berlin may have been willing to tolerate unsanctioned violence against inmates they already considered enemies of the Reich, graft that syphoned resources away from Berlin and into the pockets of individual officers would prove quite another matter. For Karl, who had engaged in petty theft as a young man, the temptations were far too great. First, the huge Buchenwald inmate population included artisans whose talents could easily be exploited for personal gain. Karl and the camp SS set up workshops where watchmakers, woodworkers, and artists were compelled to churn out luxury goods such as moldings, sculptures, and furniture for their homes, and jewelry, deluxe photo albums, and family portraits for themselves and their wives.[47] Beyond taking advantage of inmate labor, however, Karl also committed more systematic theft. Secret bank accounts were set up to spirit away the cash, jewelry, and other valuables confiscated from the thousands of prisoners that arrived at Buchenwald. To cover his tracks, Karl ordered plundered victims to sign cards stating that they had arrived at the camp without cash or valuables of any sort.[48] Meanwhile, as the death rate at Buchenwald climbed, so too did the supply of dental gold extracted from the mouths of prisoners before their cremation, and added to Karl's growing fortune.[49]

While the arbitrary and violent nature of Karl's command of Buchenwald helped to instill terror among prisoners, inmates also learned that the corruption of the SS leadership at the camp could occasionally be played to their advantage. Franz Eichhorn, a prisoner at Buchenwald who acted as barber to Karl and the SS elite, recalled how this functioned. "When, for example, a comrade was to receive a caning, the commandant would tell us about it the day before. Then we would go to the deputy commandant at the time, Florstedt, bringing him a can of caviar or some other delicacy, after which the punishment was cancelled."[50] Karl also worked in cahoots with a few prisoners at Buchenwald who arrived with preexisting contacts on the black market. With the commandant observing and pocketing the lion's share of the profits, these privileged prisoners sold desperately needed goods to other inmates at dramatically inflated prices.[51] Any such service to the commandant, however, was fraught with danger. As future investigations would reveal, those with too much knowledge of Karl's activities could be executed on the flimsiest of pretenses.[52]

Some of the more high-ranking SS men at Buchenwald might have appreciated the tolerance of corruption and embezzlement at the camp under his leadership, but Karl was deeply unpopular with his regular troops, whom he chastised on a regular basis. Official orders to his men were often accompanied with insults regarding their perceived shortcomings. Discipline was "rotten," Karl charged in late 1939, and his men too lazy and too soft, having permitted prisoner productivity to fall to "pretty much zero" in the camp. "It won't be long," Karl lamented, "before I will have to make sure everyone wipes their own asses."[53] Overbearing in his manner, Koch routinely punished his regular enlisted men with drills and subjected them to surveillance. If they were caught in improprieties involving inmates, he went so far as to threaten his men with internment as prisoners in the concentration camp.[54] For many rank-and-file personnel, the gulf between the noble and disciplined image he attempted to project to his troops and his actual corruption was tough to take and earned him great enmity. Eichhorn, the barber, recalled an incident when lemons were delivered for the benefit of the camp SS. "Koch seized the entire shipment, kept most of it for himself, and gave only a few lemons to some of the higher-ranking officers. At that time the rumor spread that I had rubbed down Frau [Ilse] Koch's naked back with lemons, but this was not the case. Still, this shows how 'popular' the commandant was with his own men."[55]

Ilse Koch at Buchenwald

However apocryphal the tales of stolen lemons, Ilse Koch benefited greatly and openly from Karl's corruption, and wore increasingly extravagant clothing he gifted her. Over time, Ilse's appearance drew unwanted attention to the ever more conspicuous wealth of her family and served to inspire potent rumors. Stories circulated that she bathed in Madeira wine and engaged in devious and sadomasochistic sexual behavior both with the camp's SS officers and with inmates.[56] So many rumors swirled around Ilse, in fact, that legal authorities would later struggle to pinpoint her actual activities at Buchenwald, and to separate the truth and the fiction of her relationship with prisoners there. It is clear, however, that Ilse made a deep impression on those who saw her, perhaps because of her alleged and oft-described good looks, but more likely because she was one of the only women that Buchenwald inmates had the chance to see. Prisoners took to referring to her as the "commandeuse," suggesting a degree of authority that rivaled that of her commandant husband. This erroneous designation clearly overstates the case, but its persistence indicates that Ilse's presence at Buchenwald was felt deeply by prisoners, despite her own postwar protestations that she had acted merely as mother and wife, confined largely to the family home and totally ignorant of what occurred within the camp's barbed wire.

Ilse's primary domain at Buchenwald was an opulent villa, larger than the other homes on the forested street, that provided the central axis of the housing settlement for Buchenwald's SS elite. Located nearly a kilometer's walk from the camp compound main entrance, the three-story Koch villa was surrounded by a rampart crowned with a single turret and punctuated by an entranceway to an underground garage. Built through the slave labor of prisoners, the house had an exterior evoking early Romantic German architecture while its interior was furnished in a largely contemporary and high-quality Art Deco style. The Koch villa was also undeniably Nazi, complete with busts of Hitler, a chandelier constructed of antlers, and a portrait of Karl in SS uniform hanging on the wall of the otherwise sparingly decorated master bedroom.[57]

Koch family photos of Ilse sunbathing in the garden that surrounded the house and bathing her children in the small concrete pool constructed for them suggest that she embraced the role of mother prescribed to her by the Nazi state. For the majority of the period that Karl was commandant at Buchenwald, Ilse was pregnant, giving birth in January 1938 to son Artwin, in April 1939 to daughter Gisela, and in December 1940 to daughter Gudrun. Yet while family photos depict Karl and Ilse as loving parents, they also reveal chilling truths about Koch family life. Photographs accompanied by the caption "First Snow at Buchenwald" show Ilse strolling in a full-length fur coat alongside Karl and directly in front of the main entrance to the camp compound, while Artwin and Gisela play happily in the snow on a picturesque winter's day. Other photos show Karl and Artwin feeding deer inside the small SS zoo built for the Koch family, which contained a concrete enclosure for bears that stood only fifty meters from the crematoria complex.[58] The presence of the family at play so near the barbed wire that kept thousands languishing in murderous conditions bespeaks a callous indifference to the suffering of Buchenwald's inmates and belies the idea that Koch family life and the camp Karl governed could remain wholly separate spheres.

The most direct and regular contact between the Koch household and the prisoner population occurred through the slave labor that Ilse used in the home. Prisoners worked in the Koch villa doing various household chores and even assisting with the children. Some of them would later testify against Ilse, reporting on her total disinterest in their well-being, and making allegations of extramarital liaisons between Ilse and other members of the SS staff that undercut her image as loyal wife and mother.[59] Beyond availing herself of slave labor in the home, however, Ilse convinced Karl to commission for her a riding hall, a massive structure built through the sweat and toil of dozens of Buchenwald prisoners, a number of whom reportedly died in the process. Built in 1939 at the substantial cost of 250,000 reichsmarks (more than a million dollars in today's terms), the wooden structure with mirrored walls stood twenty meters high and was used by Ilse for

Fig. 1.4   Karl Koch and son Artwin feed deer in Buchenwald's zoo, adjacent to the prisoner compound, October 1939. Ilse Koch Personal Album 2, Records of the Office of the Judge Advocate General (Army), Record Group 153, National Archives and Records Administration.

morning rides that seldom lasted longer than half an hour. As she rode her horse around the ring, the camp's SS band reportedly provided musical accompaniment.[60] She would later account for the construction of the riding hall with the flippant explanation that "prisoner labor was cheap, and the wood inexpensive."[61] In reality, there were substantial human and economic costs associated with the riding hall's construction, and it became a symbol of Koch family corruption, cruelty, and frivolity, for which Ilse would soon have to account.

Ilse's love of horseback riding, in fact, played a key role in some of the most persistent and damning accusations made against her by camp inmates. Though Ilse insisted that she took little interest in the Buchenwald compound and its prisoner population, many survivors later testified that she was a regular presence around the camp, usually riding "Puppe," a black horse that was a gift from Karl. Some recounted seeing her with a riding whip in hand that she used against those who dared glance in her direction or worked too slowly. Others remembered her dressing in provocative ways deliberately to draw the stares of prisoners, so that she would have grounds to punish them, whether personally or by jotting down their numbers and reporting them to SS guards. Survivor Emil Carlebach recalled how this worked: "The accusation of molesting a German woman is something she employed frequently. I myself heard her shouting several times, 'You seem to never have seen a German woman, you are going over the bock!'" The "bock" was a wooden sawhorse over which prisoners had to bend for flogging.[62] Survivor Walter Retterpath remembered watching Ilse as she rode up to a labor gang building a road, reprimanded one of the men, then bloodied his face with her riding crop. Retterpath recalled her screaming: "I dare say you are looking at my legs?"[63] More than two dozen witnesses would later testify that she was frequently seen at floggings, some sharing their impression that she derived pleasure from witnessing inmates subjected to cruelty.[64] Following the war, however, Ilse would fervently contest such accounts, painting herself instead as the victim of malicious and vindictive camp rumor. Her three pregnancies and the small children she had to raise, she insisted, made her alleged omnipresence on horseback at the camp impossible.[65]

Such accounts of brutality, even if sometimes apocryphal, exemplified how concentration camp prisoners were terrorized on a regular basis, and partly explain Ilse Koch's designation as the "commandeuse." This title, however, also reflects a perception of a more official and substantial administrative authority, which might likewise have originated in Ilse's activities. According to the account of one of Karl's men, Ilse had keys to the commandant's office and to Karl's desk, and was a frequent presence around the camp's headquarters. Ilse assisted her husband with paperwork at times, an activity that must have

Fig. 1.5   Ilse Koch at home with children Artwin and Gisela, Buchenwald, 1941. Ilse Koch Personal Album 2, Records of the Office of the Judge Advocate General (Army), Record Group 153, National Archives and Records Administration.

exposed her further to the goings-on in the camp.[66] Yet Karl clearly was opposed to any suggestion of authority on Ilse's part. Ilse's receipt of a letter addressed to "Frau Standartenführer Koch" at their Buchenwald home was enough to throw Karl into a rage.[67] While there can be little doubt, therefore, that Ilse was both aware of what happened within Buchenwald's fences and a willing beneficiary of her husband's graft, Karl Koch's authoritarian style of command and overbearing personality precluded her exercising anything approaching the sort of authority sufficient to warrant the title "commandeuse."

By the beginning of 1941, the Koch family had spent nearly four years at Buchenwald, living a life defined by prestige and luxury thanks to Karl's official position and the degree to which it could be exploited for personal gain. That the couple often projected an image of being loving and nurturing parents of three young children, even as they oversaw and witnessed unspeakable suffering around them on a daily basis, does not appear to have struck Ilse or Karl as particularly contradictory.[68] Yet behind the scenes, all was not well with the Koch family. In March 1941, four-month-old Gudrun died of pneumonia in the care of Karl's stepsister, Erna Raible, while Ilse was away skiing, prompting Raible to accuse Ilse of neglect.[69] Infidelities may also have raised tensions, as rumors swirled around Ilse's activities and Karl's extramarital liaisons were open secrets. Despite these household troubles, however, it is hard to imagine that Karl or Ilse foresaw that the lavish life they had built at Buchenwald was about to come tumbling down in dramatic fashion. While Karl continued to treat Buchenwald as a private fiefdom under his total control, his theft and embezzlement had caught the attention of local SS authorities, who refused to turn a blind eye. Karl believed his friends in high places would shield him from scrutiny or consequences, but revelations of the scale of his pilfering and fraud at Buchenwald would soon leave him dangerously exposed. And Ilse would learn quickly that her own fate was inextricably bound up with that of her husband.

2   Corruption, Murder, and the SS Trial of Ilse and Karl Koch

By mid-1941, Ilse Koch had spent four years at Buchenwald and had borne three children in the lavish family villa that broadcast the power and prestige of her commandant husband, Karl. Without concern for the sufferings of the prisoner population, Ilse raised her family on the fringes of the camp's barbed wire while taking advantage of her position to employ inmate-slaves to assist in the upkeep of her household. At the same time, Karl's efforts to forge Buchenwald into a model concentration camp had helped to make it into an infamous site of suffering for the political, racial, and religious groups deemed enemies of the Reich. Already, its program of arduous slave labor, meager rations, crowded conditions, and brutalities at the hands of SS guards had led to thousands of inmate deaths.

Yet if the Koch era at Buchenwald was marked by brutality, Karl's naked pursuit of personal enrichment helped to bring a different sort of notoriety to the camp, as a site of SS corruption, graft, and illicit enterprise. Karl made little attempt to conceal the growing opulence of his lifestyle at Buchenwald, and Ilse's expensive jewelry and furs began to raise eyebrows. And while many within the SS hierarchy viewed personal (if discreet) enrichment as an acceptable perk for those who worked in the concentration camps, the Kochs were unlucky

Fig. 2.1   Ilse in a fur coat, strolling with Karl, Artwin, and Gisela past Buchenwald's main gate and detention "bunker," December 1940. Ilse Koch Personal Album 2, Records of the Office of the Judge Advocate General (Army), Record Group 153, National Archives and Records Administration.

enough to draw the attention of one particularly fastidious senior Nazi official, the Higher SS and Police Leader under whose authority Buchenwald directly fell: Josias, Hereditary Prince of Waldeck and Pyrmont. When rumors of Karl's personal corruption reached the aristocratic Waldeck, he took the unusual step of ordering an investigation. At first, the Kochs were able to shrug off this unwelcome scrutiny as other high-ranking SS leaders intervened on their behalf. Eventually, however, Waldeck's curious and dogged pursuit would lead to the Koch's downfall—a spectacular collapse that reveals some of the greatest ironies and contradictions implicit in the ethics and ideology of the Third Reich.

Hereditary Prince Josias of Waldeck and Pyrmont might at first glance seem an unlikely character to launch an investigation into misdeeds at Buchenwald, given his SS credentials and personal involvement in the ideological crimes of the Nazi state. A highly decorated veteran of the First World War, Waldeck had joined the Nazi Party in 1929, and was quickly embraced for the perceived prestige his royal title brought the fledgling movement. By 1930 he had joined the SS, and within a year was chief of staff to its leader, Heinrich Himmler.[1] Waldeck personally campaigned in the election of 1933 alongside Hitler, who sought to draw a link between himself and the traditional and heralded German aristocracy that the prince represented.[2] In his remarkably varied career, Waldeck also served as adjutant to SS General Sepp Dietrich, as a counselor in the Foreign Office, as creator of a "Bureau for the Germanification of Eastern Peoples" that assisted in the Nazi colonization of occupied Eastern Europe, and as a member of the Reichstag for the duration of the Third Reich. He played a direct role in Nazi crimes as leader of an execution detail that dispatched a number of Hitler's opponents during the 1934 "Röhm Purge," and as head of an SS unit that attacked the Jewish residents of Bad Arolsen and destroyed the local synagogue during the 1938 nationwide Kristallnacht pogrom.[3] It was, however, during his 1939 appointment as Higher SS and Police Leader of Weimar that Buchenwald came under the prince's administrative authority, and the Kochs came to his attention.

It is no longer entirely clear what first drew Waldeck to investigate Karl's leadership of Buchenwald. While some claimed that he had been out to settle a personal grudge with the commandant, Waldeck later testified that while he had disliked Karl from the moment he met him and viewed him as a "base character," his motives had not been personal.[4] Instead, he insisted that his secondary portfolio as a judge advocate and appointing and reviewing authority for the SS and police court came with a professional responsibility to enforce the law.[5]

Fig. 2.2　Josias, Hereditary Prince of Waldeck and Pyrmont, during his US Army trial at Dachau, 1947. Courtesy United States Holocaust Memorial Museum.

Waldeck explained that rumors of Karl's corruption had been rife, and evidence of embezzlement and graft at Buchenwald became impossible to ignore:

> It started in 1941, when I heard about something going wrong financially in Karl's place. At first I didn't particularly believe this until one of his closest collaborators and co-perpetrators made a statement so concrete that I ordered Koch to my place to talk to him. . . . I proved to Koch his own illegal acts by showing him in

his own books. They were done in such a blunt manner that even I, who am not a business student, noticed it myself. So I told the fellow all of this and then simply took the pistol away from him and arrested him. Then I had him taken to Weimar in a car and quartered him with the Gestapo.[6]

Waldeck quickly learned, however, that his own administrative authority was no match for Karl's immense clout with his friends in the highest echelons of the SS hierarchy. The day after Koch's arrest on December 18, 1941, Waldeck received livid phone calls from his superiors, who accused him of having acted outside his authority to arrest "their best commandant."[7] Waldeck attempted to stick to his guns but his efforts were soon thwarted by the intervention of Himmler. Waldeck later described the furious teletype he received from Himmler as containing "phraseology which I don't care to [repeat]. In thirty-five years of soldiering I had never been talked to that way before."[8] To Waldeck's great frustration, Koch was released less than twenty-four hours after his arrest.

For Ilse, Karl's arrest was terrifying, not only because it threatened to bring to an end the privileged life they had built at Buchenwald, but also, evidently, because she feared implication in her husband's crimes. Reconstructing Ilse's reaction to Karl's arrest is difficult, however, as the only extant accounts are contradictory—despite their coming from the same source. Konrad Morgen, an SS judge who was a key Waldeck ally and investigator central to the case against the Kochs, testified at Ilse's 1947 trial at Dachau that her first reflex was to turn on Karl. Ilse, Morgen stated, attempted to distance herself from her husband by telling her circle of friends that Karl was a "criminal" and a "murderer," and exclaiming that it was he and not Buchenwald's prisoners that belonged behind the barbed wire.[9] She endeavored to present herself as a victim rather than a beneficiary of Karl's tyranny, and as shocked to learn of the wealth he had accumulated and other evidence of his malfeasance. Upon Karl's quick release, Morgen explained, Ilse then faced the serious problem of answering to her husband for this stunning about-face. This was, Morgen surmised, the reason that Ilse claimed to have suffered a nervous breakdown following Karl's arrest: saying so allowed her to disavow what she had said, pretending it was the result of a temporary descent into stress-induced delusion.[10] On the witness stand, Ilse would confirm Morgen's account of a nervous breakdown but insist it had been legitimate. She denied any memory of having denounced Karl in the process.[11]

As with many aspects of Ilse's case, an alternate and more salacious account of her behavior exists. A Nazi-era report on corruption at Buchenwald, written by Morgen in 1944, draws on testimony of various members of the camp SS to expand on the circumstances of Ilse's alleged breakdown as Karl's criminality came to light, and posits a far more nefarious scheme. According to this account, Ilse had been carrying on extramarital affairs with two SS men at Buchenwald—Protective Custody Commander Hermann Florstedt and Buchenwald Chief Physician Waldemar Hoven—and was motivated by their plotting. Allegedly, Florstedt, in an effort to pry Ilse away from her husband, had told her that Karl's shady financial activities were becoming open secrets, would soon be discovered, and would have terrible consequences. At the same time, Hoven, also trying to win her over, told Ilse of an illicit affair Karl was carrying on with a dancer in Weimar. The report contended that Ilse allegedly came to feel that it was time to save herself, realizing her husband's affections clearly lay elsewhere (as evidently did hers) and that his crimes might soon be discovered.[12]

This, Morgen wrote, was the circumstance that led to her breakdown. In front of Florstedt and Hoven, but also in the presence of a local SS police leader named Hennicke, she not only denounced Karl as a murderer, but also told them that there was money hidden throughout the Koch villa, and that she intended to go to Himmler, tell him everything she knew about her husband's corruption, and seek his protection. Florstedt and Hoven now felt the situation they had helped to create was getting out of hand. Florstedt had hoped to replace Karl as commandant, and Hoven wanted to secure Ilse's more permanent affections, but both now feared—especially as Himmler's name was raised—that unwanted attention would be drawn to their schemes and other activities of the camp SS. According to this account, Ilse's nervous breakdown was of Dr. Hoven's invention: to contain the damage of her unplanned outburst he advanced a diagnosis of hysteria and informed Hennicke that nothing Ilse said should be taken seriously. Florstedt meanwhile did his part by letting it be known that his affections for Ilse were limited, helping to convince her to reconcile with Karl and go along with the cover-up. While the report does not explicitly lay out the timing of these interactions, the presumption is that they coincided with Karl's release from prison and spurred Ilse to go back to him as he returned to a position that appeared to be safe after all.[13]

This more dramatic and sordid account of Ilse's reaction to Karl's arrest, although no longer verifiable, hints at a trend that would grow increasingly evident as Ilse's legal troubles mounted. With his 1944 report, Morgen was preparing the way for Ilse Koch's prosecution by emphasizing sexual desire and adulterous behavior as key motivators of her actions. As well as detailing her various extramarital affairs, Morgen refers to Ilse "wearing the pants" in her marriage to Karl, and describes Karl as having lived in "sexual bondage" to Ilse.[14] By attributing to Ilse a sort of omnipotent sexual attraction and insatiable sexual appetite he implied that the SS personnel with whom she was involved had merely given in to their natural urges as men. As will be seen, the tendency to cast Ilse's adulterous behavior and sexual hunger as evidence of a much deeper and more dangerous degeneracy became a common trope in her postwar trials, effectively used to bolster accusations of violent and depraved activities.

While a sparse documentary record and scant witness testimony prevent the painting of any complete picture of Waldeck's investigation and its aftermath, there can be little doubt that Karl owed his survival largely to Himmler's personal intervention. Karl's SS personnel file makes it abundantly clear that he was viewed by his superiors as a highly effective and ideologically committed commandant who had played a key and laudable role in the establishment of a number of the Reich's most infamous concentration camps.[15] That Karl may have used his post to enrich himself and his family appeared to be something Himmler was willing to overlook. Himmler, in fact, followed up his intervention on Karl's behalf with a decree that forbade any SS legal authorities from arresting the commanding officer of a concentration camp without an express order from the SS chief himself—a rule dubbed the *Lex Waldeck*.[16] In addition, Himmler's direct subordinate, SS Major General and Inspector of Concentration Camps Richard Glücks, appeared at Buchenwald to speak out on Karl's behalf and quash rumors of his misdeeds. All charges against Koch, Glücks insisted, had been the result of "malicious slander" and any who would dare speak "even the slightest word" against Koch in the future, he promised, would be punished.[17]

Despite intervening on his behalf, however, Himmler appears to have felt that having Karl continue to serve at Buchenwald under Waldeck's administrative authority would be a liability given both Karl's undeniable penchant for thievery and Waldeck's determination to stamp out corruption. As a result, Himmler forbade Karl from re-entering the Buchenwald camp compound after his release, and instead named SS-Senior Colonel Hermann Pister, former commandant of the Hinzert concentration camp, to take Karl's place.[18] Karl was reassigned to Lublin, Poland, to take charge of the Majdanek concentration camp on January 18, 1942, while Ilse and the children remained behind in the Koch villa at Buchenwald.[19] Although perhaps chastened by his transfer, Karl had good reason to believe he could still count on his SS superiors' full support as he took up his new post in Poland, and he made sure his subordinates knew it. Karl distributed copies of a letter he received following his arrest from SS Lieutenant General Oswald Pohl, chief of the SS Wirtschafts und Verwaltungshauptamt (Economic and Administrative Main Office) and the head administrator of the Nazi concentration camps. It read: "My Dear Comrade Koch: If at any time in the future any unemployed lawyer will stretch out his vicious hangman's hands after your innocent body, then I shall place myself in his way with all the strength of my personality, and woe be to him."[20]

Karl's leadership at Majdanek was marked by the excesses and cruelties that defined daily life in Nazi concentration camps. Set up in 1941 predominantly for Polish Jews, it also held Polish political prisoners, Soviet POWs, and other "enemies" of the Nazi state; Majdanek held some twenty-five thousand inmates at any given time.[21] Under Karl, most inmates at Majdanek slaved either in construction details to expand the camp or in workshops making everything from military uniforms to furniture to aircraft parts. Even though the gas chambers at the camp would not be installed until after his stint there, the death rate at Majdanek while Karl was commandant was astonishingly high. Owing to brutal conditions defined by disease, starvation, torturous slave labor, and outright mass killing, a full twenty-five percent of the camp population was dying per month by the autumn of 1942 according to existing fragments of the camp's death books.[22]

While initially Karl's governance of Majdanek raised few eyebrows, his reputation as the Third Reich's "best commandant" suffered a near fatal blow one summer night in 1942. On July 14 at around 11:15 PM, the enforced quiet of the Majdanek night was pierced briefly when eighty-six Soviet POWs rushed the barbed wire near the camp's latrine and used a ladder fashioned from scraps of wood to climb the fence and disappear into the fields of corn that surrounded the camp. Karl, who was informed of the escape by a phone call from prison compound commander Hermann Hackmann at 11:30, suddenly found himself at the center of a fiasco.[23] Hackmann initially told Karl that only fifteen to twenty had escaped, and ordered the troops to establish a roadblock to recapture the men, but none were apprehended. Perhaps trying to prevent word of the escape from getting out, Karl held off notifying the regional SS and police until five o'clock the next morning, by which time it was clear that the number of escapees had been substantially greater than first realized—and only once the escapees had had hours to flee. Two members of the camp guard had fired dozens of shots at the fleeing men, but managed to strike only two of the would-be fugitives while the rest vanished into the night.[24]

SS Authorities and the Pursuit of Karl Koch

Following the mass escape from Majdanek, a furious Heinrich Himmler ordered Karl relieved of his duties. Himmler also directed that an official investigation be undertaken to determine whether the incompetent handling of the outbreak constituted dereliction of duty.[25] In particular, Karl stood accused of failing to properly secure the camp compound, failure to provide a properly armed, trained, and competent camp guard, and failure to launch an immediate and effective response to the escape.[26] Attempting to save his career, Karl argued in his own defense that, because the camp was still under construction, the fences and guard towers were not completely ready—there was only one layer of barbed wire, and no alarm. As for his detail of camp guards, Karl insisted it was not his fault they were poorly trained, because he had received only old reservists who were barely fit for duty to begin with. Last, he argued that his slow response to the outbreak was appropriate given that he was not initially informed that the number of escapees was so high. More dubiously, Karl claimed in his favor that he had promptly discovered another escape plot among the Soviet POWs who had stayed behind—and had his guard shoot forty-one of these prisoners inside the fences of Majdanek.[27] An SS and police court in Berlin ultimately accepted Karl's defense and dismissed his case in 1943. Still, the incident helped to erode Himmler's faith in him, distancing Karl from a key ally on whose protection he depended.[28]

Following Karl's removal as commandant at Majdanek in the summer of 1942, he returned to Ilse and the children, who were still living in the villa at Buchenwald. It was there that he learned of his new and rather unglamorous assignment to command a postal protection unit near Saaz, Czechoslovakia. To his chagrin, he also confirmed what Ilse had already noticed: that Waldeck, despite all warnings from his SS superiors, had continued to snoop around and was quietly continuing his investigation into Koch family affairs. Waldeck's postwar testimony suggests that he had experienced Himmler's prior release of Koch as a humiliating rebuke to his authority that could be undone only by uncovering evidence of criminal behavior so damning that the SS leadership would be unable to brush it aside.[29] "In spite of the chewing out [from Himmler]," Waldeck later recalled, "I still left nothing untried to collect more evidence ... to get the case going again."[30]

It did not take long for Waldeck to stumble upon a piece of evidence that he hoped might implicate Karl: two suspicious entries in the Buchenwald death books concerning the apparent killing of the prisoners Walter Krämer and Karl Peix. According to various accounts of Waldeck's investigation provided after the war by both former SS men and Buchenwald survivors, Krämer and Peix were communist orderlies in the camp hospital who had treated Waldeck either for injuries sustained following an air raid or for a case of boils, depending on the account.[31] Recalling conversations with the men, Waldeck was now perturbed to see both listed as having been "shot while trying to escape" at different times on the same day. According to one account, Waldeck found the entries unconvincing because Krämer in particular had bad feet and was unlikely to flee. Another account holds that Waldeck knew both had been due for release soon and would not have risked their lives trying to escape.[32]

Though it would be more than a year before Waldeck would learn the true circumstances of the murders of Krämer and Peix, the suspicious circumstances of their deaths and a growing record of financial misdeeds at Buchenwald allowed him to build a dossier documenting "mistreatment of prisoners, gross fraud ... and further embezzlement."[33] This emboldened Waldeck to return with his new cache of evidence to Himmler, who granted permission to continue the investigation into Koch, but with a highly restricted mandate. Signaling that the reasons for killings in the concentration camps were not Waldeck's business, Himmler granted permission for an investigation "only concerning the charges about unauthorized profiteering."[34] With this official but restricted mandate, Waldeck resumed his exploration of Karl Koch's tenure at Buchenwald, limited as it also was by the fact that Karl had departed for Saaz, along with much of the evidence of his malfeasance. For the first time, Waldeck now added Ilse Koch to the list of suspects, surmising that she was knowingly benefiting from her husband's theft.

It may be that Himmler would not have been so willing to allow Waldeck to proceed anew with his investigation at Buchenwald if Karl Koch had not already done much to erode the SS chief's support, but the decision was also in keeping with a broader trend to clamp down on the sort of corruption in the ranks that generally had been overlooked until the middle years of the war. In the summer of 1942, a series of incidents indicated a new resolve to root out SS corruption in the concentration camps. The commandant at Dachau, Alex Piorkowski, was investigated for corruption, demoted, and suspended from duty on Himmler's orders; at Sachsenhausen, an investigation into the personal enrichment of commandant Hans Loritz led to his sacking as well.[35] Unfortunately for Karl, one effect of the Reich's protracted war effort was heightened sensitivity to shifting public opinion within Germany as conditions on the home front worsened and progress on the battlefields slowed. Hitler now insisted on exemplary behavior from the Reich's leading figures, concerned that revelations of corruption could further undercut the popular support the regime had previously enjoyed.[36] Himmler conveyed similar sentiments to a gathering of SS officers during a notorious speech in Posen, Poland, in 1943. Describing the mass killing of Europe's Jews as a defensive action that constituted a sacred undertaking, Himmler warned that thievery had the power to undercut the moral underpinnings of the genocide. "We had the moral right, we had the duty to our people," Himmler proclaimed, "to destroy this people which wanted to destroy us. But we have not the right to enrich ourselves with so much as a fur, a watch, a mark, a cigarette or anything else." Any SS men breaking this rule, Himmler declared, "will die without mercy!"[37]

When Waldeck resumed his investigation of Karl Koch, therefore, the mood within the SS had changed, as Himmler signaled he was now less willing to tolerate corruption within the ranks. Although Waldeck initially struggled to gain traction in his renewed efforts against Karl, his investigation received an unexpected boost in the early summer of 1943. That June, the SS and Police Court in Kassel was busy with a separate case of suspected corruption at Buchenwald and had requested that the Reich Criminal Police send someone to investigate. Under these auspices, the SS judge Konrad Morgen entered Buchenwald for the first time. Assiduous and arrogant, Morgen had entered the SS and the Nazi Party in the spring of 1933, and first served as an SS judge when he accepted a posting to the SS Court Main Office in 1940.[38] Though Morgen later would attempt to cast himself as an anti-Holocaust crusader and "fanatic for justice" who used whatever legal power he had during the Third Reich to undermine the Nazi machinery of destruction, the documentary record reveals a deeply committed SS man whose anticorruption campaign stemmed not from humanitarian impulses but from a desire to protect the "honor" of the institution he served and loved.[39] Morgen, it seemed, embodied the values espoused by Himmler at Posen.

Morgen arrived at Buchenwald with a reputation as an anticorruption crusader following his tenure as a judge in the SS and Police Court in Cracow beginning in January 1941.[40] It had been at Cracow, according to his postwar recollections, that he first witnessed the graft, rampant embezzlement, and black-marketing endemic to the local SS elite. Across a series of anticorruption cases launched by Morgen, high-level arrests were made and trials ended with more than one execution. Nevertheless, Morgen grew disillusioned in Cracow, especially when Heinrich Himmler stepped in to put an end to the anticorruption case Morgen was building against one of the SS leader's most trusted men, SS cavalry commander Hermann Fegelein.[41] For reasons that are no longer clear, Morgen was briefly demoted after leaving Poland, then reassigned by Himmler in May 1943 as a judge and "anticorruption specialist" in the Reich Criminal Police Office.[42] It was in this capacity that Morgen first arrived at Buchenwald.

The particular case that brought Morgen to Buchenwald did not concern Karl or Ilse Koch, but instead involved allegations that the SS chief procurement officer, Thilo Bornschein, had embezzled foodstuffs and sold them on the black market—a case Morgen found to be without merit.[43] Over the course of the weeks Morgen spent at Buchenwald investigating Bornschein, however, he purportedly was shocked at the evidence, discovered "by coincidence" of deep corruption, graft, and embezzlement by former commandant Koch and his cronies.[44] According to his postwar recollections, Morgen followed up on his own initiative and by questioning members of the camp SS and searching the houses of SS men on Koch's personal staff was able to discover small fortunes of cash and gold and evidence of hidden bank accounts. Though the sources of this wealth would be hard to

Fig. 2.3   Konrad Morgen's Nazi Party membership book. Courtesy Archive of the Fritz Bauer Institute, Estate Konrad Morgen, ML Morgen-49.

trace, Morgen concluded that much of this bounty must have been confiscated from inmates upon arrival. Rather than send on confiscated currency and goods to Berlin as required, Koch and his most loyal underlings had taken them as their own, living lavish lifestyles that their regular salaries, Morgen observed, would not have allowed.

Before his removal from command, Karl had even bought a fancy car.[45] Whispers of a black market at Buchenwald and an illicit trade in luxury goods produced by prisoners at Karl's behest also reached Morgen's ears.

Morgen immediately identified a number of Karl's men implicated in these schemes and had them arrested.[46] At the same time, he presented his findings to Waldeck, whose earlier investigative efforts and evidentiary materials Morgen now built upon. With Waldeck's full support, Morgen reported back to SS authorities in Berlin in July 1943 and requested permission to lead a more muscular investigation into what he described as a "corruption complex" at Buchenwald spearheaded by Karl Koch.[47] Morgen's timing, it appears, was perfect. By now, Himmler clearly had lost all appetite for shielding Karl, having recently referred to him as "tired and lazy," and openly musing about sending him to fight at the front.[48]

Morgen's findings therefore found a receptive audience in SS-Senior Colonel Bender, the high-ranking judge attached directly to Himmler's office. According to Morgen's recollections, he presented Bender with evidence of "extensive crimes being committed in the concentration camps," including at Majdanek, that warranted "the carrying out of a broad general investigation" that he now wished to lead.[49] Bender, Morgen later recalled, replied that it was a "very fortunate coincidence" that Morgen had come at that very moment, because Himmler had just decided to close all proceedings against Karl Koch. Instead, Himmler had resolved that Karl "should be made to give up his illicit bartering, should be reduced from . . . colonel to the rank of a major, and should be placed at the disposal of Lieutenant General Pitzin in the East for the construction of roads."[50] Morgen, however, persuaded Bender that Himmler should be convinced that the proposed punishment was not sufficient, given how grave the crimes discovered during his preliminary investigation actually were. In the end, the evidence of suspected financial malfeasance that

Morgen presented produced the desired outcome, and must have left Waldeck feeling immensely vindicated. As Morgen later explained, "I received, upon report to the Reich criminal police officer, to the main SS-court office, and to the SS judge attached to the Reich leader of the SS, SS Senior Colonel Bender, an order and authority to conduct a new investigation and to arrest the accused."[51]

Morgen's Investigative Commission at Buchenwald

Morgen now had official backing to investigate "unauthorized personal gains and unauthorized mistreatments and killings of inmates carried out . . . for personal reasons."[52] In his postwar testimony, Morgen sought to underscore that while this mandate put Karl and Ilse Koch in his crosshairs, his hands were tied when it came to "killings and mistreatments in the form of executions through shooting, hanging, gassing, corporal punishment, third-degree interrogations, experiments withholding food and refusal of medical care, that had been ordered by the highest Reich authorities." Such acts, Morgen explained, fell outside his authority for three reasons—because they were "political acts [that] were not under the jurisdiction of legal review," because "the actions were not wrongful according to the National Socialist system," and because the authorization for such acts ultimately lay with Hitler himself, whose decisions were beyond scrutiny. It was "only because Koch and his circle had set himself beyond the order of the concentration camp," Morgen continued, that "he became punishable and it was possible to prosecute."[53]

This rather convenient claim implies that Morgen would have stood in the way of state-sponsored murder at Buchenwald if only he had had the authority, but there is little evidence to support this idea. While Morgen's account broadly jibes with the postwar testimony of Waldeck and others involved in the investigation, it also served to provide him with an internally consistent defense of his own response to the brutality of the concentration camp system, rooting his apparent indifference in his alleged fidelity to the law.[54] In Morgen's Nazi world-view, the concentration camp had become "a thing of horror" not because of its state-sanctioned regimen of torture and deprivation, but because of the presence of "unrestrained criminals" among the SS who acted against the interests of the Reich.[55] And so, while Morgen would claim at war's end that his investigative efforts threw a monkey wrench into the concentration camp system and helped to save the lives "of thousands of prisoners," there is no evidence that concern for the general sufferings of the camp population propelled him.[56]

Driven primarily by his zeal to root out SS corruption in the interest of its more efficient operation, Morgen was rewarded with an expansive mandate and sweeping investigatory powers not only at Buchenwald, but throughout the Nazi concentration camp system as a whole.[57] This authority, officially bestowed by Himmler's office, allowed Morgen to pursue the Kochs and their accomplices free of the sort of obstruction that had hampered Waldeck's earlier efforts. He was granted a small staff and comfortable office within Buchen-wald, complete with a telex machine and use of the camp's communication systems and courier service. Later, Morgen would describe himself sitting "like a spider in its web," watching daily affairs in the camp while inviting various suspects and witnesses to converse behind closed doors and make statements.[58] Morgen also examined Karl's affairs during his tenures at other concentration camps, establishing investigative commissions at Majdanek and Sachsenhausen that were directed to send dispatches of their findings back to Buchenwald.[59] He quickly learned that Karl's unpopularity with his own rank and file led some to cooperate with the investigation enthusiastically; for others, especially among the higher echelons of the camp SS, Morgen's eight-month stint at Buchenwald generated substantial anxiety and raised fears about who might be implicated next in Koch's crimes.[60]

Morgen's first order of business was to conduct a thorough inspection of the camp. His fanciful postwar recollections of his impressions of Buchenwald again appear crafted to insulate him from moral, if not legal, complicity in the suffering and death he surely observed. Entering Buchenwald, Morgen insisted, entailed a "great surprise." The camp was "situated on wooded heights with a wonderful view. . . . There was much lawn and flowers. The prisoners were healthy, normally fed, suntanned." Morgen contended that rations were so good at Buchenwald that "the majority of prisoners certainly had it better than the majority of the civilian population."[61] "During the time I was interned in American camps [after the war]," Morgen continued, "I met many former prisoners who wished for the old days when they were in German concentration camps."[62] The fraudulence of these perverse claims is laid bare by the fact that over the course of 1943 and 1944, some twelve thousand prisoners died at Buchenwald, many from diseases linked to the horrific conditions and starvation rations Morgen refused to acknowledge.[63] Morgen's rosy picture of the camp in a period when crematory ovens burned night and day stands very much in line with his fidelity to the SS and the postwar attempts he would make to shield the SS from criticism and from implication in the Reich's most notorious crimes.[64] Morgen pursued Koch not because he had run a murderous institution but because he had hampered its effective operation, and threatened to sully the image of the "decency" and "loyalty" of the SS with his corruption.

Once Morgen had familiarized himself thoroughly with the camp, he sought to use the authority granted by his SS superiors to seek Karl's return to Buchenwald for questioning. Morgen later recalled, however, that tracking down the former commandant was no easy matter. He first wrote to Karl's superior officer requesting that Karl be ordered to return immediately to Buchenwald from his postal protection unit in Saaz. Koch never arrived. Morgen then learned that Koch was visiting Berlin, and arranged for him to be escorted to the appropriate train to Weimar, where he was to be picked up at the station. This time, Morgen was informed that Koch hadn't appeared at the appointed time, and had soon after been spotted in his car speeding toward Buchenwald. He was pursued, but then turned off the main road to the camp and managed to disappear down a forest path.

Morgen, by now furious, thought that perhaps Karl had returned to the Koch villa at Buchenwald with the intention of hiding or destroying evidence, and decided to go there accompanied by an SS and police court judge, Werner Paulmann.[65] In a rather melodramatic postwar account of Karl's arrest, Morgen described what happened next:

> We went to his villa. It was now past midnight. Pitch black. Not a sound. Nothing. His car was nowhere to be seen. All quiet. Nothing moved. I took the heel of my boot and banged on the door. Nothing! Suddenly we heard a shuffling of feet. A thunderstorm began. Lightning flashed. Very dramatic. Paulmann said, "Get your gun ready, there's going to be shooting." And then he appeared. In a dressing gown, cool and calm. He asked, "What do you want?" Paulmann said, "We're taking you for interrogation, you better get dressed right away." "Yes," he said, "I just got home and wanted to freshen up." He had driven there and wanted to hear from his wife what was going on in Buchenwald. I had had this woman's phone tapped and mail intercepted, and she had probably noticed something. . . . And then I questioned him all night. The slyest fox I've ever seen and ice cold! Without any human feeling. . . . He answered very, very cautiously and had an explanation for everything. I did not believe much of what he said so I arrested him.[66]

With no further delay, Morgen informed his superiors at the SS Leadership Main Office in Berlin that Karl had been taken into custody

Fig. 2.4   The Koch villa at Buchenwald. Ilse Koch's Personal Album 2, Records of the Office of the Judge Advocate General (Army), Record Group 153, National Archives and Records Administration.

on August 24, 1943, in accordance with the prior approval of SS chief Heinrich Himmler. "Highly suspected of embezzlement, the forgery and destruction of documents, intimidating and threatening officials, and other serious offenses," Karl Koch, Morgen's telex reported, was now in the Gestapo prison in Weimar.[67]

Though Morgen's postwar account of Karl's arrest makes no mention of Ilse's presence that night, she did not escape his attention for long. The day after Karl's arrest, Morgen returned to the Koch villa and conducted a thorough search with the assistance of Criminal Chief Secretary Heinrich Nett from the Reich's criminal police, as well as new Buchenwald commandant Hermann Pister and the camp's chief administrative officer, Otto Barnewald. As Himmler had some months earlier ordered the Kochs to vacate the residence, the contents of the household were for the most part already packed and awaiting relocation to Saaz.[68] All was now seized instead and carefully cataloged, presumably leaving the house virtually empty. Once the search was complete, Ilse was arrested as an accessory to her husband's crimes, for the possible destruction of evidence, and for an unspecified "utterance directed against the state."[69] She later testified:

> They came to me early in the morning at nine o'clock. [Morgen] said he had to search the house by order of [Himmler]. The house was turned around from top to bottom. I don't think there was a spot in it that was not searched. . . . I asked him what the cause of the search was and I did not receive a proper answer. I was arrested the same day.[70]

So began sixteen months of incarceration for both Ilse and Karl, while Morgen continued his investigation and prepared a case for trial. Chief Criminal Secretary Nett arranged for the Koch children, Artwin and Gisela, to be sent to Saaz and placed in the care of Karl's stepsister, Erna Raible.[71]

According to Nett, who assisted Morgen throughout the investigation, the real work began only after Karl and Ilse's arrests. Morgen and his team sought to interview any inmates with knowledge of the corrupt schemes Koch and his cronies had engaged in, but quickly found this to be a great challenge. With good reason, Buchenwald prisoners feared retribution for speaking up about SS corruption or denouncing the behavior of their overlords—especially to an SS judge. Morgen later claimed that he attempted to solve this problem by assuring the prisoners that "finally an office had been found which would take care of their sufferings," that they would be protected, and that "steps would be taken against the persons who were guilty with all energy and no holds barred." Morgen even professed to have received permission from Himmler to release inmates whose testimony was particularly helpful.[72] Given Morgen's postwar propensity for masquerading as an opponent of the official violence of the concentration camp system, and in the absence of any evidence that such releases occurred, such claims must be taken with a grain of salt.

Whatever inducements Morgen offered in exchange for the testimony of the handful of prisoner-witnesses who ultimately participated in his investigation, they were not sufficient to offset the risks of co-operating.[73] At first, Morgen had doubted reports of the unauthorized killing of inmates at the hands of corrupt SS men and found it very difficult to substantiate Waldeck's earlier suspicions that such killings had occurred. As Morgen later explained, he came to share these suspicions when he noticed that a number of potential witnesses he sought to question regarding knowledge of SS corruption were suddenly reported to have died:

> The files themselves offered no clues to suspect illegal killings. . . . In each case, different causes of death were given. But it struck me that the majority of these deceased prisoners had been put into the camp hospital or in the arrest [bunker] before their death. . . . Only by chance did I hit upon the first clue; it struck me that the names of certain prisoners were listed at the same time in the rolls of the camp prison as well as in those of the camp hospital. In the prison rolls, for example, it said, "Date of release 9 May, 12 o'clock." In the hospital register, "Patient died 9 May, 9:15 a.m." . . . False entries must have been made here. . . . I succeeded in getting behind this system, for it was a system, under Commander Koch. The prisoners were taken to a secret place and were killed there . . . and sick reports and death certificates were prepared for the files.[74]

With this "system" in mind, Morgen reexamined the case that had caught Waldeck's attention the previous year: the killing of the two communist inmates from the camp infirmary, Krämer and Peix. Both were marked as "shot while trying to escape" in the death register, but

Morgen discovered evidence directly linking their murders to Karl Koch. Morgen learned that Karl had ordered the camp's political department to investigate Krämer and Peix and to arrive at charges, but they had failed. As a result, Karl ordered that the men be quietly transferred to a work detail at Goslar and then executed on the flimsy pretext that they had conducted political discussions in the infirmary.[75] According to Morgen, the two men were ordered to fetch water from a well and were shot from behind by SS Master Sergeant Johann Blank.[76]

Curiously, Morgen provided two different accounts of Karl's motive for the killing. In his 1944 report on the findings of his investigation at Buchenwald that sought to underscore financial crimes, Morgen explained that Karl's reasons for the killings were unknown but likely stemmed from a need to conceal knowledge of his corruption.[77] Testifying before an American military court at Dachau in 1947, however, Morgen appears to have modified his account by incorporating the version of events that prominent Buchenwald survivor Eugen Kogon provided in his popular 1946 history of the camp, *Der SS-Staat.* As Kogon had relayed from the accounts of well-placed former inmates, Morgen now testified that Krämer and Peix had been killed because they were in possession of an embarrassing truth: the two men had successfully treated Karl with the drug Salvarsan for a case of syphilis he had acquired while in Norway.[78] Whatever the true motive for the killing, Morgen was confident that Karl was guilty of murder. As always, Morgen's primary concern was not the killing in and of itself, but the fact that the killing had been unauthorized and was committed to conceal Karl's misdeeds. On these grounds executioner Blank was also arrested, but he committed suicide rather than face the prospect of an SS trial.[79]

The lengths to which Karl's accomplices would go to silence those with knowledge of their crimes appear to have extended beyond Buchenwald's inmates to their fellow members of the camp SS. In the autumn of 1943, Morgen had sought testimony from SS-Master Sergeant Rudolf Köhler, who allegedly had knowledge of the killing of two other prisoner-witnesses by the chief camp doctor, Waldemar Hoven.[80] Upon requesting an interview with Köhler, Morgen learned that he had been found in a semiconscious state, likely having ingested poison. Morgen raced to Köhler, whom he found lying "like a shadow," and who denied any attempt at suicide.[81] He soon died. Morgen arrested Hoven on suspicion of murder, and ordered an autopsy on Köhler that detected "poisons of the alkaloid group" in his stomach.[82] Morgen's next move illustrated his utter contempt for the life of Buchenwald's inmates: he ordered that an experiment be carried out on four Soviet prisoners who were to be secretly given the same chemical compound in varying amounts, allegedly to ascertain what constituted a lethal dose.[83] In an affidavit submitted after the war, Morgen did not deny ordering the experiment, which was confirmed in diary entries by SS-Major Erwin Ding-Schuler, the doctor who carried it out.[84] Instead, Morgen sought to clarify that the men had already been sentenced to death for other crimes, and he provided the unlikely explanation that the purpose of the experiment "was not to injure the subjects, but was to show that this combination of drugs would *not* result in injuries."[85] Though Morgen and his team had been certain that Köhler was murdered, they were unable to gather sufficient evidence to warrant building a new case.[86]

The Indictment of Karl and Ilse Koch

Despite various setbacks and pitfalls, Morgen and his team managed to carry out dozens of interviews, interrogations, searches, and examinations of camp records between August 1943 and April 1944, and produced a substantial report on corruption and murder at Buchenwald. The document, purportedly distilling more than four thousand pages of evidentiary material into its eighty-seven pages, lays out the

charges against Karl Koch, Ilse Koch, and two senior SS men implicated in killings on Karl's behalf: SS captain and chief camp doctor
Waldemar Hoven, and arrest bunker chief and SS Master Sergeant
Martin Sommer.[87] Morgen later explained that while Karl "had surrounded himself with a staff of criminals," he sought the prosecution
of only the most implicated and high-ranking of his men.[88] As explained in the opening pages of his report, evidence of a huge web of
criminality at Buchenwald had been unearthed, but he had limited
his focus to specific crimes that he could most easily prove and that
were sufficient to yield for the culprits "the punishment they deserve."
Each of the suspects, Morgen wrote, was "a mass-murderer in his own
right." For Karl Koch in particular, there was "no punishment severe
enough to match his guilt."[89] The report, submitted April 11, 1944, is
the most concrete documentary record of what Morgen actually did
at Buchenwald, including whom he sought to charge, what crimes he
sought to punish, and what evidence he was able to assemble in support of his case. It established the basis for the official SS indictment
of Karl and Ilse Koch, and for the SS trial they would soon face.

The first half of Morgen's report, subtitled "The Corruption
Complex," lays out Karl Koch's financial misdeeds in painstaking
detail, while Ilse's alleged crimes appear at the document's end. Reconstructing Karl's financial history, Morgen shows that when he assumed the leadership of Buchenwald in 1937, he had a total of only
17.60 reichsmarks (RM) in his bank account. By the time Morgen's
investigation began in 1943, however, Karl had amassed a personal
fortune of over 100,000 RM, even though his annual salary never ex-
ceeded 12,000 RM. Allowing for his annual costs, and a history of
withdrawals of approximately 10,000 RM per year, Morgen concluded
that no less than 78,000 RM of Karl's wealth was unaccounted
for—the equivalent today of nearly half a million dollars.[90] Morgen
also discovered expensive collections of art, stamps, and furniture,
as well as fine wine, fine clothing, and fine perfumes for Ilse. Morgen

noted Karl's spending on lovers in Weimar and Norway, and on treatment for the syphilis he had acquired through his liaisons.[91] Karl, Morgen explained, had hastily dumped a large quantity of illicit cash when the investigation began via donations to a popular charity—the Winterhilfswerk des Deutschen Volkes (Winter Relief of the German People). Morgen, however, uncovered this ruse, while also discovering secret bank accounts that Karl could provide no reasonable explanation for keeping.[92]

The sources of Karl's wealth, Morgen explained, could be traced first of all to the November 1938 "Judenaktion"—the nationwide anti-Jewish pogrom now known as Kristallnacht—that for the first time brought large numbers of Jews to Buchenwald.[93] Morgen claimed that concentration camp authorities had been directed to confiscate all valuables that arrived with these prisoners, to catalog them in front of a witness, to put them in storage, and to provide a receipt to their original owners. Instead, Karl saw to it that these Jewish prisoners threw their valuables into open boxes unregistered and were forced to sign forms stating that they had arrived at Buchenwald with nothing of value. Beatings were used to ensure all funds were extracted and flowed directly to Karl and his men.[94]

Beyond the outright theft that occurred following Kristallnacht, Morgen detailed how Karl and his cronies sold food to prisoners at a huge markup; how prisoners were forced to make "donations" for various camp enterprises; how those deemed to be violating rules were obliged to pay fines or invited to buy their way out of beatings; how the dental gold was extracted from the dead in their ever increasing numbers at the crematoria; and how craftsmen who entered Buchenwald as prisoners were put to work making everything from fine watches to ceramics to family portraits for the SS staff.[95] Karl had even worked in cahoots with one favored prisoner named Meiners who had extensive connections with the black market. Meiners was allowed to wear tailored civilian clothes and travel as far as Munich in a car

Karl provided to buy and sell on behalf of the camp SS.[96] Karl initially denied his financial crimes under questioning, but Morgen's repeated interrogations eventually exacted a confession to the comparatively smaller crime of embezzling some 20,000 RM. "I don't have an explanation for my behavior," Morgen's report quotes Karl as stating. "Only that I have been spoiled by my superiors. Everything which I proposed and did was sanctioned. I always got praise and won laurels. No one criticized my actions. This went to my head. I became a megalomaniac."[97]

Morgen's report also leveled charges against Karl Koch of an even more serious variety, asserting his central role in the arbitrary abuse and killing of inmates. Morgen wrote incredulously about Karl's violations of the rules of conduct allegedly spelled out by SS leadership for the imposition of corporal punishments in the concentration camps and the protocol to be followed in the event of an inmate's death. Morgen's invocation of these rules reveal him to have been an SS man either remarkably naive in his presumed belief that such rules were followed elsewhere, or cynical in his invocation of these otherwise disregarded rules as he pursued Karl. Morgen repeated, for instance, SS rules stating that every death in a concentration camp must be reported to the personal staff of Himmler and to the family of the victim, and that any unnatural death required an autopsy and an investigation to ascertain whether criminal charges were warranted.[98] Under Karl's command, however, "it was common for prisoners to be continuously killed in different ways, in a clandestine fashion without central command."[99] Morgen's report lists no fewer than 160 unauthorized killings in the camp infirmary administered by Hoven, and scores in the arrest bunker carried out by Sommer, largely on orders given by the commandant.[100] Believing it unnecessary to elaborate in his report on such a large number of killings, Morgen documented Karl's role in only three particular cases: the killings of Krämer and Peix in the camp infirmary, and the killing of another prisoner named Wendel, who had assisted Karl at Majdanek and evidently had come to know too much about his affairs.

Karl, Morgen concluded, had created an atmosphere of terror at Buchenwald rich in atrocity. Morgen even pointed to the endless roll calls that had prisoners standing daily for hours and in all conditions, although this was common practice in all concentration camps. "Many people told Koch that this treatment was not justified and did not exist in other camps. Koch disregarded these people and called them sissies. He was proud to be known as the most notorious concentration camp commandant."[101]

Morgen's accusations against Ilse similarly began with financial matters and the forceful claim that she was "no better than her husband with regard to greed, arrogance, and cruelty."[102] As he had done with Karl, Morgen first laid out evidence of large sums of money that could not be accounted for legitimately. Ilse, Morgen wrote, had had only 121 RM in savings in 1938, yet bank accounts set up for her and the Koch children contained 25,000 RM when the investigation commenced in 1943.[103] According to Morgen, Ilse claimed total ignorance of the sources of the immense wealth Karl brought to her and the household and professed no knowledge of basic family finances, even regarding how much her husband earned. Morgen juxtaposed her claims with descriptions of lavish expenditures, including for the riding hall that had been built at Buchenwald at enormous cost and solely for her pleasure. Ilse, Morgen argued, "must have noticed that this immense increase in wealth . . . could not have been come by honestly."[104] Resorting to gender stereotypes that would echo throughout Ilse's legal odyssey, Morgen explained that "especially as a woman she [also] should have taken notice of . . . and been suspicious of" the fine furniture, textiles, clothes, and housewares that filled the Koch villa.[105]

To undermine Ilse's claims that she was merely a housewife unaware of her husband's affairs, Morgen provided evidence that she had owned keys to her husband's office and helped keep his working schedule. Further, Morgen wrote that intercepted letters from Ilse showed how "the criminal couple worked together."[106] Ilse had petitioned Karl's superiors to have him reinstated as commandant of Buchenwald, and had also sought to undermine the ongoing investigation against him by denouncing those who led it. Such activities, Morgen argued, unambiguously contradicted Ilse's claims to have occupied a separate sphere wholly divorced from her husband's professional—and criminal—life.

To further challenge Ilse's professions of naivete and innocence, Morgen drew her character into question, in part by reconstructing her extramarital affairs and the machinations that surrounded them. Morgen reported on her illicit relationships with Florstedt and Hoven, and how those two had sought to draw Ilse away from Karl by convincing her that his downfall was imminent. Her alleged nervous breakdown which followed had seen Ilse denouncing Karl as a murderer and a thief who had secret bank accounts and money stashed throughout the house. Although Ilse quickly recanted these claims when the charges that resulted from the initial investigation of Karl did not stick, Morgen proceeded to use these statements to challenge her claim that she had remained oblivious to Karl's misdeeds. Morgen delved even further into Ilse's family affairs, writing that her cruelty and arrogance were "especially noticeable in her behavior toward her mother," who lived in "dire conditions" and yet was "not given enough to eat" while visiting the Koch family.[107] He maintained that Ilse was "the most hated person" at Buchenwald in part because she was so arrogant that "she did not even greet the wives of other commanders."[108] Morgen's attempt to imply guilt by highlighting flaws in character unconnected to crimes under the law foreshadowed strategies that would be used later to convict Ilse in court. In Morgen's mind, criminal corruption was intimately tied to moral corruption; that Ilse violated moral standards of decency and fidelity as a wife and mother was to him all the more reprehensible.[109]

Given the violent and perverse crimes that Ilse would stand accused of in postwar American and German courts, it is worth noting the conclusion of Morgen's report that Ilse should be prosecuted only for "benefiting from the proceeds of crime, and the habitual receiving of stolen goods."[110] Although Morgen attributes acts of violence to her, he appears to have found the anecdotal evidence too sparse to support an indictment. Morgen does report that Ilse added to the terror of the Koch era at Buchenwald through her sexual provocations and targeting of prisoners for beatings. As Morgen wrote, "she tried to excite sexually deprived prisoners through sex appeal, or provocative clothes and sunbathing. Whenever a prisoner looked at her, she remembered his number and asked her husband to give him twenty-five cane strokes."[111] Morgen quotes an SS witness who had heard Ilse say to a prisoner as she was riding past, "look at me again if you want to risk your ass."[112] As the indictment of Karl Koch, Hoven, and Sommer illustrates, Morgen was perfectly willing to press charges for unauthorized abuses of concentration camp prisoners where the evidence warranted. That Ilse would emerge at war's end as perhaps the most potent symbol of the cruelties of the concentration camp system while the names of her co-accused—implicated in mass murder—remained largely unknown would surely have struck Morgen as bizarre in 1944.

On August 17, 1944, Morgen issued formal indictments of Karl and Ilse Koch, Waldemar Hoven, and Martin Sommer that set the stage for a trial before the SS and Police Court in Weimar. Karl was, the indictment stated, "highly suspected of ... particularly egregious fraud and breach of trust with his superiors through the embezzlement and concealing of funds and goods in an amount of at least 200,000 RM that he himself took or gave to third parties at the expense of the Reich." Further, Karl had, "in an especially grave manner, practiced continuous military disobedience by not obeying orders ... and thereby willfully endangered the security of the Reich, and managed the camps contrary to his orders and in a fashion undermining to public morale." Finally, Morgen charged that Karl, "with malicious intent and means dangerous to public safety" had "premeditated the murder of at least the prisoners Krämer and Peix on November 6, 1941, in Goslar and the prisoner Wendel in the year 1942 in Lublin." The charge against Ilse was briefer: "Frau Koch," the indictment stated, "is highly suspected . . . to be guilty of the habitual receiving of stolen goods, and taking for her benefit at least 25,000 RM and goods totaling 46,000 RM that she had to assume, according to the circumstances, were procured by illegal means." Both Sommer and Hoven were charged with various counts of murder, as well as breaches of military discipline.[113] Within a matter of weeks, the trial would be underway.

The SS Trial of Karl and Ilse Koch

At first glance, the idea of an SS trial focused on the prosecution of fraud, theft, and the murder and abuse of prisoners in the concentration camps may appear surprising, if not absurd. The Nazi state is often depicted as unrestrained by the rule of law, typified by arbitrary and unchecked terror. Yet while terror was undoubtedly one of the central features of the Nazi era, it would be wrong to see the Third Reich as inherently lawless. Indeed, the state-sanctioned violence and plunder that occurred between 1933 and 1945 depended not only on the circumvention of the traditional German legal code, but also on its cooption and "Nazification" to reflect the values and priorities of the new regime.[114] Murder and theft remained indictable offenses. The Third Reich, as contemporary observer and legal scholar Ernst Fraenkel influentially argued, can be conceptualized as evolving into a dual state, where the traditional legal order (including the German penal code and court system) remained largely intact, if increasingly infused with Nazi laws and personnel. This "normative" state coexisted alongside the "prerogative state," by which arbitrary power was wielded by the regime, often in pursuit of its more ideological goals.[115] This duality guaranteed that irony and contradiction would be constant features of the Nazi legal order. The case of Karl and Ilse Koch provides a remarkable illustration that this tension between the rule of law and arbitrary power extended even into the concentration camp system and through the senior ranks of the SS.

The Extraordinary SS and Police Court that would hear the case against Ilse and Karl Koch was designed expressly to hear particularly sensitive cases concerning the activities of members of the SS and police forces in Germany and throughout occupied territories. The SS and police courts were not connected to the regular Reich judiciary, but were venues unto themselves with legal jurisdiction that superseded that of any civilian court, and provided the only avenue for the trial of SS personnel for breaches of the law in the course of their duties.[116] Without a penal code of their own, these courts relied upon both civil and military legal codes, as well as less easily defined SS values, such as honor, decency, and loyalty.[117] The role of the judges who presided over SS courtrooms was therefore substantially different than what was expected of traditional judges assessing arguments and applying the law. Instead, SS judges were equally to play the role of a political and ideological vanguard, with principle often taking precedence over the letter of the law.[118] This court system therefore exemplified the tension between unrestrained ideological commitments on the one hand, and a need to fall back on statutory law on the other. The fundamental objective of court proceedings under the Nazis was similarly shaped by ideological considerations. As the Reich's propaganda minister, Joseph Goebbels, framed the purpose of a legal judgment, it was not to obtain recompense for a wrong or to rehabilitate a criminal but instead to ensure the preservation of the state.[119] In the SS and police courts, the typical preoccupation was with property crimes, which constituted 42 percent of all cases tried.[120] As Himmler had declared at Posen, SS corruption had the potential to fundamentally undercut the "moral" foundations of SS programs and to erode popular support for the regime more generally. The court proceedings launched against Karl and Ilse Koch with Himmler's blessing are symptomatic of this anxiety.

As the Koch case helps to illustrate, however, Himmler's proclaimed insistence on a "clean" SS did not mean that the SS marched in lockstep to root out corruption within its ranks. Instead, the nepotism and patronage that dominated the SS created bonds of personal loyalty that cut across lines of authority and complicated investigations. Indeed, the legal pursuit of Karl and Ilse Koch remained perilous for those involved. Few in the higher echelons of the SS hierarchy wanted to see their virtually unchecked power—especially in the occupied territories and in the concentration camps—curtailed by a new insistence on accountability and the rule of law. According to Morgen, SS-Lieutenant General Oswald Pohl, head of the SS Economic and Administrative Main Office and chief administrator of the concentration camps, led a relentless campaign to convince Himmler to halt the investigations into SS corruption that the Koch case had spurred. Pohl, after attempting to use his authority to personally stand in the way of such investigations with limited impact, argued forcefully that they sullied the good name of the SS, "agitated" the concentration camps too much, threatened the "discipline of the detainees," and obstructed the noble work of his men. The process could snowball out of control, he warned Himmler, and eventually he could be unable to guarantee security in the camps. Pohl, whom Morgen characterized as deeply corrupt and concerned only for his own position, insisted to Himmler that the Koch trial should bring an end to such investigations for the good of the SS, and that Morgen in particular should be removed from office.[121]

As the opening of Karl and Ilse's trial approached, it appears that Pohl's arguments had begun to have their desired effect on Himmler, who now began to second-guess the wisdom of pursuing such cases further. Morgen was informed in the middle of 1944 that he would be able to hold onto his position for a few more months, but that once the forthcoming trial of Karl and Ilse Koch was complete no new investigations would be permitted.[122] A date in early September 1944 was set for the trial before the Extraordinary SS and Police Court in Weimar. Morgen later remembered Himmler envisioning Karl's probable execution and how the occasion could be used to send a spectacular warning to any other SS leaders inclined toward corruption:

> Himmler wanted to make a speech at the gallows under Karl's dangling feet. All of the concentration camp commanders should gather for this. They should be urgently lectured at night under torchlight. This is how the romantic Himmler had imagined it. And then they should confess what they had committed. Those who confessed should be set free without punishment. But those who committed an offense after this point should be shot.[123]

Morgen's account of Himmler's attitude was broadly consistent with the SS leader's prior pronouncements at Posen and suggests that, despite Himmler's key role in permitting legal proceedings against Karl and Ilse Koch to proceed, he had misgivings about the benefits of a formal trial. His preference lay instead with the extrajudicial approach to criminal behavior within the SS that the totalitarian state allowed.

When the SS proceedings against Karl and Ilse Koch finally began, both already had languished in the Gestapo prison in Weimar for more than a year in conditions that codefendant Martin Sommer later remembered as abysmal.[124] Karl, Sommer recalled, managed initially to secure the only one of the six basement cells with a flush toilet, while Ilse shared a tiny and filthy cell with another female prisoner that was equipped only with a bucket. Sommer described Ilse's cell as a "hole," with two cots covered with straw mattresses and filthy blankets. It was so small, he recalled, that when Koch or her cellmate sat up on her cot, her knees touched the other's cot. The cell was artificially lighted day and night, but its window was covered by a sheet of iron stamped with holes that allowed the prisoners to see only the ankles of those passing by outside.[125] Karl, Sommer remembered, sought relief from his solitary confinement with brief visits to the prison courtyard for fresh air and exercise; this, however, led to deeply ironic and presumably uncomfortable situations when Buchenwald prisoners were occasionally brought to the Gestapo prison for extended interrogations and found themselves sharing a courtyard with the former commandant who may well have once lorded over them. In the early weeks of his imprisonment, Karl allegedly had circulated in the yard with inmates who had taken part in a clandestine ceremony at Buchenwald to mark the death of Ernst Thälmann, the Weimar-era leader of the German Communist Party murdered at Buchenwald on August 18, 1944.[126] Karl's only other outlet were the letters he exchanged with Ilse, as no personal contact was permitted.[127]

The first day of the trial, therefore, marked not only the beginning of Karl and Ilse's formal legal reckoning, but the first time the pair had seen each other in over a year. As with the conditions of Karl and Ilse's incarceration, the only substantial account of the trial's opening was given by defendant Sommer, in 1967, while serving a life sentence in West Germany for multiple counts of murder at Buchenwald. By that point, with his own legal fate sealed, Sommer had little to gain from skewing the historical record. To be sure, the paucity of corroborating witnesses and the sheer passage of time make his recollections less than authoritative, but they are nonetheless useful in reconstructing a broadly plausible narrative.

According to Sommer, Ilse entered the courtroom looking neat and fresh in a suit of red-and-grey plaid with a white blouse open at the neck. Karl entered shortly after. Meeting for the first time since their arrest in August 1943, the couple shook hands and quietly asked each other how they had been. Ilse took the first of the four chairs set up for the defendants, and was followed by Karl, who sat beside her, while Sommer took the third chair, and Hoven the fourth.[128] Presiding over the secret trial was SS-Lieutenant Colonel Richard Ende, assisted by two SS assessors. Morgen acted as prosecutor, and the Koch couple were assigned SS-Captain Dr. Piepenbrock to act as defense counsel. Defending Hoven and Sommer were two additional SS jurists. Among the other dozen or so present in the closed courtroom were several witnesses who came and went, and a handful of SS observers and auditors. These included Higher SS and Police Leader Prince Josias of Waldeck, who had first launched proceedings against Karl, SS-Senior Colonel Hermann Pister, who had succeeded him as commandant of Buchenwald, SS-Major General and Inspector of Concentration Camps Richard Glücks, and SS-Lieutenant General Oswald Pohl's representative from the WVHA, SS-Court Chief Kurt Schmidt-Klevenow.[129]

As all records of the trial were lost or destroyed, reconstructing what actually occurred once proceedings were underway depends wholly on the scant postwar recollections left by Sommer and a few other key participants including Konrad Morgen and Ilse Koch. Suffice it to say, these brief and often self-interested narratives allow only a partial picture of the SS trial to emerge. From all indications, Morgen's prosecutorial strategy relied on laying out the findings and evidentiary materials contained in his eighty-seven-page investigative report. To prove Karl's financial malfeasance, Morgen produced the documentary evidence of hidden bank accounts and records showing Karl's dramatic enrichment following the arrival of Jews at Buchenwald with the 1938 Kristallnacht pogrom. The confession that Morgen had extracted from Karl concerning his admitted embezzlements was likewise introduced. To prove that Karl had engaged in the unauthorized killing of inmates, Morgen presented evidence of the conspiracies to silence the inmates Krämer, Peix, and Wedel, and showed how false entries in the camp's death records had been designed to cover up how the victims had met their fate.[130] Morgen referred to Paragraph 211 of the Reich Penal Code to definitively state that "the killing of a human being 'in order to cover another criminal action' is murder."[131] It was the Führer alone, Morgen later recalled arguing, who could decide whether "enemies of the state" would live or die; Karl Koch had received no blanket authorization to do the same.[132] Sommer later remembered that, as Morgen presented this extensive body of evidence to make his case, Karl "appeared disheartened" and that when he was questioned "the presiding judge always had to request that he speak up."[133]

Unlike her husband, Sommer claimed, Ilse Koch provided answers that were clear and precise. According to the indictment, Ilse stood accused of receiving stolen goods and committing theft of some 25,000 RM. As would be the case in her later trials, the court's attention also came to focus on her alleged extramarital affairs and implied questions of character. The only extant account of specific dialogue from the proceedings comes from Sommer's recollection of the interaction among Ilse Koch, SS-Judge Ende, and Hoven after evidence had been presented that defendant Hoven had attempted to murder a prisoner named Kurt Titz. Morgen alleged that Titz, who worked as a domestic servant in the Koch household, had become aware of Hoven's affair with Ilse, and Hoven had tried to poison him to keep the romance secret. Titz, who would become a key witness in Ilse Koch's postwar trials, fortunately was tipped off by another prisoner, and did not consume the poisoned food laid out for him. Ende, Sommer recalled, began by probing the relationship between Hoven and Ilse, who denied the affair outright:

> *Judge Ende:* How was it really?
> *Ilse Koch:* I told my husband: Dr. Hoven is good company. He does not get to see his family too often, maybe we

should invite him over. And this is why Dr. Hoven visited us a couple of times when my husband was still [at Buchenwald], and one time when my husband was already in Lublin.

Judge Ende: Did it come to intimate relationships?

Ilse Koch: No, we had a glass of sparkling wine together, and talked about Dr. Hoven's family and my children.

Judge Ende: Did it come to an exchange of affection?

Dr. Hoven, [interrupting] in tears: This is unfair, there was never anything between me and Ilse Koch.

Judge Ende, according to Sommer, then questioned Ilse about her husband's financial misdeeds:

Judge Ende: What did you know about these frauds?

Ilse Koch: My husband never told me anything about it, and I didn't hear anything about it.

Judge Ende: Where did the money for your furniture come from?

Ilse Koch: I bought it when I was still a girl and brought it with me into the marriage.[134]

Although Sommer's recollections must be viewed as selective impressions more than direct transcriptions, the fact that trial proceedings came to focus on Ilse's extramarital affairs was confirmed by Karl's stepsister, Erna Raible, in her own postwar recollections. Raible told of a letter she had received from Karl expressing total shock at revelations that came out at trial regarding his wife's "harlotry."[135] Sommer's recollection of Ilse's testimony before the SS court is also consistent with answers she would provide in later trials. Consistently, she flatly denied all reports of extramarital affairs, while insisting implausibly that she had had no knowledge whatsoever of her husband's activities, or of the sources of his immense and sudden wealth.

Although few further details of the proceedings in the Extraordinary SS and Police Court survive, Morgen later stated that increased pressure from his SS adversaries (chiefly, he believed, from Oswald Pohl) led to his dismissal as prosecutor and the adjournment of the trial on September 10, 1944, following only three days of hearings. Morgen was reassigned to Poland, and would be replaced by SS-Major and Judge Werner Hansen when the trial resumed on December 18. According to Morgen, Schmidt-Klevenow, Pohl's representative at the trial, had successfully undermined his reputation, loudly denounced his methods, and openly questioned his loyalty to the SS and its goals:

> Every day after the trial sessions, the Court and the auditors went together for lunch, and there . . . it was inevitable that people started to talk. There, Schmidt-Kievenow more and more bitingly gave his opinion that I had exaggerated the Koch case. . . . He said that I deliberately had given false reports to [Himmler], that the whole trial was nonsense, damaged the reputation of the SS, and disturbed the concentration camps. . . . He attacked me with a raised voice and in such a fierce manner that almost all participants withdrew themselves from me.[136]

When the proceedings resumed in December, Morgen would return to the courtroom, but only as a witness. He later claimed that by then he was regarded "as a dead man" for exposing the corruption in the concentration camps, and that rumors of his imminent arrest swirled.[137]

At the conclusion of the September proceedings, the court announced that the case of Ilse and Karl Koch would be severed from the cases against defendants Hoven and Sommer. A legal opinion submitted by Morgen at the close of the September sessions reveals that the court had become ensnared in questions surrounding the authority to kill within the concentration camps and declared that more time was required to study this issue. While the case against Karl and Ilse Koch revolved around corruption and the former commandant's orders to kill to cover up evidence of malfeasance, the actions of the other two defendants were, from an SS viewpoint, more complex and less clearly criminal. Defendant Sommer argued that he had killed only according to instructions from Commandant Koch, and only because he had been deceived into believing that Koch had possessed the jurisdiction to issue such orders.[138] Hoven argued that he had acted only in the interests of the SS and had taken to heart words spoken by Reich Physician SS-Major General Ernst-Robert Grawitz, who had visited Buchenwald and addressed the SS doctors there. Grawitz had urged them to carry out their commander's requests for killings without hesitation.[139]

When the court reconvened in December, therefore, it was solely to hear the remainder of the case against Karl and Ilse Koch.[140] As Sommer was no longer present, and with Morgen appearing only as a witness, no substantial account exists of the one or two days of hearings that preceded the announcement of the court's verdict on December 19, 1944. In his closing argument, Morgen's replacement, SS-Major Hansen, demanded the death penalty for Karl Koch, whose theft and embezzlement made him a "parasite on the people" and whose responsibility for the deaths of Krämer, Peix, and Wendel made him a murderer. As for Ilse Koch, Hansen asked that the court impose a sentence of five years for her "continuous habitual receiving of stolen goods."[141] When the court was called to order for the announcement of verdicts and sentences, Judge Ende declared Karl Koch guilty and handed down the death sentence that Hansen had demanded. Ilse Koch, Judge Ende then announced, was acquitted of all charges. This, he explained, was because the prosecution had not sufficiently proven that she had known of her husband's business transactions or of the illicit sources of his newfound wealth. After sixteen months of incarceration, she was to be released immediately.[142]

Despite the looming fate of her husband, Ilse Koch viewed the trial as a personal vindication. As she later testified before an American military court at Dachau in 1947, her belief was that her innocence had been confirmed by the work of Morgen's team, which had toiled since mid-1943 to build a case against her and been unable to produce sufficient evidence for a conviction. "After sixteen months in prison pending investigation," she declared, "where all kinds of things were tried against me and where even prisoners [testified] against me . . . everything was found to be based on rumors. . . . I was acquitted unconditionally."[143] Following her release, Ilse remained in Weimar for a week, visiting Karl as he awaited his fate. According to Martin Sommer, who remained in the Gestapo prison and allegedly spoke with Karl, Ilse came to see her husband a number of times, and they conversed at great length. Ilse, Sommer recalled, "was in good spirits that he would receive parole at the front and nothing would change concerning their marriage. . . . [Karl] didn't believe that his sentence would be carried out."[144] At the end of December 1944, as the collapse of the Reich loomed, Ilse left Weimar for Ludwigsburg, where her children had moved with Erna Raible. Karl, Sommer claimed, remained positive after Ilse left, receiving regular letters from his wife and believing that his reprieve could not be far off.[145]

Although Ilse no longer languished in the Gestapo prison with her husband, the new life that she found in Ludwigsburg was far from serene. When Ilse appeared at Raible's home on Christmas Eve of 1944 to take up residence with her children, tensions flared almost immediately. Raible, it seems, had long been leery of Ilse; during visits to the Koch family at Buchenwald she had, on numerous occasions, been alarmed by what she viewed as Ilse's lack of concern for her children and tendency to drink to excess.[146] Now that Ilse was living under her roof, Raible was unwilling to tolerate such behavior. She later testified that Ilse left the children alone day in and day out, and ran around with various men late into the night—and that, when Raible complained, she reacted with fury and contempt.[147] Within six weeks, Raible had thrown Ilse out of the house, forcing her to take up residence with the children in a small, third-floor apartment of a nearby home. Soon, Ilse fought with her new landlady, Maria Klaus, who would also report that Ilse neglected her children while "men came to see her continuously" and into the early hours of the morning. Ilse, she complained, was "turning the house into a brothel." When confronted, according to Klaus, Ilse shouted that "it was none of her damn business."[148]

That postwar investigators sought out and recorded such testimony reflects how scrutiny of Ilse's criminal behavior would continue to be bound up with allegations of licentiousness and what her accusers would depict more broadly as her deep moral flaws as a woman and mother. Little could Koch have imagined that, despite the mass murder orchestrated by her husband at Buchenwald, it would be she who was cast as the embodiment of Nazi barbarism. In no small measure, the prominent place that Koch would come to occupy in the postwar imagination would be driven not only by a voyeuristic fascination with her alleged crimes, but also by an outrage at her perceived violation of accepted gender norms.

By the beginning of April 1945, Allied forces were closing in on the Reich from all sides, having recently captured Frankfurt in the west and Danzig in the east. On April 4, American soldiers stumbled upon Ohrdruf, a subcamp of Buchenwald, discovering for the first time the stacks of dead bodies that would soon become infamous and emblematic of the liberated concentration camps. That day, too, a group of SS men arrived at Karl Koch's cell. According to Martin Sommer, Koch cried out, "Help me! Where can I escape? They want to take me away to shoot me!"[149] Koch was handcuffed, brought to Buchenwald, and confined to its arrest bunker. Sommer claimed that he later heard from Hoven, who had recently returned as a physician to Buchenwald, that he had looked through the peephole of Karl's cell and saw him "pacing like a madman."[150]

On the morning of April 5, 1945, only twenty-four hours before the first evacuations of prisoners from Buchenwald would begin, Karl Koch was taken from his cell, offered a blindfold which he refused, and shot. Various sources have stated that Karl's body was then burned in the camp crematorium, but the ovens at Buchenwald had in fact ceased functioning in mid-March due to a shortage of coal.[151] Instead, his body was disposed of in an unknown location.[152] Ilse, still in Ludwigsburg with the Koch children, was never informed. According to Buchenwald survivor and chronicler Eugen Kogon, Karl's eleventh-hour execution was carried out on the orders of Waldeck, who worried that as Allied forces approached Karl might be paroled and sent to the front.[153] If that is true, Waldeck's order stands as a remarkable bookend to the crusade he had initiated four years earlier to hold Karl Koch accountable for murder and corruption at Buchenwald. As Ilse would soon discover, her reckoning was still to come.

3   American Military Justice and the "Bitch of Buchenwald"

When US forces liberated Buchenwald on April 11, 1945, Ilse Koch was living with her children in Ludwigsburg in relative obscurity, still unaware of her husband's fate. Having been exonerated by the Extraordinary SS and Police Court from charges of participating in the illegal activities that had led to Karl Koch's execution, Ilse made no attempt to conceal her identity and saw no reason why she might be sought out and held accountable for what had occurred behind the camp's barbed wire. Yet as American intelligence officers and war crimes investigators worked with survivors in the wake of Buchenwald's liberation to piece together what had occurred at the camp, the first reports surfaced of a "red-headed witch" who had tormented inmates in a most perverse and brutal fashion. Unbeknownst to Ilse, her name had joined a list of dozens of war crimes suspects to be apprehended and brought to trial, opening a new phase in her legal odyssey that would lead again to her incarceration. And even though she had had no rank in the Nazi state, an emergent popular fascination with her alleged crimes would help to transform her into one of the most hated Nazi figures in the postwar period, and into a conduit for the popular condemnation of the Third Reich's ugliest atrocities.

The Liberation of Buchenwald

The final days of Buchenwald concentration camp were marked by chaos, atrocity, and death. On Easter Sunday, April 1, 1945, Allied forces pushed through the Fulda Gap and approached the town of Eisenach less than sixty kilometers from Weimar.[1] While buoying the hopes of Buchenwald's prisoners who now learned that liberation was near, the Allied approach fueled the anxieties of the camp SS, prompting a series of last-ditch maneuvers to cover up evidence of systematic atrocity and eradicate or evacuate the surviving inmate population. On April 6, Heinrich Himmler ordered the wholesale evacuation of Buchenwald.[2] That day, three thousand of the camp's Jews were forcibly assembled and marched out of the camp on foot under SS guard.[3] Soon, however, the Kochs' old nemesis, the SS and police leader Prince Josias of Waldeck, grew impatient at the pace at which the commandant, Hermann Pister, was emptying the camp and personally stepped in to speed the process. Over the course of two days, fifteen thousand additional prisoners were marched from the camp or crammed into cattle cars that left Buchenwald on April 8 and 9 for other camps still beyond the reach of the Allied advance.[4] One in three of these evacuees would die.[5] The quickening pace of these murderous evacuations prompted members of the underground resistance at the camp to send out a desperate Morse code message on a clandestine shortwave transmitter built by a fellow inmate. Sent twelve times and in English, German, and Russian, the message read "To the Allies. To the Army of General Patton. This is the Buchenwald concentration camp. SOS. We request help. They want to evacuate us. The SS wants to destroy us." Reportedly, the prisoner operating the transmitter fainted when, against all odds, he received a reply: "KZ Bu. Hold out. Rushing to your aid. Staff of Third Army."[6]

With the Allies closing in, killing at the hands of the SS continued. On the night of April 10, the inmates in the camp jail were murdered.

Meanwhile, in the crematorium complex, incriminating documents were burned and, in the execution cellar, most of the forty-eight noose hooks were removed and a fresh coat of paint applied to cover blood stains on the walls.[7] American forces, however, advanced faster than the SS could work. When the sound of combat was heard in the distance on the morning of April 11, Pister attempted to placate the increasingly restive inmate population, announcing that control of the camp would be handed over to prisoner leadership. Near noon, loudspeakers at the camp barked out an order that all SS personnel were to report to their stations outside the camp enclosure immediately, leaving only those in the guard towers. By 3:00 PM, the first American tanks from the reconnaissance battalion of the Sixth Armored Division, Third US Army, had rumbled past Buchenwald, prompting the SS to withdraw and the guards in the towers to flee into the surrounding forest.[8] A previously clandestine prisoner militia stepped in to fill the power vacuum left by the SS, seizing control of the camp. Other inmates pursued and managed to apprehend and detain no less then seventy-eight of the fleeing German personnel.[9] When the first American troops from the Eightieth Infantry Division entered the camp compound at 5:30 that afternoon, therefore, they were met not by German resistance but by greetings from a committee of organized prisoners now in control of the camp, and by the cheers and desperate handshakes of the healthier among the camp's surviving inmates.[10]

Nothing, however, had prepared US troops for what lay beyond the camp's main gate. A week prior to the liberation of Buchenwald, American soldiers had entered the recently abandoned subcamp Ohrdruf, revealing evidence of atrocity never before encountered by western Allied forces. There for the first time, American troops discovered hundreds of naked corpses stacked "like cords of wood" and still more in pits half charred amid burnt timber and ash.[11] So astonishing was the scene that Generals Dwight D. Eisenhower, Omar Bradley, and George S. Patton visited Ohrdruf to bear witness. The evidence of "starvation, cruelty and bestiality," Eisenhower cabled back to Washington, was so overwhelming as to "beggar description." Before leaving the camp he announced, "I want every American unit . . . to see this place," knowing it would strengthen their resolve. "We are told that the American soldier does not know what he is fighting for. Now, at least, he will know what he is fighting *against*."[12] Yet after the horror uncovered at Ohrdruf, the soldiers who liberated Buchenwald the following week discovered something that American troops had never encountered before: a massive surviving inmate population of approximately twenty-one thousand people in desperate need of food, medical care, and other basic necessities of life.[13]

"When I walked through that gate," recalled US Army private Leon Bass, "I saw in front of me . . . the 'walking dead.'"[14] "Some just had a piece of blanket covering them," remembered Ventura De La Torre, a twenty-year-old soldier from California. "And their knees were nothing but skin and bone. Their ribs. . . . A terrible sight to see."[15] Paul Bodot, another of the American soldiers arriving earliest at Buchenwald, was first to witness the scene inside a barrack inhabited by prisoners too sick to greet their liberators:

> I could hardly believe my eyes. The air was unbreathable; mistrustful gazes turned toward me. . . . Most of them were lying in groups of four or five on plank beds intended for one inmate each. The misery of the entire world could be read in their gazes. Most of them were not even conscious of the fact that they had been liberated. But slowly a spark brightened their faces. They wanted to convince themselves that it was not a dream, and tried to touch my uniform. . . . Eyes filled with tears, some dropped to their knees.[16]

Unlike Ohrdruf, Buchenwald was not only a crime scene at the time of its liberation, but a still-unfolding humanitarian catastrophe. American forces were wholly unprepared for the massive needs of the liberated prisoner population and the horrific working conditions, made all the worse by the retreating SS who had destroyed the pumps that provided the camp's water supply and drove its sewage system. While American personnel from the Medical Corps began to arrive in substantial numbers forty-eight hours after the liberation and set to work alongside an organized administration of former prisoners to feed, clean, clothe, and provide medical attention to the camp's most desperate survivors, the death toll continued to climb for some time. Between five thousand and six thousand survivors were deemed critically ill, mostly with dysentery and typhus.[17] A tally of the camp population on April 16 counted twenty thousand survivors, a thousand fewer than were counted at liberation only five days earlier.[18]

As former prisoners worked in tandem with American personnel to stem the death rate and to bring a semblance of order to the liberated camp, the US Army sought to chronicle and make known the unprecedented crimes committed at Buchenwald. Because it was the first major concentration camp liberated by western Allied forces, and because General Eisenhower had insisted that the evidence of atrocity discovered there be widely publicized, Buchenwald received more attention than any other concentration camp. Delegations arrived from the US Senate, US House of Representatives, and British Parliament, while a team from the US Army Signal Corps led by famed Hollywood director Billy Wilder filmed the aftermath of the liberation. Within days of its liberation also, dozens of reporters descended on Buchenwald, dispatching stories, often paired with frightful photographs, that made the front pages of newspapers around the world and turned Buchenwald into a household name. Many struggled to find words for the macabre scene that greeted them. Percy Knauth, a war correspondent for *Time* and *Life*, wrote that the sight of the liberated, "emaciated beyond all imagination or description," had forever changed him. In a 1946 book full of scenes of suffering and death, he put it starkly: "Until the day when I saw Buchenwald, I respected men."[19] In an emotional account on CBS radio, Edward R. Murrow implored his audience to "believe what I have said about Buchenwald," but also to understand that the horrors went further: "I reported what I saw and heard, but only part of it. For most of it, I have no words."[20]

War Crimes Investigators and First Murmurs of the Name Ilse Koch

On April 16, 1945, American soldiers marched twelve hundred citizens of the neighboring city of Weimar through Buchenwald on a compulsory tour to see firsthand the evidence and aftermath of human indignities and murders committed in the name of National Socialism. With their faces at times betraying shock, numbness, or abject defeat, the men, women, and children in the procession made mandatory stops to view the still-occupied sick barracks, the dissection lab, the gallows, and the crematoria courtyard, where stacks of decomposing bodies remained. Some fainted, others used handkerchiefs to cover their noses and mouths.[21] Military personnel also guided these involuntary visitors past something new that day: a table on which some newly liberated inmates had displayed objects attesting to the depraved and barbarous activities of the camp SS. Among these were two shrunken heads, various preserved organs in glass containers, a plaster death mask, more than a dozen pieces of preserved, tattooed human skin, and a lamp with a stitched shade reportedly also made of human skin.

As objects of atrocity, the impression they made was deep. In a *New York Times* article, "Nazi Death Factory Shocks Germans on Forced Tour," journalist Gene Currivan described how "men went white and women turned away."[22] Currivan's report, published April 18, was the first in the American press to mention Ilse Koch, though it did not refer to her by name. The tattooed skins, Currivan explained, had been collected by the wife of the commanding officer: "This woman,

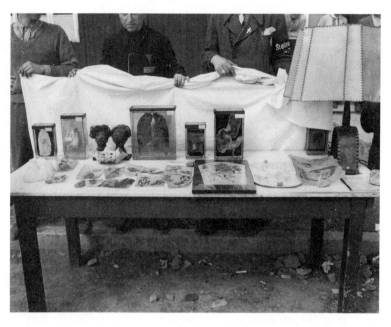

Fig. 3.1   Liberated prisoners display shrunken heads, tattooed skins, preserved human organs, and a lampshade allegedly made of human skin, Buchenwald, April 1945. US Army Signal Corps, Record Group III, National Archives and Records Administration.

according to prisoners, was an energetic sportswoman who . . . had a mania for unusual tattoos, and whenever a prisoner arrived with a rare marking on his body, she would indicate that that would make a valuable addition to her collection."[23] For much of the newspaper-reading public, these crimes epitomized Nazi barbarism and demanded swift retribution.

Though Currivan may have been the first to report a connection between Ilse Koch and the grisly artifacts displayed by liberated inmates at Buchenwald, murmurs of Koch's name and allegations of atrocities of a most shocking nature had reached Allied authorities even prior to the camp's liberation. She first appeared in a February 1945 report marked "secret" and entitled "Information on the Infamous Concentration Camp at Buchenwald, Germany." Based on accounts by a German informant who had spent more than seven years at the camp as a political prisoner, the report detailed the slave labor, starvation, and brutality that defined daily life at Buchenwald. It also devoted a section, under the heading "The Acme of Sadism," to Ilse Koch's rumored activities. According to the report,

> The wife of Commandant Koch . . . was at least partly responsible for, if not the instigator of, the most extraordinary act of sadism. An order came from the commandant . . . to run through the lists of men who had been reported . . . as having tattoo marks on their body. . . . After 40 to 50 . . . had been killed and the corpses delivered to the Pathological Department, the tattooed skins were removed and tanned. . . . Frau Koch had lampshades made out of them. Some of the pieces . . . were made into a kind of chamois leather cloth, which Frau Koch used for wiping her windows. . . . [The informant] was further told, but did not actually see, that she had a chandelier made of three human feet.[24]

While the report's unnamed author acknowledged that such accounts "appear incredibly fantastic," American military personnel at Buchenwald soon discovered that similar stories were not uncommon.[25] Few survivors would claim they directly encountered Koch, but their accounts, while differing in the details, indicated how prominently Ilse Koch figured in the collective memory of the camp's liberated inmates.

Shocking reports of Ilse Koch's alleged crimes continued to surface following Buchenwald's liberation, as both US Army war crimes investigators and personnel from the Psychological Warfare Division arrived at the camp to gather evidence and witness statements that chronicled the camp's history of murder and brutality. While the former built dossiers in anticipation of future legal proceedings and the latter gathered materials deemed useful for the reshaping of German public opinion, both worked alongside survivor-volunteers to craft extensive reports on Buchenwald built largely on the testimonies of dozens of liberated inmates. From the outset, accounts of tattoo collections, human-skin lampshades, and the malevolent presence of Ilse Koch were remarkably persistent. Edward A. Tenenbaum and Egon W. Fleck from the Publicity and Psychological Warfare section of the US Twelfth Army Group were the first to submit a major report on Buchenwald. Dated April 24, 1945, their eighteen-page document repeats the claim that Ilse Koch had selected tattooed inmates for death so that she could have their skins made into "extraordinary objects." Tenenbaum and Fleck added allegations of sexual deviance, as SS judge Konrad Morgen's 1944 indictment had also done. According to their report, "both [Karl Koch] and his wife were perverts, the husband a homosexual and the wife a nymphomaniac. Both satisfied their desires on the hapless inmates. The wife would walk through the camp, pick a likely partner, take him for the night, and then invariably have him shot."[26]

The most comprehensive report on Buchenwald (published later as *The Buchenwald Report*) was compiled by a small team from the Psychological Warfare Division led by Second Lieutenant Albert G. Rosenberg and designed to serve the overall intelligence needs of the US Army.[27] Rosenberg deputized the Austrian survivor and antifascist resistor Dr. Eugen Kogon to write the lion's share of the report, which quickly grew to more than four hundred pages and included 168 individual sub-reports and the testimonies of 104 survivors.[28] While the report mentioned various acts of violence attributed to Ilse Koch, including instigations of inmate beatings, it also provided an early indication that concrete evidence tying Ilse to the collection of tattooed human skins was scarce. It described, for example, the practice of collecting tattooed skins. However, Kogon, who had gained extensive knowledge of the activities of Buchenwald's SS medical personnel while working as a prisoner-clerk for SS camp doctor Erwin Ding-Schuler, named not Ilse Koch but an SS doctor named Erich Wagner as the primary culprit:

> Dr. Wagner wrote a doctoral dissertation on tattooing, had the entire camp searched for people with tattoos, and had them photographed. The prisoners were later called to the gate by Commandant Koch, selected for the splendor of their tattoos, and sent to the infirmary. Soon after the best examples of skin appeared in the pathology department . . . Koch had an "artistic" table lamp made for himself out of human bones stretched over with human skin. Hundreds of prepared skins were sent to Berlin on orders of the chief doctor for the concentration camps, SS Colonel Dr. Lolling.[29]

Another similar account in the report comes from Gustav Wegerer, who had acted as kapo in the pathology department. Wegerer identifies Dr. Wagner as having summoned tattooed prisoners to the camp hospital where they were killed with lethal injections and "the tattoos . . . peeled off and tanned."[30] Appended to the report was a full copy of Dr. Wagner's 1940 dissertation, "Ein Beitrag zur Tätowierungsfrage" (A Contribution to the Tattoo Question).[31] Completed at Buchenwald and accepted by Friedrich Schiller University in Jena, it purported to demonstrate a link between criminality and the practice of tattooing one's body. Kogon also included the testimony of a survivor named Stefan Heymann, who had worked for the camp SS keeping statistics, saying that Ilse Koch had had items of tattooed skin. His recollection, however, was that such objects were given as gifts by the highest-ranking SS men at Buchenwald. "Frau Koch," Heymann remembered, "had a lady's handbag made from the same material. She was as proud of it as a South Sea woman would have been about her cannibal trophies."[32]

More than any other crime committed at Buchenwald, the collection of tattooed skins and their alleged use in the production of decorative items stoked the public's imagination and deepened its sense of indignity and thirst for justice. The descriptions of these atrocities in the Psychological Warfare Division's reports contributed to the public's growing knowledge of the barbarity of the Nazi concentration camps, not only in the United States but also in Germany. The US Army's war crimes investigators, however, were the ones tasked with assembling the hard evidence and witness testimony that would facilitate the arrest and future prosecution of those responsible for all that had occurred at Buchenwald. This task fell to a small team from the war crimes branch of the Third US Army led by Lieutenant Colonel Raymond C. Givens. Based in the Hotel Elefant in Weimar, the team succeeded in collecting signed and sworn affidavits from 177 camp survivors of fourteen nationalities.[33] As Givens gathered mountains of evidence concerning the totality of the crimes committed at Buchenwald, he too worked to verify the shocking accounts of Ilse Koch and her alleged predilection for tattooed human skins. First, to confirm that such atrocities had actually occurred, Givens submitted for scientific analysis three samples of tattooed parchment handed over to American personnel by camp survivors. The US Army's chief of pathology reported back to Givens on May 25, 1945, that microscopic investigation of the skins had shown they were indeed human.[34] The focus now shifted to the more challenging task of determining who was responsible.

Though rumors of Ilse Koch's role in the collection of human skins swirled at Buchenwald, the evidence gathered by war crimes investigators pointed in various and sometimes contradictory directions. As Givens reported, the survivors with whom he spoke "were closely confined and passed information from one to the other as the investigation got underway."[35] Hugo Beher, a German communist who had spent seven years imprisoned at Buchenwald, told investigators, for example, that "from the window of [Ilse Koch's] private home she would watch the new victims who were brought in and stripped naked. If she saw a tattoo design . . . that pleased her, she . . . had him killed and the skin brought to her."[36] The Koch home, however, was nearly a kilometer from the camp and far removed from view. The affidavit of Second Lieutenant William Powell, an American soldier imprisoned at Buchenwald for two months in late 1944, explained that Russian POWs at Buchenwald often had tattoos of eagles on their chests, and that the commandant's wife "evidently thought they would make a good decoration of some sort for a lampshade, and had them cut out."[37] According to this account, the victims bore terrible scars but were not, in fact, killed. Yet as Powell had arrived at Buchenwald more than a year after Ilse Koch had left the camp following her arrest in August 1943, he too was testifying to what he had heard but not to what he had seen firsthand.

In his final report on war crimes at Buchenwald, Givens acknowledged that the testimonies collected by his team seldom provided unimpeachable connections between atrocities and those responsible, but he asserted that such evidence was not required. "An attempt to show what perpetrator killed which victim is with few exceptions impossible and furthermore unnecessary," Givens wrote. Foreshadowing the strategy that US Army prosecutors would use against concentration camp personnel and against Ilse Koch, he argued that all were clearly guilty of participating in the broad "Nazi plan" to kill, starve, and torture those deemed enemies of the Reich.[38]

As the role of war crimes investigators was to compile, not critically evaluate, these varying accounts, dealing with the vexing issues of hearsay testimony and camp rumor in the evolving case against Ilse Koch would be a task for prosecutors in the future. War crimes investigators and prosecutors recognized that, for certain types of crime at Buchenwald—mass murder among them—there were unlikely to be eyewitnesses beyond the perpetrators and the dead. Instead, knowledge of such crimes would have to be built from the rumors that had circulated in camp and been verified to some degree by the frequency with which they were recorded. In taking this view of camp rumor, the war crimes investigators echoed the approach of a previous joint investigative committee from the US Senate and House of Representatives. Having toured Buchenwald and gathered its own eyewitness testimonies on behalf of the American government, that committee argued in its report that, along with both hard documentary evidence and the accounts of eyewitnesses, camp rumor or hearsay also deserved to be given substantial weight:

> A third kind of evidence was what may be called the common knowledge of the camp, that is to say, evidence of things done in the camp which were not done publicly but which, nevertheless, all prisoners were aware of. This is similar to certain knowledge possessed by prisoners generally in legitimate institutions like State penitentiaries. These prisoners, from custom and experience, from the conversation with the guards and among themselves, and from a very plain and almost mathematical kind of circumstantial evidence, have accurate knowledge of certain things which they have not actually seen with their own eyes. The prisoners at the camps speak about these things as though they had actually seen them. . . . [This] kind of evidence was often as accurate and reliable as the two kinds of evidence above referred to.[39]

Much of the evidence investigators gathered against Ilse Koch lay within this category of inmates' "common knowledge." It soon would fall to US Army prosecutors to test the contention that such testimony was fundamentally reliable and could form the foundation of a successful criminal prosecution.

The war crimes investigation at Buchenwald concluded at the beginning of June 1945 with the submission to American military authorities of seventy-eight boxes of documentary evidence and the signed and sworn affidavits of 177 survivors.[40] For the regimen of slave labor, starvation, abuse, and murder that led to fifty-six thousand deaths at Buchenwald, the evidence was overwhelming and damning. Together, the materials gathered by investigators provided a remarkable and expansive chronicle of Nazi criminality at Buchenwald and facilitated the arrests and trials of dozens of perpetrators. Over the course of the weeks and months that followed, American military authorities took into custody some 250 war crimes suspects accused of atrocities at Buchenwald, among them Ilse Koch.[41] Although her co-arrestees included such figures of power and authority at the camp as the higher SS and police leader Prince Josias of Waldeck, the commandant Hermann Pister, and chief physician Waldemar Hoven, it would be the prosecution of Koch's alleged crimes that would dominate newspaper headlines—indeed, that would create a scandal sensational enough to spur hearings in the United States Congress.

Arrest and the Prospect of a Buchenwald Trial

By June 1945, news of the liberation of scores of concentration camps had made headlines around the globe, sparking widespread shock and outrage and lending credence to the Allied characterization of the war effort as a crusade against unprecedented barbarism. And while the world learned of the millions murdered in the name of National Socialism, reports of lampshades and other items made of human skin drove home the sheer depravity of Hitler's twelve-year Reich. It is remarkable, therefore, that even with wide-ranging reportage, including the distribution both inside and outside Germany of a newsreel prepared by the US Army titled "Ilse Koch's Lampshade," Ilse Koch herself had continued to live quietly with her two children in the city of

Ludwigsburg. As Koch later claimed at trial, she had remained oblivious to news reports linking her to atrocities at the camp, and was shocked to learn that American authorities designated her a war crimes suspect. "It would have been easy," she later testified, "for me to obtain false papers and live somewhere with a false name. It also would have been easy for me to have disguised myself. But . . . I had no reason whatsoever to disappear. I never even conceived of the possibility of being put to trial."[42]

On June 16, however, Koch was summoned to appear at Ludwigsburg City Hall for questioning by US war crimes investigators, after a former inmate of Buchenwald had recognized her on the street and reported her to occupation authorities.[43] Koch's initial interrogation likely reinforced her own purported view that she had little reason to fear prosecution. At no point did war crimes investigators make mention of human skins, or of any other atrocity she was later accused of having had a hand in; instead, they asked only general questions before homing in on the activities and whereabouts of her husband, Karl. Yet despite Ilse's insistence that she had not feared prosecution, the fact that she lied repeatedly to investigators suggests that, at the very least, she felt some need to cover her tracks.

Seeking first to conceal her 1932 entry in the Nazi Party, she declared that she had "belonged neither to the NSDAP [Nationalsozialistische Deutsche Arbeiterpartei] nor to any of its affiliated organizations," and to the contrary had been "liberally-minded."[44] To questions regarding her years spent at Buchenwald, she responded with the blanket and wholly implausible answer that she would parrot for the rest of her life: she had been wholly ignorant even of the most basic goings-on at the camp, despite living on the fringes of its barbed wire and interacting daily with inmate slave-laborers. "I lived . . . only for my children," she insisted. "My husband . . . never informed me about anything connected with his duties, and therefore I know nothing about conditions in the camp. My husband told me nothing about the

camp administration or the living conditions and labor methods. . . .
I was never admitted into the interior of the camp." In a further departure from the truth she explained that, after Karl's removal from command at Buchenwald, "he was not assigned to any other concentration camp," despite the fact that he served as commandant at Majdanek.[45]

The falsehoods that punctuate Ilse's interrogation may in part have been provided to prevent further incrimination of her husband, as she was still uncertain that his death sentence had been carried out. She did not know where he "could possibly be," she claimed. "The last place where my husband was kept was the Police prison in Weimar. During the last months I repeatedly tried to obtain information on the whereabouts of my husband. I did not succeed, however."[46] In a rather clumsy personal attempt to ingratiate herself to her US interrogators, she concluded by explaining that she had American relatives, once considered a life in the United States, and had a Jewish dressmaker who could attest to her good character.[47]

Though US authorities did not detain Koch following her interrogation, she was again summoned to City Hall on June 30, 1945, and this time, to her shock, placed under arrest. According to Koch, she had believed at first that her arrest had only to do with her husband, as no mention was made of charges stemming from her own activities at Buchenwald. "I was merely told," she later testified, "that I would have to be held as a hostage because I could not say whether the death sentence of my husband had been carried out or not."[48] It was only in October 1945, she claimed, four months after her detention had begun, that she read with great alarm an article in *Life* that included a full-page picture of her and a caption stating that she had had prisoners killed to collect their tattooed skins.[49]

US authorities would not formally charge Koch for another eighteen months. In the meantime, she joined eleven hundred detainees in a Ludwigsburg internment camp for women known as "Lager 77" that contained mostly "political suspects" who had been members of various Nazi organizations.[50] As rumors of Koch's alleged crimes spread, it appears that even her co-inmates viewed her with suspicion, especially as she interacted little with others. Anna Fest, a former guard at Ravensbrück concentration camp also incarcerated at Lager 77, recalled that other prisoners found Koch "spooky," as "one knew who she was." As Fest later recalled, "I always had the feeling . . . as though a beast of prey were skulking. She never walked in the middle of the hallway. She was always against the wall, and if anyone else walked down the hall, she jumped back quickly to her room. . . . She closed herself up."[51] As would become increasingly evident, Koch found incarceration nearly unbearable, and steadfastly insisted that she had done nothing to deserve it.

As Koch languished in what were in reality modest but comfortable conditions in Ludwigsburg, American authorities debated what to do with her, and with all those suspected of crimes at Buchenwald. Unlike other major camps liberated by American forces, Buchenwald wound up within the Soviet zone of occupation following the delimitation of German territory by the European Advisory Commission in June 1945. A joint declaration of the United States, the Soviet Union, and Great Britain made November 1, 1943 at Moscow had stipulated that war crimes suspects (with the exception of the highest-ranking members of the Nazi state, tried later by the International Military Tribunal at Nuremberg) were to be "brought back to the scene of their crimes and judged on the spot by the peoples they have outraged."[52] Because US authorities had ceded Buchenwald to the Soviets on July 4, 1945, because thousands of Soviet POWs had died at the camp, and because many of the witnesses and suspected perpetrators were now also in the Soviet zone, it initially appeared that the Soviets were best poised to prosecute Buchenwald's personnel. Yet, while the Soviet Union initially expressed interest, persistent stalling and an unproductive series of negotiations with American occupation authorities concerning the sharing of evidence and witnesses led the United States to take on the Buchenwald case in the autumn of 1946.

The court that would try Ilse Koch and others accused of atrocities at Buchenwald was not an international tribunal like that established at Nuremberg to try the senior surviving figures of the Reich. Instead, Buchenwald defendants would be tried by an American military commission court established on the grounds of the former concentration camp Dachau. The US Army granted jurisdiction to the Dachau court to try those accused either of war crimes involving American nationals as victims or of committing mass atrocities in the American area of control or in concentration camps liberated by US forces.[53] In repurposed barracks at Dachau that once had held victims of National Socialism, American authorities detained as many as fifteen thousand war crimes suspects—a number that, after careful screening, yielded some thirty-five hundred slated for trial.[54] Alongside arrestees from Buchenwald were personnel from the concentration camps Mauthausen, Flossenbürg, Dora-Nordhausen, Mühldorf, and Dachau itself.

The sheer number of war crimes suspects indicted at Dachau represented a judicial undertaking that was, according to the US Army, "without parallel" in its magnitude.[55] As a result, efficiency would be the underlying goal of the trial program; military authorities instructed these commission courts to adopt "simple and expeditious procedures to accomplish substantial justice without technicality."[56] The composition of the courts made an overly legalistic or pedantic approach to the trials unlikely: on each panel of five to seven judges, only one was required to have legal training, and the rest had merely to be senior officers regarded as "men of stature in their professions." Conviction required a simple majority vote; those found guilty by the court had no avenue for appeal, but instead had their cases subjected to a mandatory review by the deputy judge advocate for war crimes—the same authority who appointed the court as well as the prosecution and defense teams in the first place.[57]

William Denson and the Indictment of Ilse Koch

Assigned to prosecute the Buchenwald case was a thirty-three-year-old West Point and Harvard Law graduate named William Dowdell Denson. Raised in Alabama, Denson's outlook was shaped by a strong Christian upbringing and by the prominent legal careers of his father and grandfather, the latter of whom had served on the Alabama Supreme Court and had defended black Americans in an era when it had required substantial courage and conviction to do so.[58] Fond of quoting the Bible, Denson prided himself on having committed to memory no fewer than 215 verses of scripture.[59] Though Denson emanated a warm southern charm, he viewed his service at Dachau as contributing to a moral crusade against the evils of Nazism and had no qualms about calling for those found guilty to be sent to the gallows. Preparation for the Buchenwald trial got underway at the beginning of 1947, and by that time Denson had already prosecuted a total of more than 150 concentration camp personnel in three major trials for the Dachau, Mauthausen, and Flossenbürg camps. With all but three defendants found guilty, Denson succeeded in having the court impose the death sentence more than a hundred times.[60]

The "nervous and physical strain" exerted by the cases he had prosecuted following his arrival at Dachau in the autumn of 1945, however, had caught up with Denson.[61] "I looked like a concentration camp inmate myself," he later recalled. "I was 117 pounds—before I was 165–170 pounds. I was physically drained. I had the shakes. I was in bed for three weeks." Denson had hoped to return to the United States as a result of his exhaustion. Instead, the US Army insisted he prosecute one last major concentration camp case before hanging up his

Fig. 3.2   Chief Prosecutor William Denson at the Buchenwald Trial, 1947.
Courtesy United States Holocaust Memorial Museum.

hat. "They needed me to try one more," he remembered. "The final case was Buchenwald."[62]

Denson had built his remarkably successful prosecutorial record at Dachau on an innovative legal strategy that permitted the indictment and rapid trial of large groups of perpetrators—and he would use this strategy again to prosecute Ilse Koch as part of a broader Buchenwald case. Unlike prosecutors at Nuremberg, who used novel legal charges such as "crimes against humanity" and "crimes against peace" to encapsulate the atrocities committed by the Nazis, Denson used only "violations of the laws and usages of war," a charge based on traditional definitions of war crimes spelled out in the Geneva and Hague Conventions. Denson's indictments of Buchenwald suspects, however, would not be for direct perpetrations of war crimes, but for "participating in a common design" to commit war crimes. This meant that defendants did not have to be shown to have committed specific acts of violence or killing. It needed only to be shown that they, through their actions and duties, contributed to the upkeep of a criminal enterprise—in this case, the concentration camp. To prove his case, it would be sufficient for Denson to establish that there was in place at Buchenwald a system to ill-treat and murder prisoners, that the defendants were aware of this system, and that each of the defendants in some fashion aided, abetted, or participated in enforcing this system. The extensive evidence of atrocity presented to the court would not only be used to illustrate the deeds of specific defendants, but to show that it would have been impossible for any defendant to have served at Buchenwald without being aware of the daily regimen of torture and death that gave the camp its raison d'être. Having successfully employed this approach at the Dachau, Mauthausen, and Flossenbürg trials, Denson recalled feeling he "could try [the Buchenwald case] by falling off a log—nothing to it."[63]

Despite numerous accounts in the press and in the reports filed by American war crimes investigators tying Ilse Koch to the abuse of inmates and to the items of tattooed skin found at Buchenwald, it was not an obvious decision for Denson to include her in the group of thirty-one defendants selected for trial. In the various investigative reports completed by US authorities at Buchenwald there were conflicting accounts of Koch's role and alleged crimes, and few of the people offering them claimed firsthand knowledge. Camp survivor Dr. Eugen Kogon, who had written much of the Buchenwald Report submitted by the US Army's Psychological Warfare Division, also submitted a report to Denson in February 1947 to familiarize him with the evidence and names of those "who carry the main responsibility for concentration camp Buchenwald" as well as individuals responsible for specific egregious acts. While Kogon's report details the role of others Denson would choose for trial, such as Pister and Waldeck, it makes no mention whatsoever of Ilse Koch or of the tattooed skins.[64] The fact that Koch had had no official role at the camp or in the Nazi state, moreover, would make it challenging to tie her to the alleged "common design" to commit war crimes at Buchenwald. Koch was also an unusual choice for another reason: she was the only female perpetrator ever chosen by Denson to stand trial, and one of only four ever to appear before a Dachau court.

Denson, nonetheless, was deeply impressed by the accounts he read and with the survivor-witnesses with whom he spoke. Through such interactions, he came to describe Ilse Koch as "a sexy-looking depraved woman who beat prisoners, reported them for beatings, and trafficked in human skin."[65] Denson was clearly sympathetic to the conclusions of investigators at Buchenwald who had determined that the "common knowledge" of inmates was generally both reliable and sufficient, even when details varied. Later, Denson would also remember struggling to accept as true some testimonies of atrocity, fearing that the witnesses he encountered were "drawing on fantasy rather than reality."[66] Over time, however, and having seen incontestable evidence of murder and cruelty in the concentration camp system as a whole, Denson recalled getting to the point where he "could believe almost anything."[67] Indeed, Denson appears to have put aside all caution in his evaluation of rumors he heard and secondhand testimonies provided by the witnesses he interviewed. Looking back many years later, he reflected on his initial impressions of the Koch case:

> I didn't believe it. Truthfully, when I was first exposed to this thing I thought, "Shucks, innocent people had been mistreated and now they want to come back with a little vengeance." These stories were

just too fantastic, too far out of line for normal behavior.... But when you listen to one witness recite the facts about what happened, and then the next witness testified about the same event, and they didn't have a chance to get together ahead of time and fabricate the stories, there was enough dovetailing of the important elements of what had happened to make anyone who is reasonable realize that it had happened. You couldn't have gotten two minds to come up with a fantastic set of circumstances that each of them had described separately.[68]

Corroborating witness testimony of this nature would be key in the case Denson built against Ilse Koch. The permissive rules of evidence that governed proceedings in the Dachau court substantially eased Denson's burden, as the prosecution could present any testimony to the court that had "probative value to the reasonable man" including hearsay and "the statement of a witness not produced."[69] In preparation for trial, Denson and his team screened dozens of witnesses, paying close attention to their body language, how clearly they spoke, and their overall ability to appear "calm and objective" and to make a "good and honest impression."[70] Denson's case against Ilse Koch would hinge on the testimony of the thirteen he thought best fit this bill.

On March 7, 1947, following two months of intensive preparation, Denson announced the indictment of Ilse Koch and thirty co-accused from Buchenwald for "Violations of the Laws and Usages of War." The indictment names the highest-ranking defendant first, lists remaining defendants in alphabetical order, and spells out the particulars of charges against them:

In that Josias Prince zu Waldeck [et al.] ..., acting in pursuance of a common design to commit the acts hereinafter alleged, did, wrongfully and unlawfully, encourage, aid, abet, and participate in the operation of Concentration Camp Buchenwald and its sub-camps and out-details, which operation included the wrongful and unlawful subjection of citizens of the United States of America, Poles, Frenchmen, [etc.] and other non-German nationals who were then and there in the custody of the then German Reich . . . to killings, beatings, tortures, starvation, abuses, and indignities, the exact names and numbers of such persons being unknown but aggregating many thousands.[71]

Just how Denson and his team intended to tie Ilse Koch and each of her co-accused to this expansive charge was revealed in an illustrated information booklet prepared by the prosecution staff and released with the indictment. Presumably distributed as a primer for official observers and members of the press, the booklet provided a photo of each of the defendants alongside the alleged activities the prosecution argued would secure their conviction. Ilse Koch, as defendant number fifteen, was described fantastically as having "commanded [Buchenwald] together with her husband." The booklet, remarkably prejudicial in providing unproven, pretrial assessments of the accused, stated that the prosecution would show that Ilse Koch:

(1) As commandeuse of Buchenwald Concentration Camp, indulged in personal sadism against inmates.
(2) By virtue of her position, caused the deaths of many hundreds of inmates.
(3) Indulged in the sadistic practice of using human skin of inmates for such personal items as gloves, book covers and lampshades.[72]

The prosecution's designation of Koch as "commandeuse of Buchenwald" is striking not only because of the extraordinary degree of authority it attributes to Koch, but also in its departure from the more measured conclusions of war crimes investigators. William Denson and his team, it seems, were setting themselves a very high bar. Having overcome his struggle to believe, however, Denson had accepted as fact the most extreme accounts of Koch provided by the witnesses he selected. He came to view Koch as nothing less than a mass murderer who embodied the most monstrous and perverse elements of Nazi evil—a contention he would now have to prove to the court.

The release of the Buchenwald indictments and the sensational accompanying information booklet helped to excite the interest of the press in the case and fueled a macabre fascination with the crimes attributed to the so-called "Bitch of Buchenwald."[73] And while earlier reports of nymphomania and sexual deviance were not reflected in the indictment of Ilse Koch, a stunning revelation only two days before court proceedings were set to begin guaranteed that salacious questions about her "moral character" would remain prominent throughout her trial: Ilse Koch was three months pregnant. According to Robert Kunzig, the assistant prosecutor who, with fellow lawyer Solomon Surowitz, rounded out Denson's prosecution team, a French officer serving for the defense had appeared in their office and asked whether they had had Ilse examined lately. "Examined why?" Kunzig asked. Later he would recall how the officer responded: "In his best English he answered—I can still hear it now—'She ist wiz zee babee.'"[74] Denson and his team at first assumed this to be a hoax, given that Koch had been in US custody for nearly two years, but to their deep chagrin soon learned it was true.

As embarrassing rumors arose that Koch had been impregnated by an American or Polish guard and an investigation was launched, she herself steadfastly refused to betray the identity of her lover. The official explanation that eventually emerged—that a war crimes detainee and former acquaintance of Ilse's named Fritz Schaeffer had tunneled into her quarters from the mess hall where he worked—was absurdly unlikely.[75] As murky as the circumstances remained, however, the implications were immediately clear to Denson and his team.

Whereas they had intended to ask the court to impose the death penalty for Koch's crimes, the judges would not condemn a pregnant woman to hang on the gallows. While Koch's pregnancy would confirm for some trial observers that she lacked "good womanly virtue," the prosecution recognized it might well be a cunning strategy she employed to save her neck.[76]

The United States versus Ilse Koch

The Buchenwald trial opened on April 11, 1947, two years to the day after the camp's liberation by American forces. The courtroom, which during the Third Reich had contained a slave-labor workshop producing shoes for the German Army, was decorated only with a large American flag that hung above the table at the head of the room where the eight-member panel of judges sat. The prosecution team occupied one side of the room, while on the other stood a table for the defense team, and three rows of risers to seat the thirty-one accused. In the middle of the room sat a single wooden chair on a raised wooden block for those testifying before the court; at the back, rows of chairs constituted a spectators' gallery that at the trial's opening was full to capacity with three hundred observers. As film cameras droned and an array of bright spotlights shone, Ilse Koch took up a position in the middle of the second row while her codefendants shuffled awkwardly into their seats. With everyone present save for the members of the court, all rose as the president of the court, Brigadier General Emil C. Kiel, entered, followed by his seven fellow judges. At 10:00 AM, the court was called to order.

Proceedings began with a series of challenges to the jurisdiction of the court concerning the fact that Buchenwald lay outside the American zone of occupation and that some crimes to be considered by the court had occurred before the United States had entered the war on December 8, 1941. The court quickly dismissed these challenges,

Fig. 3.3   Ilse Koch enters the Dachau court, April 11, 1947. US Army Signal Corps, Record Group 111, National Archives and Records Administration.

accepting the prosecution's argument that the United States had both the authority and vested interest as a member of the community of nations, to prosecute violations of international law wherever and whenever they had occurred. US Army captain Emmanuel Lewis, part of the court-appointed American defense team that represented Ilse Koch and her thirty codefendants, then attempted to present a "challenge for cause," arguing that the overwhelming and damning press coverage of the accused and their alleged crimes prior to the opening of the trial—spurred in part by the "information booklet" issued by the prosecution—had eroded any possibility that the defendants would be tried by an impartial panel of judges. Although Lewis spoke on behalf of all the defendants, this challenge applied first and foremost to Ilse Koch:

> The prosecution ... has not missed an opportunity to brand these people as arch criminals without giving them the opportunity of answering the charges in the same manner of communication that the prosecution had. ... This case has been tried in the papers before it has been brought to this court of justice. ... Several of the accused have been vividly pictured in the newspapers and over the radio as being arch criminals of the worst type. We contend that all this publicity has tended to create an opinion in the mind of the court as to the guilt or innocence of the accused.[77]

The court, however, swiftly dismissed the challenge, declaring that it had formed no opinion as to the guilt of the accused, and could hear the evidence "without bias."[78] With proceedings allowed to continue, the president of the court now asked each of the defendants to rise, and to state their name, age, residence, nationality, and status. As Ilse Koch stood to respond, she, like each of her fellow defendants, received a numbered identification card on a string to wear around her neck for the duration of the trial. Finally, before a pause for lunch, the president read out the charges, prompting the defense to enter a blanket plea of not guilty on behalf of each of the thirty-one accused.

Before presenting his first witnesses to the court, Chief Prosecutor Denson delivered a brief opening statement to remind the judges that the charges leveled at Ilse Koch and her thirty co-accused did not require evidence tying specific defendants to specific acts of atrocity, but only to the existence of a "common design" at Buchenwald to mistreat and murder prisoners that each of the defendants had in some fashion aided and abetted. Justice for those shown to have participated in this common design, Denson concluded, could "only be satisfied with the hangman's noose."[79] Denson's first order of business, therefore, was to present evidence attesting to the murderous conditions at Buchenwald. This, he decided, could be best achieved by screening for the court two short War Department films shot at the camp days after its liberation. In these films, various forms of mistreatment, torture, and murder by the Buchenwald SS were described, but the only defendant referred to explicitly was Ilse Koch. Describing evidence of atrocities discovered at the camp, the narrator lists a "lampshade made of human skin at the request of an SS Officer's wife."[80] While the impact of the film's screening is not noted in the trial record, Denson must have hoped that it would be similar to the effect of the film compilation "Nazi Concentration Camps" shown during Nuremberg proceedings. There, even the most senior figures of the Third Reich had covered their faces or looked on in shock as images from the liberated camps helped to create a deep sense of moral indignation in the court.

Once the film had laid the groundwork for the members of the court to understand the depth of the horrors that had occurred at Buchenwald, Denson introduced the first of dozens of witnesses who would testify over the course of the coming months against one or more of the accused. The presentation of the prosecution case against Ilse Koch, however, was complicated by the fact that she had had no official position at the camp. As a result, it would not be sufficient for Denson to apply his standard strategy of illustrating guilt merely by showing that the concentration camp in question was a criminal enterprise, and that the accused, by virtue of their service and position, had participated in its upkeep and function. Instead, Denson would have to illustrate that despite her civilian status she nonetheless contributed to the common design to murder and abuse Buchenwald's inmates. To do so, the prosecution called to the stand witnesses who could testify that Ilse Koch had substantial power of command at Buchenwald despite lacking an official SS position; that she personally had abused, or requested the beatings of, Buchenwald prisoners; or that she had collected objects fabricated of tattooed skins and had selected certain prisoners to die for their production.

As the presentation of witnesses began, all eyes were on Ilse Koch. The press, whose interest in the Koch case had been stoked both by salacious rumors of her behavior that had been reported on in the weeks following Buchenwald's liberation, and by the information released by the prosecution team, raced to find adjectives that combined her alleged evil with her supposed beauty, sexual prowess, and perversity. In a manner never used when reporting on Koch's male codefendants, many stories began with descriptions of her looks and sometimes of her body. Journalists referred to her variously as the "Bitch of Buchenwald," the "Witch of Buchenwald," and, in *Stars and Stripes,* even as the "sex-hungry witch of Buchenwald." They noted her "voluptuous body," or described her as "hard-faced and red-haired," or "red-headed and quick-witted."[81] The most extensive report, in *Newsweek,* featured photos of Ilse in her bathing suit and playing with her son, Artwin, juxtaposed with photos of emaciated concentration camp inmates and the Buchenwald gallows. Under the headline of "Witch of Buchenwald: Record of a Sadist," it described Ilse's search for tattooed inmates and her "nymphomania," and then her appearance in court:

> She is still attractive, despite her rather blowsy brown sack suit, her short socks, bare leg, and saddle shoes. Flaming titian hair, emerald-green eyes, and a school-girlish complexion belie that she is 40. On a prison diet she has reduced 40 pounds, until her figure, despite a too-prominent derriere and a still-conspicuous bust, is almost boyish. She listens to the evidence intelligently and intently.

Every once in a while she raises a girlish hand to stroke her slightly double chin. One can read an occasional sullenness in her face, but little to suggest that she is the fiendish character the mounting piles of evidence prove her to be.[82]

Combining sexualized imagery, gender stereotypes, and sadistic or fetishized violence, such reports served to satisfy a growing thirst for details of her trial in the United States, where the reading public began a long and eager wait for a guilty verdict and commensurate punishment.

The first witness Denson selected to testify against Ilse Koch was former prisoner Dr. Eugen Kogon, whose Buchenwald Report had chronicled the history of the camp for the US Army and whose credibility was bolstered by his high level of education, his expertise, and his demeanor. Neatly dressed in a dark suit and tie with combed-back, receding brown hair and silver spectacles, Kogon related to the court the authority and power that he and his fellow inmates attributed to Koch, and the fear that she had inspired in them:

> Ilse Koch was known to me as the Commandeuse of the camp during the time of the Commandant Koch. In the eyes of the prisoners she was just as dangerous as Koch. . . . Prisoners in the work details were reported [to the SS guards for punishment] by the Commandeuse whenever she went by on horseback or walked by. Outside of that prisoners were sent to the bunkers or sent on outside [work] details whenever they had a conflict with the Commandeuse. . . . I heard from comrades that prisoners who had been reported by the Commandeuse did not reappear, that they disappeared, that they were dead."[83]

Kogon's testimony and his use of the term "commandeuse" bolstered Denson's contention that Ilse Koch exercised significant authority at

Buchenwald yet his account also provided an early indication that the prosecution would have difficulty producing for the court reliable first-hand testimony. Kogon, under cross-examination, confirmed that he had "never had any direct contact" with Koch. Rather than through personal experience, he had learned of the alleged crimes he described on the stand through the reports of fellow prisoners. Further, Kogon admitted that he had never seen Koch within the camp's barbed wire enclosure in the seven years he spent at Buchenwald, but only caught glimpses of her in the distance on two or three occasions. He explained that he was able to identify Koch in the dock only because of the many photos he had seen of her in the press in the months preceding the trial.[84]

Following Kogon's testimony, Denson introduced a series of witnesses who recounted more specific incidents of violence alleg-edly inflicted, ordered, or inspired by Ilse Koch. Most accounts, like Kogon's, were based on hearsay, but the prosecution hoped that such evidence, so long as it was consistent, would convince the court of Koch's complicity. Former inmate Paul Schilling, for example, testi-fied that he had seen Ilse and Karl Koch walking along the road leading to the camp one day in late 1941. When they passed two Polish Jewish inmates pushing a heavy cart, he reported, "Frau Koch told her hus-band, 'This dirty Jewish pig dared to look at me,'" and Karl promptly beat one of the men to the ground. Under cross-examination, how-ever, Schilling confirmed that he had been forty to fifty meters dis-tant from the incident and had not himself heard Ilse utter these words; rather, a "comrade" of the victim had told him in a conversation two hours afterward what Ilse had uttered.[85] While Shilling's account at-tested to Ilse's knowledge of, and moral complicity in, the abuse of prisoners at Buchenwald, therefore, it could not confirm that violence had occurred at her instigation.

In similar testimony, witness Ernst Blanck recalled an incident during which Karl Koch had beaten a prisoner, allegedly after Ilse had complained that the man had ogled her. Under cross-examination, Blanck, too, confirmed that he had been too far away when the incident occurred to hear whether or not Ilse had in fact demanded the beating.[86] Former inmate Josef Broz testified that while he was working as part of a labor detail in the Koch garden, Ilse had appeared and furiously accused the men of having picked her berries. When the eleven men of the detail returned to the camp compound at the end of the work day, they received beatings from the SS, leaving Broz to surmise that Ilse must have reported the incident to camp authorities.[87] The accounts of Broz, Schilling, and Blanck highlighted the difficulty of proving that Ilse Koch had spurred others to acts of violence, given that it required firsthand knowledge, which few witnesses possessed, of conversations or comments between Koch and the camp SS.

The only witness to testify that he himself had been physically abused by Koch was former inmate Max Kronfeldner. According to Kronfeldner, he and two fellow prisoners were returning from the camp hospital when a redheaded woman on horseback approached them and struck each of them with a riding crop. While Kronfeldner had personally experienced this beating, the authority of his firsthand account was undercut to a degree when he explained that he had not known who had administered the whipping at the time, but was only told later by his camp comrades that the perpetrator must have been the wife of the commandant.[88]

Even if the prosecution's attempt to establish Ilse Koch's responsibility for the physical abuse of inmates had to rest largely on hearsay or conjecture, Denson and his team believed they could connect her more conclusively to the practice of collecting tattooed human skins by calling to the stand a number of prisoners who had worked in Buchenwald's pathology department and seen for themselves the objects in question. Witness Dr. Peter Zenkl, who prior to his incarceration at Buchenwald had served as mayor of Prague and who at the time of his testimony at Dachau was deputy prime minister of Czechoslovakia, recounted his experience working in the pathology department. "During the time I was there," Zenkl testified, "human skins with tattoos on them were taken from the dissecting room. The skin was cleaned, dried and stretched on frames there."[89] Zenkl further testified that various SS men took the dried skins and were attracted in particular to those pieces containing the most obscene tattoos. Zenkl, however, could not testify to Ilse Koch's role, and confirmed that he had worked in the pathology department in late 1943 and early 1944, when she was no longer at Buchenwald.[90] Witness Pierre Biermann similarly described for the court the practice of collecting human skins that he witnessed while working as a prisoner clerk in the pathology department, but provided nothing to place Koch at the scene. While Biermann testified that he had seen a pile of dried tattooed skins, and that fellow prisoners had told him that this collection originated because Ilse Koch "had expressed a desire to own certain objects made of human skin," he confirmed that he had only worked in the pathology department from early 1944, months after Koch's departure.[91]

Spending much more time on the stand than Zenkl and Biermann was Dr. Kurt Sitte, a Czech physicist who was the "leading prisoner" in the pathology department from mid-1942 until the camp's liberation and who testified at length on the activities of his SS overseers and Ilse Koch. Sitte began by testifying that no fewer than thirty thousand dead bodies passed through the department during his tenure there, and that orders had been issued that particularly colorful or lewd tattoos were to be removed from corpses when found.[92] Sitte testified that seeking out living prisoners and murdering them for their tattoos "was not done" while he was at the camp, although he had heard a rumor that it had occurred in connection with SS Dr. Erich Wagner's dissertation research before his arrival in 1942.[93] When asked to describe Ilse Koch's role in the collection of skin, Sitte could only testify that he had heard "from prisoners with whom we [played] ... handball" that Koch had had a human skin lampshade delivered to her from the pathology department, but that he had never seen it himself.[94] Elaborating on widely circulated rumors at Buchenwald, Sitte testified further that "it was common knowledge that in the camp it happened that prisoners were called to the hospital from commandos where Ilse Koch had passed by the day before.... These prisoners later on were killed in the hospital and the tattooing stripped off."[95] Before leaving the stand, Sitte identified for the court a number of pieces of skin, which were then formally entered as exhibits by the prosecution.

Knowing that allegations that Koch had collected tattooed human skins were key to her prosecution, and to the public's morbid fascination with the "Bitch of Buchenwald," defense counsel Captain Lewis labored to expose the myriad weaknesses in the evidence presented in court. Lewis underscored the testimonies of Biermann and Zenkl, who both had said the practice of collecting tattooed skins continued at Buchenwald in Koch's absence, undercutting the prosecution's insistence that this macabre activity was primarily prompted by and undertaken for her. More fundamentally, Lewis emphasized that Biermann, Zenkl, and Sitte all relied on hearsay and camp rumor; none could tie Koch directly to the practice. Thus, with regard to this most sensational charge, the testimony of the witnesses introduced by the prosecution left little doubt that tattooed skins had been collected at Buchenwald in some fashion, but was insufficient to implicate Koch.

After introducing the testimony of the former inmates who had worked in the pathology department, Denson and his team focused much of their time and energy on eliciting information from two key witnesses who allegedly had extensive firsthand knowledge of Ilse Koch's activities and who, the prosecution hoped, could more directly tie her to atrocities at Buchenwald. The first was a German farmer named Kurt Titz who had arrived as a prisoner in 1939 and worked as an orderly in the office of commandant Koch, and then as a domestic servant in the Koch household. Titz testified that, during his tenure working for Karl Koch, Ilse had visited her husband frequently and sometimes reported prisoners for punishment. "Mrs. Koch and her husband, they sort of ruled together," Titz recalled. "If she did not want to see a man anymore, then she simply said, 'I can't stand the sight of this man anymore,' and the man wouldn't be there anymore. . . . Any desire she would express, her husband would take care of."[96] Titz testified that he himself had had a run-in with Ilse when she appeared in Karl's office and found Titz drinking a glass of the commandant's wine in his absence. Although Titz asked Ilse not to report his transgression to her husband, she told Karl nonetheless, with the result that Titz was beaten by defendant Anton Bergmeier and consigned to the arrest bunker, where he was hanged up by the arms.

Titz explained to the court that, despite the beating he received, he was ordered six weeks later into service as a domestic servant in the Koch home, where he would see Ilse on a daily basis. Arriving at five o'clock each morning, Titz kept the house orderly and clean, and woke and dressed the Koch children.[97] Titz testified that on two occasions, as he worked in this capacity, he observed Ilse taking down the numbers of prisoners working outside the house to facilitate their punishment. He recounted an incident when Ilse saw a prisoner sweeping the street who had turned up his collar, and threatened the man that she would have his "ass beat up" if he didn't turn it back down; she then wrote down his number and handed it to SS Captain Florstedt.

Of most interest to the prosecution, however, were Titz's recollections of the furnishings of the Koch home, and in particular, of two lampshades that he dusted daily in the lounge. At the request of assistant prosecutor Kunzig, Titz described these lampshades to the court:

> They looked like parchment. One of them was smooth, and the other, standing on the desk, had sort of tattoos on it. It was explained to me that those lampshades were made out of human skin. There was a dead skull between these two lampshades. Little Edwin [sic] was playing around with this dead head and pulling out the teeth. I had to put the teeth back in.[98]

Following these recollections, Titz was cross-examined aggressively by Captain Lewis, who sought to call into question the veracity of his memory and the validity of the inferences he had drawn:

> *Lewis:* You testified that you saw the two lamps that were made of parchment. . . . One of these lamps appeared to you as it had a tattoo on it, is that correct?
>
> *Titz:* Yes. . . . I don't remember the exact tattoo there because it was always horrible for me to look at them knowing they were made of human skin. Every time I had to look at these lampshades, it was a horror to me.
>
> *Lewis:* How often did you see those lampshades?
>
> *Titz:* I saw them every day.
>
> *Lewis:* You cannot tell us today what picture was on the lampshade?
>
> *Titz:* I cannot say exactly . . .
>
> *Lewis:* You dusted them every day didn't you?
>
> *Titz:* Yes. . . . All I remember was that a sailing boat was on there.
>
> *Lewis:* So you do remember what pictures were on the lamp, don't you?
>
> *Titz:* Yes. Well I don't have an exact picture but around the edges there were dots or squares or stars.

Lewis: There was a sailing boat on there, is that right?

Titz: Yes.

Lewis: When you went to the pathology department, it was there that you were told about the nature of these lamps, is that not correct?

Titz: Yes.

Lewis: Before that, you did not know, did you?

Titz: I did not know. I am not a doctor and could not discern it. I only know from the pathology that there was one lamp shade to be made of a lower part of a person's leg with the toes to be used as a switch and that work was refused by the prisoner who was supposed to do it.

Lewis: That never got into Mrs. Koch's house, did it?

Titz: I never saw it . . .

Lewis: Had you ever seen any lamp similar in material to the one that you saw in Frau Koch's house?

Titz: The big standing lamp was entirely without tattoo. Of course, not being an expert I cannot say whether that was human skin, all I know is that I was told so in the pathology department . . .

Lewis: As far as you could see, that lamp was no different than any ordinary lamp you had ever seen before or since, was it?

Titz: No.[99]

After underscoring for the court that Titz's belief that human skins had been used in the production of the lamps in the Koch household was based purely on conjecture or hearsay, Lewis took on Titz's claim that Ilse had "ruled" Buchenwald alongside her husband:

Lewis: Did you hear Mrs. Koch tell her husband how to run the Camp Buchenwald?

Titz: Mr. and Mrs. Koch were for all practical purposes one
and anything that Mrs. Koch desired, Koch would do
cheerfully and gladly because he loved her above all.

Lewis: Did you ever hear Frau Koch in her husband's office tell
him how he should run Camp Buchenwald?

Titz: Rather frequently I heard in the office that Mrs. Koch
complained about this or that prisoner.

Lewis: Did you hear her tell her husband what should be done
with those prisoners?

Titz: I did not hear that directly, but after all she knew from
several other cases what those prisoners could expect. . . .

Lewis: Outside of that, you never heard Frau Koch discuss any
camp matters with her husband?

Titz: No.

Lewis: So in that manner, you state to this court that she
regulated the camp, is that correct?

Titz: Yes. [100]

Having drawn to the fore the assumptions that informed Titz's
testimony, Lewis concluded his cross-examination by calling Titz's
character into question, asking the witness to recall the bizarre incident that had purportedly resulted in his dismissal from service in
the Koch home. In his prior testimony, Titz had admitted that Ilse
had caught him drinking wine in Karl's office, but claimed that this
was the only alcohol he had had the opportunity to consume while at
Buchenwald. Under cross-examination, however, Titz now recounted
how he also broke into a case of wine in the Koch cellar in Ilse's absence and got "terribly drunk." He admitted that, before slipping into
a state of total unconsciousness, he had "smashed up everything that
was in the house," but denied a particularly salacious detail that had
been reported: that when he was discovered by Ilse and sent to the
bunker he was wearing her underwear. [101]

In his own defense Titz explained that, rather than reckless debauchery, the incident was spurred by his desire "to make an end" to his life, having reached the point that he "couldn't stand it any longer."[102] Nonetheless, his credibility had been damaged. Also inconvenient for the prosecution was that Koch had called for Titz to be punished, not killed, after his rampage—a fact that was hard to reconcile with claims that she routinely had prisoners beaten to death merely for casting glances in her direction.

Following Titz to the stand was another key witness whose sensational and shocking accounts of Ilse Koch's activities at Buchenwald appeared at first to confirm the central pillars of the case that Denson and his team had built. Herbert Froboess, a draftsman from Dresden, explained that he had been sent to Buchenwald as a prisoner of conscience in 1937 because he had once resided in a Franciscan monastery.[103] An inmate until liberation, Froboess described working both on labor gangs and as a cartographical draftsman preparing family trees, photo albums, and other decorative items for the camp's higher-ranking SS officers. Asked to describe for the court his first encounter with Ilse Koch, Froboess recalled an incident on a work detail that combined allegations of physical violence with sexual perversity:

> We were working in the so-called falcon's yard, digging a line for cables, and I was working together with a Czech chaplain. This chaplain loosened the soil, and I was throwing it up with the shovel. Suddenly somebody was standing on top of the ditch and was yelling, "Prisoner, what are you doing down there?" [She was] standing with her legs straddled over the ditch (demonstrating). We looked up to see who it was and recognized Mrs. Koch. She was standing on top of the ditch without any underwear and a short skirt. As we did this, she said, "What are you doing looking up here?" and with her riding crop she beat us.[104]

As Froboess continued, he showed what the defense would describe as a suspicious knack for appearing at just the right time and place to witness incidents or overhear conversations that deeply implicated Koch. Froboess recounted, for instance, how he had come to learn that Koch had once had an affair with a man she met in a Leipzig restaurant; when her former lover subsequently arrived as a prisoner at Buchenwald, she went out of her way to punish him. The most serious incident Froboess recalled involved a column of Jewish prisoners who were carrying stones in front of the Koch home at a speed Ilse allegedly deemed insufficient. Ilse, Froboess testified, used her riding crop to hit some of these exhausted workers with such fury that they fell to the ground, knocking down other prisoners in the process. Koch did this alone and yet so violently that, as Froboess put it, "whole columns of severely injured Jews were carried into camp through the course of the day."[105]

Aside from Froboess's identification of Koch as the direct perpetrator of brutal and perverse violence, the prosecution also elicited testimony from him that supported the other components of its case: that Ilse had co-commanded Buchenwald, and that she had sanctioned the killing of inmates for the collection of their tattooed skins. Asked to describe the scope of Ilse's authority at Buchenwald, Froboess testified that he had seen an order issued by Karl Koch to the camp SS stipulating that "Mrs. Koch is to be addressed and respected as Mrs. Colonel Koch at all times, and any of her orders will be obeyed in the same manner as if he himself had given them."[106] He testified also that he had seen in Ilse Koch's possession a document briefcase, a pair of gloves, and a photo album made of human skin and had personally witnessed Ilse's selection of a tattooed prisoner for death. The incident, Froboess explained, occurred when Ilse observed members of a construction detail slaving shirtless on a particularly hot day:

There was a comrade there—his first name was Jean . . . and he was known throughout the camp for his tattoos. . . . On his chest he had an exceptionally clearly tattooed sailboat with four masts. Even today I can see it before my eyes very clearly. Mrs. Koch rode over to him [on horseback]. . . . And then she told him, "Let's work faster, faster." . . . and then she took his number down. . . . the camp comrade was then called to the gate at evening formation. . . . We didn't see him anymore.

Six months later, Froboess testified, he visited the pathology department and saw samples of human skin. "And to my horror," he testified, "I noticed the same sailboat that I had seen on Jean."[107] He claimed to have seen the tattoo yet again later, this time on the cover of an album that Karl and Ilse Koch gave him with instructions to prepare a "family journal" for the family. When Ilse handed him the album, he noticed also that Ilse was wearing gloves of what he claimed to recognize as "whitish-yellow" human skin "with a star tattooed on the back of the left glove."[108]

The accounts elicited from Froboess were the most implicating, gruesome, and sensational to be heard by the Dachau court, prompting the defense to engage in a rigorous cross-examination that left his credibility in tatters. The defense first confronted Froboess with a series of inconsistencies in his testimony for which he could not properly account. Captain Lewis had Froboess confirm, for instance, that it had been in the summer of 1940 that he had seen Koch riding on horseback and writing down the numbers of prisoners for punishment. He then pointed out that Koch had been pregnant at that time—her daughter Gudrun was born in December—making horseback riding a highly unlikely pastime.[109] Further cross-examination compelled Froboess to admit that, contrary to his initial testimony, he had never actually seen Karl Koch's alleged official order to his men concerning Ilse's title and authority, but only heard of its existence.[110]

Turning to Froboess's account of Ilse targeting the tattooed prisoner Jean, Captain Lewis first had Froboess clarify that he had never actually heard the exchange between Ilse and Jean, and so he did not know for certain why Jean was called out at roll call that evening. Froboess further confirmed at the prompting of the defense that prisoners were forbidden to remove their shirts, a fact at odds with his description of Jean laboring with his tattooed upper body exposed. Next, having pressed Froboess to confirm again that he stood by certain details of his testimony, Lewis worked to discredit it by pointing to conflicts with an interview Froboess had granted to a journalist regarding the same incident:

> *Lewis:* Can you tell us what you told this reporter about the case, particularly with reference to the tattooed skin?
>
> *Froboess:* I don't know exactly any more today . . .
>
> *Lewis:* Did you tell this reporter concerning this incident with your friend that your friend was called away from the job and never came back?
>
> *Froboess:* No, this can't be right because he was called away during the evening roll call.
>
> *Lewis:* Do you recall telling this reporter that several weeks later you went into the pathology department and found the skin of your friend?
>
> *Froboess:* Yes.
>
> *Lewis:* But in this court you said it was six months or more when you went into the pathology department and saw that skin, is that not so?
>
> *Froboess:* That is possible.
>
> *Lewis:* Which was it then?

Froboess: Because of the long incarceration in protective
    custody, I lost all conception of time. One cannot give
    exact dates, one can only say that it happened around
    this time or that time . . .
Lewis: I ask you now whether you saw the skin six months or
    more later or within several weeks, as printed in the
    newspaper?
Froboess: At any rate, there were several months between.[III]

If cross-examination raised doubts about the veracity of Froboess's
account, his general credibility suffered further damage when Captain Lewis revealed both that Froboess was currently employed by the
prosecution team as a draftsman in the preparation for the trial and,
more troubling still, that he had fraudulently presented himself as a
Franciscan friar. Questioned on the stand, Froboess testified that he
had never claimed to be a friar and always insisted to all who would
listen that he was not. Later in the trial, however, defense counsel introduced a witness named Frieda Förschner who testified that Froboess, dressed in a monk's robe, had accepted more than 3,000 RM
from her in exchange for an unfulfilled promise to testify on behalf
of her husband, Otto, who was tried at Dachau and subsequently
sentenced to death and executed.[112] Finally, when Lewis produced a
postcard from August 1945 depicting Froboess dressed in a monk's
robes, the witness's claim that he had never posed as a man of the cloth
was definitively impeached. The card's very title proclaimed him to
be "Father Herbert Froboess, Ancient Prisoner of the Concentration
Camp Buchenwald."[113]

Although defense counsel had succeeded in casting doubt on much
of the testimony connecting Koch directly to acts of atrocity, the prosecution still had reason to feel confident as it rested its case on May 13,
1947. Chief Prosecutor Denson had secured more than a hundred

convictions of concentration camp perpetrators in the cases he had previously argued before the military commission courts at Dachau. Experienced at using the lax rules of evidence and expansive common design charge to his advantage, Denson bargained that the military men who comprised the court would be sufficiently impressed with the consistency of the testimony against Koch to find her guilty, even if the evidence was largely secondhand and circumstantial and did not conclusively show her involvement in specific incidents. The prosecution had failed to link Koch to the collection of tattooed human skins by anything more than camp rumor, but whether her conviction would be hampered by this remained to be seen.

The Defense Presents Its Case

After the prosecution had rested its case, the Dachau court granted defense counsel a two-week adjournment of proceedings to prepare their response on behalf of Ilse Koch and her thirty co-accused. When the court reconvened on May 26, defense counsel Major Carl Whitney introduced a motion demanding that the court declare all the defendants not guilty on the grounds that the prosecution had not sufficiently proved that a "common design to commit war crimes" existed at Buchenwald as the charges alleged. Following the court's summary dismissal of this motion, Whitney prefaced the introduction of his first witness with a statement to the court that pointed to the media frenzy that had swirled around Ilse Koch in particular and had resulted in the publication of salacious and unsubstantiated claims that the defense feared would influence the court: "The newspapers have been filled with inflammatory stories concerning camp Buchenwald and these defendants have been waiting patiently for two years to present their side of the story ... and they welcome this opportunity to show the court that what has appeared in the newspapers concerning their activities is not true."[114]

With that, the defense called to the stand its first witness, former Buchenwald commandant Hermann Pister. For the most part, Koch's codefendants were not questioned about her activities by either prosecution or defense counsel; instead, their testimonies focused on their own doings at Buchenwald. Pister, however, was an exception. He testified that he had never heard that Koch beat prisoners and never would have permitted such behavior. He insisted that Koch "wouldn't have dared" to report prisoners to him for punishment, and recalled that when she appeared outside the family home she was usually in the company of her children.[115] Protective custody camp leader Max Schobert, the only other defendant to testify about Ilse Koch, echoed Pister's account, maintaining that she never contacted his office to report prisoners for punishment and that, while Karl Koch may have, he would never "have taken orders from his wife."[116]

The defense, eager to discredit accounts of violence by Ilse Koch as mere prisoner hearsay, proceeded to call to the stand a series of former inmates who provided exculpatory accounts on her behalf. Witnesses Ludwig Eichhorn, Heinrich Albrecht, and Josef Siebeneichler had arrived at Buchenwald as prisoners of faith, and all testified that, having each spent at least six years at the camp and having seen Ilse Koch on numerous occasions walking with her children or on horseback, none had ever seen her mistreat prisoners or ever heard that she was involved in such abuse. As prompted by the defense, each testified that, if she had beaten prisoners, they undoubtedly would have heard about it.[117] While the testimony of Eichhorn and Albrecht stopped there, Siebeneichler's was elicited further by the defense to distance Koch from the practice of collecting tattooed skins and to suggest that rumors of her involvement were partly the result of misinformation spread by American authorities in the wake of the liberation. Asked to recount for the court his experience working in Buchenwald's photographic department, Siebeneichler first recalled an order he received in late 1943, after Koch's departure from the camp, to photograph thirty tattooed prisoners for "the compilation of scientific research."[118] Siebeneichler testified that, while he saw skins in the pathological department at Buchenwald, he had never heard Ilse Koch's name mentioned in connection with their collection until US authorities arrived at the camp, addressed the press, and forced the civilians of Weimar to witness the aftermath of the liberation. As Siebeneichler recalled, "An American non-commissioned officer was standing on a vehicle in a crowd of assembled people and was giving a lecture about the activities of Buchenwald. . . . He had a table lamp which he explained had been manufactured out of tattooed human skin. . . . It was said that this lamp belonged to Mrs. Koch."[119]

Siebeneichler's testimony raised an implicit question concerning the provenance of the lamp: if it had been discovered and displayed by American authorities at Buchenwald in 1945, who had possessed it since Ilse's arrest and departure from the camp in September 1943? With Siebeneichler still on the stand, defense counsel Captain Lewis asked why an object so central to the trial had not been entered into evidence by the prosecution. He demanded that Chief Prosecutor Denson and his team "produce before this court the lampshade that was in the possession of the American forces at Buchenwald, or explain to the court the reason why such lampshade cannot be produced." Given that descriptions of the lampshade had varied, its examination by the court would have been instructive. In response to Lewis's demand, however, Denson claimed that, while "there was nothing we would like to do better than to produce that lampshade," it had been turned over to judicial authorities at Nuremberg in exchange for a receipt. When the prosecution team requested its return in preparation for trial, Denson explained, they were informed that this particular exhibit could no longer be located.[120] The lampshade had mysteriously disappeared, and it would never surface again.

Seeking to further draw into question Ilse Koch's alleged ownership of the lampshade, defense counsel next called to the stand

Dr. Konrad Morgen, the SS judge who had carried out the investigation and arrest of the Kochs in 1943. A civilian internee of the US occupation authorities at the time of his appearance, Morgen now appeared as a key defense witness, testifying for two full days beginning on June 11, 1947. Captain Lewis first had Morgen describe the genesis of the investigation he had led at Buchenwald and the key role that Ilse's codefendant Prince Josias of Waldeck had played in launching it. Morgen recounted at length the extensive corruption he uncovered, Karl Koch's attempts to conceal it through the murder of inmates Peix and Krämer, and the obstruction he encountered from Himmler and higher SS authorities. Depicting himself, as always, as a humanitarian whistleblower, Morgen emphasized his independence and the lengths to which he had gone to ensure Karl Koch's removal from command.

At the prompting of defense counsel Lewis, Morgen described for the court the thorough search of the Koch family home he had led in August 1943:

> *Morgen:* I, together with Criminal Secretary Nett, Colonel Pister, and Major Barnewald searched the house very thoroughly from the cellar to the attic. There wasn't a desk drawer that was left unopened. The house was then sealed . . . and after that every single piece of furniture was moved down to Saaz and an inventory of everything that had been in the house was again taken . . .
>
> *Lewis:* Now in this investigation and search you made in August 1943, did you find any lampshades made of human skin on Mrs. Koch's premises?
>
> *Morgen:* No, not one . . .
>
> *Lewis:* During your investigations at camp Buchenwald after the arrest, and even before the arrest of Mrs. Koch, until

> May of 1944, was any report made to you by anybody
> that Mrs. Koch had a lampshade or gloves or a photo
> album or a book made of human skin in her possession?
> *Morgen:* No, I didn't even hear a rumor of any such thing.[121]

Given the extent of his efforts to uncover incriminating evidence against the Kochs during the eight months he investigated their affairs at Buchenwald, Morgen's insistence that he had never encountered evidence concerning Ilse Koch and objects of human skin was notable. It cast serious doubt on her connection to the lampshade, especially as it appeared that the entire contents of the Koch household had been removed by the summer of 1943. Morgen further eroded the reliability of Kurt Titz's testimony concerning Koch's alleged lampshade by drawing attention to an inconsistency: while Titz had eagerly participated as a witness in Morgen's 1943 SS investigation and had "brought out all kinds of things against Mrs. Koch," he had never mentioned any objects of human skin at the time.[122]

Yet, while Morgen's testimony dealt a further blow to the prosecution's most inflammatory charge, defense counsel quickly learned that his testimony could be a double-edged sword. Morgen concluded his account of the Buchenwald investigation by confirming that the SS court that had heard the Koch case and sentenced Karl to death had not found sufficient evidence to convict Ilse of any crime. Under cross-examination, however, Morgen verified for the prosecution that in the course of his investigation he had often heard that Ilse had abused prisoners and reported them for punishment, that she frequented her husband's office and had access to his files, and that she was known at Buchenwald as the "commandeuse."[123] Asked if he had ascertained during his investigation that she made "obscene remarks to prisoners, as for example, 'Just look in this direction if your ass is worth twenty-five to you,'" Morgen replied that "Mrs. Koch loved to make remarks of this type," and indicated that her behavior toward the prisoners "was a scandal." Prompted by defense counsel to explain further, Morgen described how she had treated her domestic help poorly, refusing to let them use the bathroom and providing them with little or nothing to eat. Corroborating a key contention of a number of prosecution witnesses, Morgen continued:

> Toward the prisoners who she met in camp, she wore clothes which were deliberately chosen to be inciting for the prisoners. She was made up typically for sex appeal. Whenever a prisoner looked at her, then it was a pleasure for her to see to it that the prisoner was punished severely. It is my opinion also, though I have no proof for that, that through the illegal beatings which occurred as a result of these reports, prisoners also died.[124]

Recognizing that the prosecution had succeeded in eliciting testimony from Morgen that supported key components of Ilse Koch's indictment, Captain Lewis followed up Morgen's cross-examination with a series of questions designed to draw into question the witness's firsthand knowledge of these behaviors. Lewis first asked Morgen whether he himself had ever seen Koch wearing the sort of provocative clothing he described; Morgen responded that he had not, because "after the removal of her husband from Buchenwald, Mrs. Koch became very conservative."[125] Yet, while Morgen confirmed that he had learned of her ill-treatment of prisoners only from interviews with other prisoners, he also claimed that Koch herself had confessed to him that she had repeatedly reported to her husband prisoners who "had conducted themselves toward her in an indecent or insulting manner."[126] Lewis then asked Morgen whether he knew for certain that Ilse had asked for the punishment of the prisoners whom she reported. Morgen admitted that he did not, but defended his own conjecture by asserting that "if a woman in a mad voice reports to her husband the alleged misconduct of a prisoner towards her, then asking for a punishment is included in that without expressing it explicitly."[127] Finally, Lewis concluded his examination of Morgen by casting into doubt any importance given to the title "commandeuse" as an indicator of Koch's authority. Asked how the title was used, Morgen explained that this was merely a "nickname," and one applied to her "in no favorable sense."[128]

Before finally calling Ilse to the stand to testify on her own behalf, Captain Lewis summoned a few final witnesses whose testimony fortified the accounts of the key witnesses the defense had already presented to the court. First was former Chief Criminal Secretary Heinrich Nett, who had assisted Konrad Morgen with his investigation at Buchenwald and helped to execute the search of the Koch home. Nett testified that, expressly because rumors circulated at Buchenwald concerning the collection of tattooed skins, he had carefully inspected all objects in the home including the lampshades and photo albums; he had concluded, however, that these were "regular lampshades," made of nothing more than "imitation pig skin or some sort of cardboard."[129] Nett's well-documented enmity toward Ilse Koch, like Morgen's, added authority to his exculpatory testimony, and further undercut the testimony of Titz and Froboess. Captain Lewis also called to the stand Koch's brother-in-law, Arthur Schmidt, and her sister-in-law, Erna Raible, with whom she had feuded; both testified that, while they visited the Kochs on numerous occasions and for extended periods, neither had ever seen Ilse abuse prisoners.[130]

Ilse Koch on the Stand

On July 10, after three months of court proceedings and the introduction of dozens of witnesses, Captain Lewis called Ilse Koch to the stand to testify in her own defense. In marked contrast to images in the press that described her as the embodiment of sexual prowess and licentiousness, she appeared both modest and stern in a light, knee-

Fig. 3.4   Ilse Koch testifies before the Dachau court, July 1947. US Army Signal Corps, Record Group III, National Archives and Records Administration.

length, plaid dress and a dark blazer, and was visibly pregnant. Lewis first asked Koch whether she had been a member of the Nazi Party, prompting her to perjure herself as she had done under interrogation at Ludwigsburg City Hall. Though documents would later surface to prove Koch's 1932 entry into the Party, she flatly denied any such association in court. This lie, not revealed until her subsequent trial at Augsburg in 1950–1951, betrayed her fear that discovery of her membership would undercut a central plank of her emerging defense strategy: that she had been nothing more than an apolitical wife and mother unaware of what went on behind Buchenwald's barbed wire.[131] The fraudulence of Koch's denial also illustrates that she was willing to lie under oath when she felt that her alibi was in jeopardy.

As Captain Lewis's questioning continued, Koch took every opportunity to emphasize her preoccupation with family life, and in so doing, to imply that her scope of action as a woman had been proscribed by the deeply conservative and restrictive gender roles of the Third Reich. Asked whether she ever had carried a riding crop, she replied that she had no use for one, given that she "had little children," and "had to take a baby carriage along" when she walked near the camp.[132] Asked whether she exercised authority at Buchenwald and influence over Karl, she answered with incredulity: "I was the mother of the children and the housewife. . . . I didn't marry any henpecked husband, but rather a man who knew what his job was."[133] She responded similarly to a question from Captain Lewis regarding whether she had ever reported prisoners for punishment for violating camp rules:

> The operation of the camp didn't concern me, neither the work nor internal matters. I was a housewife and I think my power is being overestimated because if I have three children . . . then I am so preoccupied all day long that I have neither the intention nor the time to take care of camp matters. . . . In [my husband's] eyes, my primary job was to be the mother of our children. I tried my best to prepare a comfortable home for my husband in the evenings.[134]

Although she did admit to reporting prosecution witness Kurt Titz to camp authorities, she explained that she had done so only because he had thoroughly violated her domestic domain while employed as her servant. Confirming earlier testimony that had undercut Titz's credibility, she recounted how he had vandalized the Koch home in a state of drunkenness and had subsequently been discovered unconscious in the cellar wearing Ilse's underwear, housecoat, and shoes.[135]

Aside from posing questions that allowed Ilse to present herself as a dedicated mother confined largely to the domestic sphere, Captain Lewis also inquired about the SS investigation of her and her husband's affairs at Buchenwald, prompting Ilse to emphasize the reasons why her resulting trial had ended in acquittal. She described first how Konrad Morgen and his assistants had made a surprise visit to the Koch home and had searched it "from top to bottom" before taking her into custody. Confirming Morgen's testimony, she explained that the entire content of the Koch home was then cataloged and sent on to Saaz. It was therefore "impossible," she declared, that the lampshade shown in newsreels following the liberation of Buchenwald belonged to her, given that the house had been empty since her departure from the camp in 1943.[136] Had Morgen discovered any such object in her home, she argued, it would have been used as "a corpus delicti" to convict her.[137] Instead, Koch reminded the court, Morgen's attempt to prosecute her failed:

> After 16 months in prison pending investigation, where all kinds of things were tried against me, and where even prisoners were interrogated against me ... I was tried before an SS court. . . . I was acquitted unconditionally. . . . If any proof had been brought in at that time that I had behaved anywhere near the manner described ... then I would have been convicted without any doubt. I'm sure that one can tell from the testimony of Dr. Morgen and Dr. Nett, who you must remember were not my friends, after all that prisoners were sufficiently incited against me ... but nothing could be found except rumors and talk.[138]

"When, for the first time," Lewis asked, "did you ever hear that anything was said concerning you in any way about tattooed human skin?" Koch explained that she was already in American custody when she discovered an article in *Life* in October 1945 and immediately attempted to set the record straight:

> There was a full page picture of me in there with a caption that I had issued orders to have prisoners with tattooed skin killed so I could get the tattooed skin. Of course I was very excited and tried to see somebody with the [Counter Intelligence Corps] but I never succeeded in doing so in spite of repeated attempts. I was interrogated only once and the interrogating officer informed me that it was not he who had written that report and that I should see the journalist concerned. Of course since I was a prisoner, I could not do that.[139]

Regarding witness Kurt Titz's claim that there were two lampshades made of human skin in her home, Ilse declared his testimony to be a "deliberate lie." She was equally dismissive of witness Froboess's testimony regarding photo albums made of human skin and insisted that, in this case also, she had tried to counter what she stressed was a baseless rumor. As Captain Lewis had done, she pointed out that the prosecution had not entered any human-skin objects as exhibits:

> I never owned any such photo album. Furthermore it would be an easy thing for the Prosecution to produce this photo album in evidence since the American Military Government has it in its possession. The same is true about the lampshade that was found in my house. I did not know the witness Froboess. I saw him for the first time when he appeared on the witness stand here. . . . The first time I read the papers that I was supposed to own a family chronicle bound in human skin, I tried to smuggle a letter out of prison asking somebody to bring the family chronicle which I had at home and which I had not known at that time that it had been seized by the military government over here.[140]

Before submitting herself to cross-examination, Koch concluded her testimony with an impassioned statement that reemphasized her motherhood while expressing indignation at the allegations against her. Her fury at the press was palpable:

There has been a lot of talk about myself in the press for the last two years. I do not think there is any expression in the German language too vulgar to have been used against me.... I as a mother cannot peacefully stand by when my children are now in such a state that they dislike going to school . . . , that they are extremely shy, and that they do not have the courage to talk to anybody about their real troubles. In the papers I am described as the pinnacle of sadism, perversion and corruption. . . . The expressions in the newspapers are of the most vulgar type and the way it is stated is not that I was under any suspicion but that it is a fact that I own lampshades made out of human skin without any trial having taken place. . . . I never even conceived of the possibility of even being put to trial because I never did any of the things that have been presented against me.[141]

With those words, Koch indicated that she wished to add nothing further, prompting Captain Lewis to yield the floor to the prosecution team to permit her cross-examination. As quickly became clear, Koch would make little attempt to stem her anger but would instead meet many of the questions posed to her with blanket denials spoken with a thinly veiled contempt that would have done little to warm the court to her.

Chief Prosecutor Denson wasted little time in posing pointed questions concerning the most dramatic charges against Ilse and the most sensational and disturbing testimony the court had heard since the trial had begun. Asked first whether she had ever heard of human skin being collected at Buchenwald, and then whether she had ever seen objects of human skin or the shrunken head of an inmate that Denson now held up for the court, she explained that she had learned of all of these things for the first time when in American custody and at trial. Yet, while circumstances suggest that this may have been so, Koch's answers to Denson's subsequent questions attempted to convey such complete ignorance of camp affairs that they significantly eroded her credibility. Asked whether she had ever heard of a prisoner being beaten at Buchenwald, or "being mistreated in any form or fashion," she answered no. "My husband never told me about it," she added, "and I didn't come into contact with anybody else."[142] Denson easily cast these denials into doubt, following up with questions about her relationships with other SS men in the camp such as Florstedt and Hoven, who many had testified were with her regularly and perhaps intimately. Denson prompted her to confirm, too, that she was hardly isolated from the prisoner population, as she acknowledged that prisoners had worked in her garden, right on her doorstep, and that they could be seen at work at various stations as she walked near the camp.

Koch undermined her own credibility most with her responses to questions Denson asked about her regular walks to her husband's headquarters, just outside the main gate of the camp. Taking the route she described, she would have found herself only meters from the barbed wire of the camp compound, walking directly past the bunker in which prisoners languished and were routinely murdered. Nonetheless, Koch insisted that she was unable to confirm whether one could see through the fence because she never bothered to look, she "didn't ask about it and wasn't interested in it," and her "interests were confined" to her home."[143] The absurdity of her denials was only heightened when she confirmed for Denson that she had taken her children at least twenty times to visit the camp zoo, mere meters away from the barbed wired and the crematoria complex just inside, yet denied ever noticing either. She claimed no knowledge at the time that there was a crematorium at Buchenwald, despite the prominence of its ever-smoking chimney, and to have "only heard about it here."[144]

Denson was able to present his initial questions regarding crimes attributed to Koch, and the knowledge she had had of all that had occurred at Buchenwald, without interruption, but a second line of questioning designed to impugn her moral character brought strenuous objections from her defense team. In a thinly veiled reference to the circumstances of her pregnancy, Denson asked whether she had "maintained the same standards of moral conduct" while in American confinement as she had maintained while living at Buchenwald.[145] Before Koch could respond, Captain Lewis objected to the question as immaterial to the criminal charges currently being heard by the court. Denson, however, refused to back down, insisting that, given Koch's attempt to present herself as "an adoring, loving mother whose interest was in her home," his question was material. "The point is this," Denson continued, "a raven doesn't change its colors overnight."[146]

In response to Lewis's objection, Lieutenant Colonel John S. Dwinell, the only lawyer among the court's judges, declared that the prosecution was permitted to "examine her with respect to all her activities up to the time of her arrest," presumably including her activities in the two years that followed her departure from Buchenwald in 1943. Captain Lewis responded passionately, criticizing the court for suggesting that Koch's personal behavior after she had left Buchenwald was relevant to adjudicating whether she was complicit in the war crimes that had occurred there:

> I take the position that this woman is not being charged in this court as not having been a loving and adoring mother. She is charged with having conspired in a common design to kill and mistreat the prisoners. Her morals are of no concern of the court or anybody else under the sun but herself. If the prosecution

intends to prove by this woman's subsequent conduct, that she killed and mistreated prisoners in Buchenwald and the court is willing to hear such testimony and connect it up with such acts, then I have nothing further to say.[147]

After ordering a forty-minute adjournment to consider the issue, Court President Kiel sustained Captain Lewis's objection and, in so doing, rescued the court from an error of judgment that would have undercut the legitimacy of trial proceedings. At least officially, Ilse's personal life was off the table.

With Denson's line of questioning rejected by the court, the prosecution used its remaining time redoubling its efforts to undermine Koch's claims of ignorance in the hopes that her activities could still be encapsulated within the expansive "common design" charge, even while evidence tying her to the shocking crimes for which she had become known was appearing increasingly weak. She was asked to leave the witness chair, walk over to a large map of Buchenwald mounted on the wall behind the prosecution table, and use a pointer stick to trace her various walking and riding routes through the camp. As she did so, she was asked to explain how she could possibly have failed to notice substantial sections of the camp perimeter fence, camp quarry, isolation barracks, and execution ground. Koch, however, remained steadfast, insisting that she simply had seen nothing. Though she was compelled to admit that she had often passed prisoners working only meters from her, she similarly could not say whether any had looked emaciated, as she "never had a close look at the prisoners," and "didn't particularly search out the prisoners to observe them."[148] Following a few further questions that were met with similar claims of total ignorance, she was dismissed from the witness stand. As the *New York Times* aptly concluded, Koch's denials amounted to a plea to the court to believe that, despite her position and place, "she heard no evil, saw no evil, spoke no evil."[149]

More than a month passed following the conclusion of Ilse Koch's testimony while the court heard from eighteen more defendants taking the stand on their own behalfs. It was not until August 11, 1947, that defense counsel rested its case. In a marked and unexplained departure from the major concentration camp cases tried at Dachau thus far, the prosecution and defense waived their right to make closing arguments, allowing the court to close shortly after 2:00 PM. As the court's eight judges retired to consider the merits of the cases against all thirty-one defendants, and to sift through the mountains of evidence and hundreds of hours of testimony presented in the preceding four months, the task before them must have appeared daunting. Chief Prosecutor Denson had demanded that the court impose the death sentence on each and every one of the accused, insisting at the outset of the trial that the heinous crimes committed at Buchenwald could only be redressed on the gallows.[150] Given the dozens of executions that had already resulted from previous judgments handed down by the military courts at Dachau, it must have been starkly apparent to all present that the lives of thirty-one people now hung precariously in the balance.

Court President Kiel and his team of judges kept no record of the deliberations that followed, but it is safe to assume that the case against Ilse Koch was among the most vexing. The prosecution team had declared at the outset of the trial that it would show that Koch, as "commandeuse" of Buchenwald, had "caused the deaths of many hundreds of inmates," and had "indulged in personal sadism," including "using the human skin of inmates for such personal items as gloves, book covers and lampshades."[151] Certainly, the press had latched onto these sensational allegations and stirred a keen and morbid public interest in the case against the defendant dubbed "Lampshade Ilse." Yet the evidence presented in court to support these claims had been thoroughly undermined by defense counsel. The testimony of the numerous prosecution witnesses presented to connect Koch to the alleged collection of tattooed human skins had been hearsay, or had been contradicted by other prosecution witnesses, or had been, in a few key instances, impeached during cross-examination. Meanwhile, the lampshades and photo albums so frequently invoked by the prosecution had mysteriously disappeared and could not be produced in court. Beyond secondhand testimony that spoke to the "common knowledge" of the prisoner population at Buchenwald, therefore, the judges had little to tie Koch directly to the alleged crimes that had earned her such infamy.

As Chief Prosecutor Denson frequently reminded the court, however, the case against Ilse Koch and her thirty codefendants did not require the prosecution to prove any specific act of violence or killing by the accused. Instead, the defendants had been charged only with participation in a "common design" to mistreat or murder inmates. If the court's judges were to conclude during their deliberation that evidence connecting Ilse Koch to the killing of prisoners and the collection of their tattooed skins was lacking, this would not necessarily exonerate her from the formal charges they were tasked with adjudicating. The prosecution had argued that each defendant need only be shown to have aided and abetted the regime of terror at Buchenwald to be guilty of participating in this common design. At least according to this prosecutorial theory, the cook was as liable as the hangman, assuming that both knowingly helped to maintain the criminal enterprise that was Buchenwald. A central question therefore remained before the judges: Did Ilse Koch, a woman without formal rank or duty at Buchenwald beyond her position as the former commandant's wife, participate sufficiently in the camp's functioning to be found guilty of the common design charge?

To arrive at a verdict, the eight judges would have to consider what the prosecution *had* definitively shown. That Ilse Koch was a deeply flawed, morally compromised, and ideologically complicit defendant was irrefutable. Her blanket denials of even the most elementary knowledge of Buchenwald's reason for being, and of the suffering of its inmates, defied belief. The fact that the cross-examination of Ilse Koch was consumed to a large degree by questions of her knowledge of camp affairs suggests that the prosecution placed great importance on illustrating the fraudulence of her purported naivete. Denson and his team succeeded in showing the myriad ways in which she routinely came into contact with inmates and members of the camp's SS staff, as well as the frequency with which she visited Karl's office, only meters from the camp's barbed wire and main gate.

The testimony of various survivors, as well as that of the former SS judge Konrad Morgen, also made it clear that Koch had materially benefited from her husband's corruption while he commanded Buchenwald, that she had used inmate slave labor in her house and garden, and that she had likely used her influence at times to have inmates reported for punishment. Nevertheless, the evidence presented by Denson and his team clearly fell short of the prosecution's original claims—in this case, that Koch had "commanded [Buchenwald] together with her husband."[152] Precisely how the judges weighed the evidence against Ilse Koch, and what they found to be compelling or dubious, was not documented and will never be known. A verdict, albeit without reasons or explanations, nonetheless came quickly. Just hours after retiring for deliberations, Court President Kiel called the court back to order and, while the cameras of an expectant press clicked and flashed, asked Ilse Koch and her thirty codefendants to rise to receive their judgments.

4   Clemency, Controversy, and the Koch Case in the US Senate

By the time the US Army trial of Ilse Koch and her thirty codefendants drew to a close in August 1947, Buchenwald concentration camp had seeped deeply into the postwar consciousness. The overwhelming evidence of systematic cruelty and murder presented by the prosecution over the course of the preceding four months had made front-page headlines around the world, as had the sensational and grotesque crimes attributed to the "Bitch of Buchenwald." Yet while oft-printed stories of Ilse Koch collecting tattooed human skins had helped to arouse sustained public interest in trial proceedings, such accounts rarely noted the serious questions that defense counsel had raised about the credibility of this most shocking claim. With great anticipation, the American public now awaited the announcement of a verdict and punishment commensurate with the atrocities allegedly committed by a woman broadly viewed as epitomizing Nazi barbarism. Few could have imagined that, even after the judgment of the Dachau court, the Ilse Koch case would be far from closed, and would instead ignite an explosive controversy that would play out in the press, in the street, and in the highest offices of the US government.

When Court President Brigadier General Emil C. Kiel reopened the Dachau courtroom at ten o'clock on the morning of August 12,

1947, to announce the verdicts reached against the Buchenwald trial defendants, less than twenty-four hours had elapsed since the defense had rested its case. That the court's eight judges had spent only minutes on average arriving at verdicts for thirty-one defendants on trial for their lives was a stark reminder of the expedient nature of the legal proceedings in the US military courts. Kiel turned to the defendants in the dock and asked them to rise as their names were read out in alphabetical order. The verdict, delivered without explanation or elaboration, was encapsulated in a single sentence: "The court in closed session, at least two-thirds the members present at the time the vote was taken concurring in each finding of guilty, finds you and each one of you Guilty of all of the Particulars and the Charge."[1]

Allowing those in the dock to retake their seats, Kiel asked whether the accused desired "to introduce evidence of extenuating circumstances or to make any other statement to the court."[2] Of the ten defendants who accepted this opportunity, Ilse Koch was the last to speak. "After she was pronounced guilty and took the stand," Kiel later recalled, "she was an entirely different woman. The fire just blazed out of her eyes."[3] Koch declared first that she had had no intention of ascending the witness stand again, but that she now felt duty-bound to clear up misconceptions that continued to be published in the press and that, based on her guilty verdict, the court evidently still believed. In language that seethed with frustration and contempt, she drew the attention of the court to an article that had appeared in *Newsweek* at the end of July, some weeks after she had testified on the witness stand. Titled "Witch of Buchenwald: The Record of a Sadist," it was saturated with sexual clichés, describing Ilse as a "nymphomaniac" of "Dresden-china prettiness gone fleshy."[4] The article also repeated claims that she had collected the tattooed skins of inmates, but Ilse could not bring herself to repeat these statements in court. "It says there, amongst other things," she declared, "that I had admitted—well, you can read it. It is not my way to use that type of words. . . . It is the most vulgar lie I have ever read about myself in any paper."[5]

Ilse also pointed out that, beyond its text, the article was illustrated with photos from the personal photo albums that Herbert Froboess had testified were bound in human skin but that the prosecution had been unable to produce in court. She contended that this proved that the albums were in American hands and should now be examined to exonerate her of this charge. To conclude, she invoked her family, imploring the judges to understand that it was not her alone but her children who were suffering from the "outrageous propaganda" that continued to swirl around her. "I was a housewife and a mother of the children," she finished. "I had nothing to do with concentration camps, and my husband never told me about it, and I never saw nor heard of any of these things that are being talked about here."[6] Following this all-too-familiar refrain, Koch was asked to retake her position in the dock, allowing the court to close to consider sentences for each of the thirty-one trial convicts.

With little fanfare and few words, President Kiel reopened the court at 9:45 AM on August 14, having deliberated with his fellow judges on appropriate sentences for the accused over the course of the previous thirty-six hours. Once Chief Prosecutor William Denson had confirmed that all members of the prosecution and defense teams, as well as all personnel of the court were present, Kiel read out the sentences. Prince Josias zu Waldeck, the highest-ranking of the defendants, under whose administrative authority Buchenwald fell and under whose authority the investigation of Koch family corruption had first taken place, was called to stand before the judges' bench and to receive his sentence: "Josias Prince zu Waldeck, the court in closed session, at least two-thirds the members present at the time the vote was taken concurring, sentences you Josias Prince zu Waldeck to life imprisonment, commencing forthwith."[7] That Waldeck was spared the noose may have briefly heartened his thirty codefendants still awaiting sentencing, yet as Kiel now proceeded to call the remaining defendants alphabetically it quickly became clear that the court found the death penalty the only commensurate punishment for the crimes of which the majority of the defendants had been convicted. Buchenwald Administrative Leader Otto Barnewald, the second defendant called forward, was informed that he was "sentenced to death by hanging at such time and place as higher authority may direct."[8] In all, twenty-two of the defendants called forward that morning were read the same words. Of the nine not sentenced to hang, four received life sentences and the remainder received periods of imprisonment and hard labor ranging from ten to twenty years.[9]

It is hard to imagine what Ilse Koch could have thought as Court President Kiel's recitation of sentences approached the middle of the alphabet and reached her name. In the well-worn language, steeped in derogatory sexual imagery, that had defined both Koch's prosecution and the reportage in the press, *Time* magazine described the moment:

> The dirty-legged slattern in the prisoner's box squinted nervously at the six U.S. officers on the Munich [sic] dais. In staccato tones, US Brigadier General Emil Kiel read her sentence. . . . Justice had caught up with the red-headed, 40-year-old Witch of Buchenwald, who had prisoners at the Nazi concentration camp flogged at her pleasure and who had made gloves and lamp shades from their skins after they died of torture.[10]

Contrary to this description, however, newsreel footage that captured the moment of sentencing shows Koch in a rather conservative gingham dress and dark blazer, looking exhausted and resigned and yet not without a shimmer of the defiance that had characterized her presence in court over the preceding four months.[11] As Kiel looked down from the bench at Koch, who stood before him flanked by white-helmeted military policeman, he spoke:

> Ilse Koch, the court in closed session, at least two-thirds the members present at the time the vote was taken concurring, sentences you, Ilse Koch, to life imprisonment, commencing forthwith, at War Crimes Prison Number 1, Landsberg, Germany, or such other places as may be designated by competent military authority.[12]

According to the *Washington Post*, "her face reddened when she heard the verdict, but she gave no other outward sign of loss of composure."[13] The MP to her left immediately tapped her on the shoulder to indicate that she was to retake her seat, prompting her to turn sharply and march back to the dock as the next defendant was called to receive his sentence. As the reading of sentences concluded with defendant Franz Zinecker, alphabetically last among the accused, Kiel turned to thank the members of the court and, with few additional words, officially drew proceedings to a close.

Because the Dachau court issued no written judgment and provided no insights into its findings, one can only speculate on how the judges arrived at Ilse Koch's life sentence. Given the nature of the routinized brutalities and atrocities committed by the other defendants now condemned to die, a life sentence for Koch would appear lenient if it were true the court believed she had selected prisoners to die so that she could collect their tattooed skins. On the other hand, if this most serious claim were discounted by the judges and they aimed to punish only her more general participation in the "common design" alleged by the prosecution, then a life sentence would be severe in comparison to the sentences of other codefendants not condemned to the gallows. Prince Josias zu Waldeck had received only a twenty-year sentence despite having had administrative authority over Buchenwald and having organized the murderous evacuation of the camp's inmates

Fig. 4.1   Dachau court president Brigadier General Emil C. Kiel issues Koch's life sentence, August 14, 1947. Courtesy United States Holocaust Memorial Museum.

as American forces approached. Assistant camp physician August Bender had been sentenced to ten years for his role examining prisoners for allocation to slave-labor gangs. Wolfgang Otto, who as first sergeant of headquarters staff admitted to having participated in as many as fifty executions at Buchenwald, received only twenty years. Labor Service Leader Franz Zinecker, who did also receive a life sentence, had coordinated slave-labor battalions and beaten inmates.[14] These disparate punishments make it all the more difficult to infer the reasons for Ilse Koch's life sentence. Yet there remains a factor unique to her case that almost certainly influenced the judges: Koch was by this point seven months pregnant. If the suspicions of Denson and his prosecution team were correct, Koch's pregnancy, revealed just days prior to the trial's opening, had been no accident, but was rather a shrewd—and successful—act of self-preservation based on the assumption that the court would find her guilty as charged but would not condemn an expectant mother to die.

Reviews and Recommendations

Because the American military trial system provided no avenue for appeal, the verdicts and sentences pronounced by the Dachau court were instead subject to a series of automatic reviews. First, the US Army's deputy judge advocate for war crimes scrutinized the trial record and the evidence presented by the prosecution and defense teams to submit his "review and recommendations" to his superior, the judge advocate (European command). In turn, the judge advocate weighed the report of his deputy, confirming or rejecting the recommendations it contained while adding any additional modifications he deemed appropriate. Because the Buchenwald case involved the death penalty, the judge advocate's findings required the final approval of General Lucius D. Clay, American military governor of occupied Germany. In the meantime, Ilse Koch and her fellow trial convicts joined hundreds of other convicted Nazi war criminals in Landsberg prison, the very place where Hitler had dictated *Mein Kampf* to his deputy Rudolf Hess while both served time for the abortive 1923 Beer Hall Putsch.

Even though it would take nearly a year for Ilse Koch to hear the final conclusions reached by American judicial authorities, her appointed military counsel wasted little time assembling a petition for clemency in response to a peculiar incident that had occurred at trial's end. According to a sworn affidavit given by defense counsel Captain Emanuel Lewis, less than half an hour after the pronouncement of sentences, he and the members of his team had been approached by prosecution staff and handed the two "notorious" Koch family photo albums that Froboess had testified were bound in human skin. Incredulous that the prosecution had possessed the albums all along when they had insisted at trial that they could not locate them, Lewis immediately recognized that the albums were ordinary in construction and contained only photographs of Koch playing with her children or socializing in her garden. Lewis viewed the albums as "vital evidence" withheld by the prosecution that helped to show the spurious nature of the allegations concerning Ilse Koch's supposed collection of tattooed human skins.[15]

The subsequent petition for clemency, submitted by Lewis and defense counsel Major Carl Whitney on September 18, 1947, asked Clay to accept the albums into evidence and to see the photographs within. Contrary to the diabolical portrait painted by the prosecution, they showed Koch to be a "home-loving woman, [and] a good mother to her children" who would not have committed the crimes with which she was charged.[16] To add urgency to their petition, Lewis and Whitney included medical certification that Koch was now eight months pregnant and would soon give birth. Though the petition concluded with a reminder that defense counsel had never attempted to gain advantage by exploiting Koch's pregnancy during trial, or ever mentioned it during proceedings, it now requested that Clay also consider her condition "as a basis for the granting of clemency."[17]

In spite of the imminent birth of Koch's child, a prompt response to her counsel's petition was not forthcoming. In the meantime, Major Whitney, Captain Lewis, and five other lawyers rounding out the Buchenwald trial defense team now labored to compose a broader "petition for review" that would not only critique the trial as a whole, but specifically challenge the judgment and sentence pronounced against Koch and each of the other Buchenwald defendants. According to the opening pages of the petition, the defense team would "challenge the legality of the entire court proceeding," while showing that the guilty verdicts were "not sustained by the evidence" and that the sentences pronounced by the court were "excessive."[18] This petition began by elaborating on legal arguments already presented at trial—challenging the jurisdiction of the court and the validity of the common design charge—but added to those the argument that the case against the Buchenwald defendants was hopelessly prejudiced by improper actions on the part of the prosecution. Included as evidence was a copy of the information pamphlet distributed by prosecution staff prior to the opening of trial, which had provided pictures of each defendant beside a list of "exaggerated claims" concerning their alleged crimes. The petition highlighted that the prosecution did not prove many of the pamphlet's most serious allegations, including the claim that Ilse Koch had "caused the deaths of many hundreds of inmates." Circulating this "gruesome dossier" before proceedings began likely influenced the judges, the press, and the witnesses set to testify, argued the defense team, and placed the accused in a fundamentally unjust position "from which they were helpless to extricate themselves."[19]

There was no better case than that of Ilse Koch, the petition continued, to illustrate "the power of propaganda and mass suggestion." Koch, her counsel wrote, "had already been publicly convicted as the 'Bitch of Buchenwald'. . . . Stories about her were avidly spread around from person to person, embellished by garish accounts in the public press, each new recital adding fancier details to the picture." When it came to proving these accusations in the courtroom, the petition argued, "the evidence was totally lacking in substance. The same piece of skin with a tattooed sailboat was seen by one witness on a photo album, and by another witness on a lampshade in her home."[20] As they had in the earlier petition for clemency, Koch's lawyers again demanded that the photo albums be taken into evidence. The prosecution had kept secret its possession of the notorious albums because it knew "as a fact" that "there was never any question of human skins being used as bindings," the petition claimed. "From the highly colorful narratives of . . . tattooed human skin, it was only a step to the lurid descriptions of other misdeeds—whipping of prisoners, reporting them for punishment . . . and a host of other accusations."[21]

Finally, the petition explained that, even if Koch had committed misdeeds while at Buchenwald, her actions would not be subject to the common design charge of which she had been convicted:

> [Ilse Koch] held no official position in the camp, she was not a member of the dreaded SS, she did not participate in the formation or execution of any of the inhuman policies existing in the administration of the concentration camp. Whatever she may have done wrongfully was done of her own volition. . . . By no distortion of the evidence can her presence at Buchenwald be the basis of the charge that she was an integral part and participated in the common plan or scheme to operate the camp to the injury of its inmates. In view of all of the foregoing, the finding of guilty . . . is erroneous and should be set aside.[22]

Once Koch's defense team submitted its petition for review, there was little more it could do as the official review process was conducted by the US Army's judicial branch. Koch remained in her cell in the women's section of Landsberg prison awaiting further news. At the end of October, newspaper headlines announced the birth of her child, a seven-pound baby boy whom Koch used her maiden name to christen Uwe Köhler.[23] According to former Buchenwald doctor and codefendant August Bender, Koch had hoped to give birth within the prison, over which the American flag flew. Bender, who worked as an inmate doctor at Landsberg and who was able to visit Koch frequently, claimed to have advised her that Landsberg was for all intents and purposes American territory, and that, were her son born under its roof, he would be entitled to US citizenship.[24] If Ilse hoped, however, that this rather far-fetched scheme would bring her advantage in her quest for clemency, it was not to be. When Koch's labor began, prison officials transferred her out of Landsberg prison to the city's central hospital, and immediately after delivery, turned Uwe over to Bavarian child welfare authorities. Following a brief period of convalescence, Koch returned to Landsberg and whatever distraction could be had from mending the clothes of fellow inmates in the prison's garment workshop.

The office of Lieutenant Colonel C. E. Straight, deputy judge advocate for war crimes, began its review of the Buchenwald trial at the beginning of October 1947. Assigned to pore over the thousands of pages of trial materials and prepare a draft review for the deputy judge advocate were two attorneys, Harold A. Kuhn and Richard A. Schneider, who worked under the supervision of Major Thomas C. Marmon. Although the two lawyers had little hesitation recommending the confirmation of the death sentences pronounced against many of the Buchenwald trial convicts, their conclusions concerning Ilse Koch were striking in their departure from the findings of the court and in their concurrence with the petition for review submitted by Koch's counsel. Kuhn and Schneider found unequivocally that the most serious and shocking charges leveled at Ilse Koch were supported by scarcely more than rumor and hearsay. Schneider wrote that, "In spite of the extravagant statements made in the newspapers, the record contains little convincing evidence against the accused," and that "In regard to the widely publicized charges that she ordered inmates killed for their tattooed skin, the record is especially silent."[25] The testimonies of key witnesses Froboess and Titz, he concluded, were based on presumption and "of doubtful veracity."[26] Though Koch was shown to have beaten a few inmates, "no deaths or serious injuries are shown to have resulted."[27]

Kuhn was equally critical of the verdict. Focusing on the nature of the common design charge, Kuhn concluded that the prosecution had failed to illustrate how Koch had "aided and abetted" the operation of Buchenwald, given that "she had no official position or connection with the camp other than as wife of the camp commander."[28] The few acts of violence she was found to have committed were insufficient "to make her responsible for the results of the entire opera-tion of the camp."[29] After completing their review of the testimony against Koch, Schneider and Kuhn reported to Marmon that they had no choice but to recommend that the findings and sentence handed down in her case be disapproved. Koch, they advised, should be released.

Schneider and Kuhn had come back with dramatic findings, but it remained Straight's duty to accept or reject his staff's conclusions on the Buchenwald case and sign off on the official review and recom-mendations document. Marmon, who had supervised Schneider and Kuhn and who now advised Straight on their findings, felt compelled to report that he, too, had read over the evidentiary materials and had no choice but to concur with his legal team that the findings against Ilse Koch should be disapproved.[30] Over the next two weeks, Straight made numerous corrections and additions to the draft review as he continued assessing the evidence and seeking input from Marmon, Schneider, and Kuhn. Straight concurred with his advisers on various shortcomings of the case against Koch; nonetheless, he accepted the prosecution's argument that she had participated in a "common de-sign" to commit war crimes. He therefore requested that his advisers set aside their doubts concerning the nature of the charge itself, and instead suggest to him what they felt would be a reasonable sentence for those acts of violence Koch was shown to have committed at Buchenwald.

After some discussion with both Schneider and Kuhn, Marmon proposed a sentence of four years.[31] Satisfied with their suggestion, Straight declared Koch's sentence "excessive" and recommended a four-year term. Concurring with his advisers, he emphasized that the evidence had shown only that Koch "had beaten an inmate on at least one occasion" and had reported others for punishment. Contrary to the initial findings of Schneider, Kuhn, and Marmon, Straight allowed that the charge that Koch had participated in the common design at

Buchenwald was justified. He concluded, however, that "the extent and nature of her participation do not warrant life imprisonment."[32]

Straight's review and recommendations, though dated November 15, 1947, did not reach the office of judge advocate Colonel J. L. Harbaugh, Jr., until early March 1948. Harbaugh immediately forwarded the report and copy of the trial record to the War Crimes Review Board, an advisory body made up of military and civilian lawyers that functioned within his office to provide him with independent advice on the findings of the Dachau courts. Harbaugh would base his own recommendations on the review board's report, which he received on April 30. In lockstep with Straight, the board reported to Harbaugh that the proposed four-year sentence for Ilse Koch was "legal, fair, and just," and should be "approved and ordered executed."[33] It found that the most grave charges against Koch were without merit, there was no reliable evidence that she had prisoners killed, and "nor is there any evidence in this record of any kind that she at any time ever ordered any article made of human skin."[34] After some further consultation with the members of the review board, and with its report and the review and recommendations of his deputy in hand, Harbaugh penned his own recommendations, which were subject to the final approval of the American military governor, General Clay.

The notes Harbaugh generated as he deliberated over Ilse Koch's fate confirm the remarkable consensus emerging among the senior authorities in the US Army's judicial branch that their highest-profile case was deeply flawed. Harbaugh's worksheet indicates that he found there to be scant evidence that Koch had directly reported prisoners for beatings, and that the firsthand accounts of beatings and other atrocities from key witnesses Froboess and Titz were "exaggerated and improbable."[35] Even if taken at face value, Harbaugh noted, the accounts of beatings did not substantiate the common design charge, given that such actions "stem from the accused's personal malice, and are not shown to have been connected with the operation of the camp."

Harbaugh further noted that he had personally examined the photo albums entered into evidence upon request by the defense, and that they were "clearly not made of tattooed human skin." As he had concluded with regard to the allegations of beatings, Harbaugh likewise reasoned that, even if Koch had collected human skins, she would have done so on her own "personal whim," which stood outside the common design alleged by the prosecution.[36] His notes conclude with an unequivocal and perceptive assessment of how the press and prevailing gender norms played their roles in Koch's zealous but problematic prosecution: "I can't see anything on which we can honestly hold accused. There is no question but that she was tried in the newspapers, and suffered both before and during the trial from her unique position as the only woman at the camp."[37]

When Military Governor Clay received Harbaugh's formal recommendations on May 7, 1948, he was in the midst of navigating the dramatically escalating diplomatic tensions that would culminate at the end of June in the Soviet blockade of Berlin. Clay would go on to win accolades in both Germany and the United States for the hard line he took in this first major international crisis of the Cold War. His handling of the Koch case, by contrast, would provoke accusations that, in finding the nerve to stand up to Stalin, he had gone soft on those who had stood for Hitler.

The brief document Harbaugh prepared for Clay confirmed that the evidence presented at the Buchenwald trial "shows that each accused participated in the execution of the common design . . . [and] is sufficient to support the [court's] findings."[38] In concurrence with the reports of both the deputy judge advocate for war crimes and the War Crimes Review Board, however, Harbaugh recommended that Clay commute six of the death sentences imposed by the Dachau court to life in prison, and reduce the duration of seven of the prison terms. Ilse Koch's life sentence, Harbaugh stated, should be reduced to a term of four years. Though Clay felt compelled to scrutinize elements of

Fig. 4.2   General Lucius D. Clay, American military governor of occupied Germany and final authority over the US military trial program in Germany. US Army Signal Corps, Record Group III, National Archives and Records Administration.

the trial record himself before providing the final signature required to impose the modified roster of sentences proposed in Harbaugh's report, he formally accepted its recommendations *in toto,* on June 8, 1948. Less critical than Harbaugh of the role that gender and sexuality had played in Koch's conviction, Clay later reflected on the reasons he had signed off on her reduced sentence: "As I examined the record, I could not find her a major participant in the crimes at Buchenwald.

A sordid, disreputable character, she had delighted in flaunting her sex, emphasized by tight sweaters and short skirts, before the long-confined male prisoners, and had developed their bitter hatred. Nevertheless these were not the offenses for which she was being tried."[39] Clay further recollected that he had been aware, as he signed off on Koch's sentence reduction, of the strong reaction this was likely to bring.[40] It is hard to imagine, however, that Clay fully understood the explosion of outrage that would greet the announcement of Koch's reduced term, and the depth of the controversy his signature would touch off.

Clemency and Controversy

On June 19, 1948, some three months before the public announcement of Clay's decision, Ilse Koch herself learned of her dramatic sentence reduction. In a letter to defense counsel Lewis penned that very day, Koch expressed little relief or joy, but instead insisted that her counsel now push for her immediate release. "Today I was informed of the result of the review proceedings in my case," she began, "and I learned that the sentence was reduced to four (4) years imprisonment.... Today I should like to ask you to try and get the sentence reduced again by way of clemency." Her four-year sentence, she contended, was being counted unjustly from October 18, 1945, when she was transferred to Ludwigsburg detention camp, rather than from her arrest on June 30, 1945, yielding a release date she hoped "was determined by mistake." Every month mattered, she emphasized: "I have been separated from my children for four and a half years including the time of imprisonment during my husband's trial. I do not need to point out what that means . . . [or] to explain how much my children need maternal love."[41]

On August 16, Koch also submitted a direct appeal for clemency to American judicial authorities that demanded her "immediate release from confinement, in the interest of my children." Devoid of any expression of contrition, her appeal restated her belief that her prosecution was the result of "tremendous propaganda ... in the national and international press ... based on the testimony of witnesses who were absolutely untrustworthy." In a long, rambling paragraph, she defended herself against the charge of collecting human skins, pointing to the photo albums that had finally emerged, and attacking the credibility of key witnesses Titz and Froboess. "In conclusion," she wrote, "I ask for immediate release from captivity because 1) my children are in the most urgent need of me [and] 2) that there is no proof whatsoever that I committed a punishable offense."[42]

When the War Crimes Review Board officially rejected Koch's request for further clemency on September 14, 1948, General Clay's original decision to commute her life sentence to four years still had not been announced.[43] American judicial authorities would later deny that the delay in making Clay's finding public was motivated by political considerations, but there is no question that the early summer of 1948 would have been an inopportune time for such an announcement. At the end of March, Clay had signed off on the commutation of thirty-one of the forty-three death sentences handed down by a Dachau court against the perpetrators of the massacre of unarmed American troops at Malmedy during the Battle of the Bulge. This act of mass clemency, spurred by allegations that questionable tactics had been employed to obtain confessions from the accused, created its own controversy that would, like the Koch case, lead to substantial public outcry in the United States and culminate in hearings in the US Senate. It was in this context that Clay's decision about Ilse Koch would go unannounced until the autumn of 1948. While Judge Advocate Harbaugh would later testify that the holdup in the announcement was merely the result of an "administrative error" on his part, the delay conveniently provided some time for passions evoked by the Malmedy case to cool somewhat.[44]

In the end, it was not General Clay's office but *Stars and Stripes* that first revealed Koch's sentence reduction. Its report, published September 17, 1948, prompted the release of the official announcement later the same day. The contrast between the language of the article and the content of the statement from Clay's office provides a striking measure of the gulf between popular perception of the Koch case and the understanding of American judicial authorities who had considered the evidence presented at trial. While *Stars and Stripes* did not hesitate to describe Ilse as having "issued orders to subordinates to graft human skin from the inmates to be made into lampshades," Clay's office reported that "there was no evidence that she possessed any articles made of human skin or that she selected inmates for [that purpose]."[45] This tension between the diabolical image of Ilse Koch the press helped to create and the reality that emerged from the evidentiary record and led to the commutation of her life sentence now provided the fuel for an explosive controversy. An expectant American public had followed the Koch case closely and now felt deprived of the perceived justice it had awaited.

"Incredulity followed by indignation greeted the news from Berlin," wrote the *Washington Post* of Koch's sentence reduction.[46] Dozens of editorial pages across the United States questioned whether the US Army had lost its nerve or capacity for sound judgment, and demanded on behalf of the American people a fuller explanation for Koch's reduced sentence. The *Asheville Citizen-Times* asked pointedly, "Why in the name of outraged justice and humanity was this done?"[47] The editors of the *Miami Herald* demanded to know "in the name of basic human justice and decency, what 'further' does the army need to slap Ilse into jail and keep her there?"[48] The *New York Post* went further, labeling Koch's commutation "Clay's counter-atrocity," and describing it as "almost beyond credence."[49] Papers like the *Memphis Commercial Appeal* emphasized a need for a full accounting of Clay's actions, insisting that the "American Military Government . . . owes the American people . . . a complete and immediate explanation."[50] Others aired suspicions of what lay behind the commutation. The editors of the *Philadelphia Enquirer* wrote that "the Army's action in this case inevitably leads to a suspicion that there has been a softening of attitude toward war criminals."[51] Ed Sullivan, writing for the *New York News*, wondered cynically whether "the Army reduced [Koch's] sentence . . . so she could get back into the lampshade business." Two days later he wrote, "The commutation of this sentence has given the Commies a fine reason to taunt us, as befrienders of the Nazis."[52] The *Asheville Citizen-Times* put it bluntly: "The act of clemency smells," given that "Ilse Koch made crimes against humanity her very career."[53]

Such editorials reveal that, for many, the caricature of Koch as the perverse, mass-murdering "Beast of Buchenwald" was impervious to the evidence-based reality that had emerged from her trial and its review. Few showed any impulse to question the monstrous and sexualized image of Koch that made her such a popular lightning rod for the condemnation of Nazi crimes. In a display of this steadfast and undiminished desire to publicly denounce Koch as a beast of unsurpassed depravity, ABC's Earl Godwin declared on his radio show that "she made Bluebeard look like Peter Pan."[54]

Typically, editorials critical of Koch's sentence reduction provided few indications that their authors understood the Buchenwald case or the evidence brought out at trial in any depth. The same could not be said about a series of lengthy and impassioned opinion pieces written by Chief Prosecutor Denson. Reprinted in newspapers throughout the United States, these fanned the flames of the growing controversy and laid the groundwork for a deeper and even more heated public debate. Denson's first and most measured response to Clay's decision appeared in the *Washington Post* on September 23, 1948. Describing the news of Ilse Koch's sentence reduction as a "surprise and a shock," Denson depicted the evidence he had presented against Koch as "overwhelming," and properly reflected in the life sentence handed down by the Dachau court. It was a gross injustice, he wrote, that this sentence would be reduced through a review process in which American military jurists who were not present at trial and could only depend on "the cold print of the record" proceeded nonetheless to judge the credibility of his witnesses. In fact, the problem that reviewers had found with much of Denson's evidence was not so much that the witnesses were not credible per se, but that the testimony they provided was based to a considerable degree on hearsay and conjecture. Denson, however, failed to clarify this and simply declared that, by second-guessing the judgment of the Dachau court and extending clemency to Koch, American judicial authorities in Germany had made "a mockery of the administration of justice."[55]

As the clamor in the press continued to grow, Denson penned a longer and more vitriolic piece, also published in dozens of papers across the United States, promising to shed light on the "extent, the quantity and the quality of the evidence." Describing Koch in the most demeaning and inflammatory terms, Denson insisted that she "was no woman in the usual sense but a creature from some other tortured world." She was, he wrote sensationally, nothing less than a "sadistic pervert of monumental proportions unmatched in history." Marveling at the commutation of Koch's sentence as "one of the mysteries of the year," Denson enumerated elements of the "overwhelming case against her." Remarkably, Denson then shared evidence and testimony that had been wholly discredited either during trial or by reviewing authorities. He recounted, for example, the story of the tattooed prisoner Jean, and how Koch had allegedly selected him for death for the production of the very photo album the prosecution had failed to present in court. Denson named the witness as Herbert Froboess, but made no mention of the fact that US authorities had labeled him an "unreliable witness" after it was discovered that he had fraudulently posed as a Franciscan friar.[56]

Denson's description of Ilse's influence at Buchenwald took further liberties with the evidentiary record to place her at the pinnacle of power even after Karl's arrest in December 1941. Ilse, Denson wrote, "reigned from the commandant's quarters at the foul place until June 1943." In a particularly odd turn, Denson wrote that "on the stand, Ilse Koch maintained that she acted at Buchenwald as a 'mother' to the prisoners," yet the trial transcript provides no trace of this claim. Perhaps intended merely as a setup to attack Koch's moral character and flawed maternity, Denson's claim was followed by a sarcastic quip that "these maternal instincts were much in evidence at her trial as she became pregnant during her incarceration." Denson concluded his piece with a direct attack on Clay and a repetition of his argument that the post-trial reviewers had no business judging the credibility of his witnesses. "But perhaps the man responsible," Denson finished, "merely forgot that the most credible witnesses of Ilse Koch's depravity and perversion weren't at the trial, having left this world through the crematory smokestack."[57]

Denson's incendiary and at times misleading campaign in the press served to further arouse the outrage of those shocked by the announcement of Ilse Koch's reduced sentence and to entrench rather than complicate the diabolical image of Koch presented at trial. It did not, however, go unchallenged. Leon B. Poullada, a US Army lawyer who built a successful postwar career serving as an American diplomat, ambassador, and economic adviser, had both prosecuted cases at Dachau and acted as chief defense counsel at the Dora-Nordhausen concentration camp trial.[58] In a lengthy and scathing response to Denson published October 2, 1948, in the *Washington Evening Star*, Poullada declared that Denson "transcends the proper bounds even of a zealous prosecutor when he takes it upon himself to criticize publicly the findings of the reviewing authority, which, after all, in these cases is the equivalent of the appellate court." Poullada insisted that a robust review process was required because the Dachau courts were not akin to those at Nuremberg, where "the judges were professional jurists with a lifetime of judicial experience." Although the officers who made up the military courts at Dachau were "honest, competent men trying their best to discharge an onerous military duty and trying to dispense justice to the best of their ability," their lack of experience left them proceeding against dozens of defendants "often by rule of thumb and trial and error." Describing the Dachau trial system as a "mass-production, assembly line technique of dispensing justice," Poullada painted a less flattering picture of American justice where "nearly all the safeguards and guarantees which an accused enjoys . . . were either stripped away, or so abridged as to render them useless."[59]

In a more forthright assessment of the evidence Denson had presented to make his case, Poullada contended that most of the testimony against Koch contained "very little of substance that would have stood up in an American court." The testimony, Poullada continued, "was of the type so familiar to all of us who worked at Dachau; hearsay once or twice removed, camp rumor, prejudice . . . gossip, desire for revenge." Having attended Buchenwald trial sessions and having read over the complete trial record, Poullada allowed that Koch "was a morally depraved and callous woman not fit company for decent people anywhere," but cautioned, "these traits are not of themselves considered crimes in America and are certainly not 'war crimes' in international law." Therefore, the guilty verdict in the Koch case was not the product of overwhelming evidence, as Denson had insisted, but instead reflected the inexperience of judges who had been "swayed more by emotion than legal principles." According to Poullada, it was thanks only to the "very complete and eminently fair system of reviews" conducted by experienced lawyers in the US Army Judge Advocate General's Corps that the inexperienced Dachau trial judges were prevented from enacting a gross miscarriage of justice.[60]

In the week that followed the publication of Poullada's article, public debate in the United States only intensified. Some, like the political columnist John O'Donnell, were substantially swayed by the informed account that Poullada had provided, and wrote pieces critical of the Dachau trial system and supportive of General Clay and the military review system's checks and balances. Describing Koch's trial as a "sadistic farce" and the reaction to Koch's sentence reduction as a "noisy and bloodthirsty uproar," O'Donnell derided the popular narrative around Koch as "a gruesome atrocity tale" that "fits with the World War I propaganda lies when Americans were solemnly told (and many believed) the bloody chilling tales of the mutilated nurse, . . . the ravished nuns, and that fantastic story of the German 'corpse factory' for manufacturing soap from human remains."[61] In a lengthy feature for the *New York Herald Tribune* titled "The Evidence Against Ilse Koch," foreign correspondent Edwin C. Hartrich proposed to offer his readers "a guide through the legal maze" that would expose the lack of proof to support the Dachau court's findings.[62] Hartrich was taking his cue, he said, from the American legal authorities in Germany responsible for Koch's clemency, who responded to the outcry they had created by saying, "if you do not believe us to be correct, look at the record and judge for yourselves." Supporting the Army's findings, Hartrich questioned the integrity of Denson's witnesses and demanded to know what had happened to the human-skin objects the prosecution had made so much of but had not produced in court. Like Poullada, Hartrich inverted Denson's concerns, insisting that justice in the Ilse Koch case was achieved not at trial, but as a result of the US Army's thorough and principled review process.[63]

The journalists who expressed support for the commutation of Koch's sentence were nonetheless in the minority and found themselves targets of withering editorial criticism that conflated backing Clay's decision with placating America's communist critics, with coddling war criminals, with betraying the memories of those who died fighting Nazism, or merely with hopeless naivete.[64] As criticism of Koch's clemency mounted, General Clay himself felt obliged to enter the fray when his own motives and methods, already publicly questioned by Denson, came under attack in the press. The popular journalist Walter Winchell had suggested that "great influence behind the scenes" might have been exerted to have Koch's sentence reduced. "Whose lady friend is Frau Koch," he wondered, "in [Clay's] very high office in Berlin?" Helen Kirkpatrick, writing for the *New York Post*, speculated that Clay must have reached his decision without bothering to examine the evidence in the Koch case himself.[65] At a news conference in Washington, DC, held on October 21, 1948, Clay felt compelled to reaffirm that he himself had thoroughly assessed the documentary record and the reports of his judicial staff before reaching his conclusion in the Koch case, and had deliberated with great care and concern. The charges against her, he determined, had been based on "hearsay and not on actual evidence." In the end, Clay reflected, "my judgment may be wrong, but it is in accordance with my conscience."[66]

Clay may have hoped that his public comments on his moral obligations and the earnestness of his efforts would cool his critics, but they only served to fuel a wave of public protests targeting him directly. Even prior to Clay's trip to the United States, some papers had told readers angered by the Koch commutation that it was up to the public at large to express its rage in the streets and to push for change. The *Wichita Beacon,* for instance, insisted that "only public opinion can reverse the decision for freedom for this inhuman woman," and the editors of the *New York Worker* declared that "the Ilse Koch style of justice will cost America dear if it is not stopped by public protest."[67] Clay learned firsthand what this could mean on the day after his press conference, when he was greeted by protesters outside a charity dinner where he was to speak. Arriving at New York's Waldorf Astoria Hotel at the invitation of Governor Thomas Dewey, Clay was confronted by forty picketers demanding his removal from European command. Led by Representative Leo Isacson (American Labor Party-New York), some carried lampshades and other placards with messages that included "General Clay, Have You Forgotten 6,000,000 Murdered Jews?" and "Stop Pampering the Nazis and Start Building Peace." Addressing the gathered crowd, Isacson condemned Clay and the current administration in Washington, DC, who were "forsaking every principle for which the last war was fought."[68]

Clay returned to his post in Germany shortly after, but eighteen months later, further protests overshadowed what was supposed to be a celebratory visit lauding his efforts organizing the Berlin Airlift and thwarting Soviet attempts to assert total control over the German capital. Outside New York's Town Hall, eight hundred picketers gathered as Clay was set to address a rally organized by Common Cause, Inc., in support of democratic forces in divided Berlin. When Clay approached the lectern, a heckler rose and shouted, "Let's ask General Clay about Ilse Koch and the human skin!" As the protester was removed by police, some hundred others took up the cry before also leaving the hall. The *New York Times* reported that Clay looked "white and obviously shaken by the outburst" as he stepped forward to announce that he would not be delivering his prepared address.[69] Shocked at the aggression and radicalism of the protesters, Clay instead addressed them, explaining that "what is important is that the people give their minds and hearts to listening and to finding the right answer. . . . I would say to them that the way they acted tonight is the way I have seen freedom perish in Europe."[70]

Presumably by coincidence, Chief Prosecutor Denson himself had accepted an invitation to address a protest organized by the American Jewish Congress at the Brooklyn Jewish Center on October 22, 1948, the very night that Clay's talk at the Waldorf Astoria was picketed. The posters advertising the event asked "Shall Ilse Koch Go Free?" and demanded both that the United States "Stop Coddling Nazis" and that concerned citizens write directly to President Truman to demand action.[71] The day of the event, however, Denson withdrew

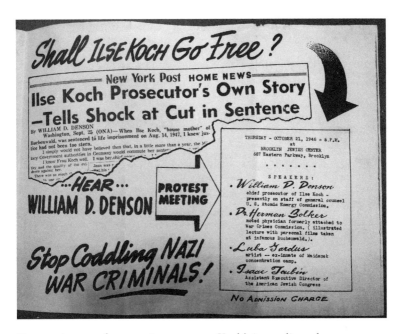

Fig 4.3 A poster for a meeting to protest Koch's impending release, October 1948. William Dowdell Denson Papers, Yale University Library, Manuscripts and Archives.

his offer to appear as one of the evening's featured speakers, having received a letter from the House Un-American Activities Committee speciously charging that the American Jewish Congress was "highly infiltrated with communists."[72] Protests elsewhere, however, continued unabated. Outside Carnegie Hall, some two hundred picketers from various organizations, including the Jewish War Veterans and American Veterans Committee, forced the eleventh-hour cancellation of a concert to be given by German pianist Walter Gieseking. Alleging the famed pianist was a Nazi sympathizer, they expressed their displeasure waving placards, one of them reading "Ilse Koch plays next Saturday."[73] At an industrial fair at the Rockefeller Center organized by the American Military Government of Germany to showcase the innovations of some five hundred German manufacturers working in the Western-occupied zones, picketers blocked the front entrance, carrying placards that read, among other things, "How Much for Ilse Koch's Lampshades?"[74] For protesters concerned with American postwar relations with Germany and the war crimes issue, the name Ilse Koch had become potent shorthand to register outrage at any perceived softness in dealing with the Nazi past.

The public protests surrounding the Koch affair also found their parallel in contemporary culture. Woody Guthrie, the folk troubadour whose guitar famously bore the phrase "This Machine Kills Fascists," took up his pen on August 8, 1948, to compose lyrics in protest of Koch's commutation written from the perspective of an inmate of Buchenwald:

I'm here in Buchenwald.
My number is on my skin.
Old Ilsa Koch is here.
The prisoners walk the grounds.
The hounds have killed a girl.
The guards have shot a man.
Some more have starved to death . . .

I see the chimney smoke.
I see their ashes hauled.
I see their bones in piles.
Lamp shades are made from skin.
I'm choking on the smoke.
The stink is killing me.
Old Ilsy Koch was jailed.
Old Ilsy Koch went free.[75]

Combining the most potent charge against Koch with searing images of Buchenwald drawn from the widespread reportage that followed the camp's liberation, Guthrie's song illustrates how deeply Ilse Koch had sunk into the postwar consciousness. The fact that Koch had become the embodiment of the savagery of the concentration camps explains the prevailing view that Clay's decision to commute her sentence was the most repugnant of injustices. It was perceived as an affront to all those who had suffered under the yoke of Nazism—and all those who had fought for its defeat.

The US Senate Investigation

From the outset, the feverish public response to the reduction of Ilse Koch's sentence was matched by a growing political controversy in Washington, DC, as the United States Congress and eventually the office of President Truman learned of General Clay's decision. Leading the charge first was Senator Raymond E. Baldwin (R-Connecticut), who responded to the news with a pointed letter to Secretary of the Army Kenneth C. Royall demanding that he account for Clay's decision. When Royall replied with a defense of Clay that expressed support for the reduced sentence and reiterated its finality, Baldwin called for an official investigation.[76] Senator Homer S. Ferguson (R-Michigan), who chaired an investigations subcommittee in the Senate, promptly heeded this call, sharing the concern that Koch's sentence reduction indicated a weakening of American resolve to punish those responsible for Nazi crimes.[77] A former judge and professor of law, Ferguson had been one of twelve senators who had sponsored a 1943 resolution calling for "immediate action designed to save the surviving Jewish people of Europe from extinction at the hands of Nazi Germany."[78] In 1945, he had toured the recently liberated Dachau concentration camp as a member of a US government delegation and been horrified by the evidence he had seen of Nazi atrocity. According

Fig. 4.4   Senator Homer S. Ferguson, Chairman of the Investigations Subcommittee of the Committee on Expenditures in the Executive Departments. United States Information Service, Record Group 84, National Archives and Records Administration.

to Ferguson, the intention of his subcommittee's investigation would be to clear up "the mass of misstatements and misapprehensions concerning the trial of Ilse Koch," given that "conflicting statements from the participants in the trial and the review tended to be self-serving and generally failed to clarify the facts in the public mind."[79]

Acknowledging that the committee had no jurisdiction to formally appeal or overturn Clay's decision to reduce Koch's sentence, Ferguson stated that its aim was to investigate what had occurred both at trial and during the review process "with impartiality and detachment," in the belief that a public disclosure of its findings "itself might have a beneficial effect." Ferguson's stated intention to lead an objective investigation appeared to be undercut, however, by the tacit presumptions that Ilse Koch was guilty and the US Army's judicial review process was at fault. Describing what he called the committee's "principal function," Ferguson said it needed to ensure that "every effort be made to bring Ilse Koch to justice."[80]

The first meeting of the investigative subcommittee occurred on September 28, 1948, behind closed doors, conducted by Senator Ferguson and Senator Herbert R. O'Conor (R-Maryland), with the aid of the Senate's chief counsel, William P. Rogers, and assistant chief counsel, Francis D. Flanagan. Aiming to account for the dramatically different assessments of the Koch case reached by the Dachau court and by judicial authorities upon review, the committee first summoned Denson, Royall, and Colonel Edward H. Young, chief of the War Crimes Branch, Civilian Affairs Division. Questioning Secretary Royall first, Ferguson requested that he briefly outline to the committee the setup of the Dachau court system. In the exchange that followed, the committee revealed its near-total ignorance of the American military trial program. Royall was forced to explain that the Dachau courts were *not* international, that there was no jury, and that the judges were all military men. He also outlined the court's jurisdiction and the basic chain of command of its personnel.[81]

Seemingly dissatisfied with Royall's insistence that General Clay was "the final authority in war crimes acting under the President," the committee appeared to search for a loophole that would allow for a reversal of Clay's decision.[82] "Have you any memorandum showing that the jurisdiction does not allow a change?" Ferguson asked. "Do you know, Mr. Secretary," Chief Counsel Rogers followed up, "whether there is authority now to cancel the reduction in sentence?" And probing further: "Would General Clay have the authority to increase the sentence?"[83] Though Royall insisted at each turn that he saw no avenue to reversing the final decision pronounced by Clay, the committee persisted with versions of these questions throughout the hearings that followed. For Royall, the bottom line remained that, no matter how he or the members of the committee might disagree with Clay's decision, it had been adjudicated fairly and was final. "The fact that one case where we may have made a mistake has aroused all of this prejudice and passion which it has, is unfortunate," Royall concluded. "There is nothing you can do about it, for this is democracy."[84]

The testimony of Colonel Young began with a series of relatively banal questions concerning the review process, but Ferguson and his colleagues grew increasingly agitated as they sought to understand how exactly General Clay had arrived at his decision to commute Koch's sentence. The review and recommendations furnished by Secretary Royall, they quickly discovered, contained a summary of the evidence against Koch, but no accompanying analysis. "I do not see how anybody," Chief Counsel Rogers exclaimed, "General Clay or anybody else . . . would have any idea what the reviewing authorities thought, because they don't in any way justify the reduction that they recommend."[85] Referring to the shocking accounts of atrocity the review recapitulated, Rogers asked Young pointedly how, "if any of these things are true or substantially true, you could possibly reduce the sentence to four years?"[86] Young's explanation that the clemency order had stemmed from doubts about the credibility of key witnesses drew Ferguson's ire; he wondered aloud how a legitimate system of review could permit lawyers not present in court to judge the credibility of witness testimony they had not heard firsthand. The committee's agitation only grew as Young explained that there was no way to know what evidence Clay did or did not find credible, given that military regulation had not required that he provide written justification for his decision, and had conducted much of his deliberation over Koch's commutation orally with his legal advisers.

As Ferguson and his colleagues expressed their astonishment that a legal judgment of such magnitude could be issued without accompanying explanation, Young felt compelled to remind the committee that the courts at Dachau were created for expediency first. "I am sorry that the rules don't provide for what you wish," Young explained, "but I will say that in military law . . . we stress a lot the time limit, that is promptness of action. We stress the lack of technicalities that you have in your civil courts. . . . The procedure is different."[87] Young explained, however, that "the record itself stands for the reasons for the reversal" and concluded his testimony with a promise to furnish the committee with a copy of the trial record they had yet to access or read.[88]

The testimony of Young and Royall had made it clear that the committee had been ill-prepared and could not proceed much further without a significant adjournment to consider the voluminous trial record itself. Still, Ferguson called Chief Prosecutor Denson before concluding the day's proceedings. The committee's initial questions simply called on Denson to confirm and elaborate on the criticisms of the Koch case review he had already laid out in his lengthy opinion piece published the previous week. After restating his objections to the reviewing authorities' evaluation of his witnesses' credibility, Denson engaged in a revealing exchange concerning the nature of the evidence in the Koch case. Ferguson first asked Denson whether he was satisfied that he had proven his case "beyond a reasonable doubt," and whether indeed that was the standard required for conviction at Dachau. Denson responded that he had argued his case *as if* this had been the necessary burden required of the prosecution, but he also explained that, in the Dachau courts, "there was some question . . . as to whether that was a rule to be applied."[89]

Given Denson's explanation that hearsay evidence was permitted in military law, Ferguson wanted next to understand the nature of the specific evidence tying Koch to the collection of tattooed human skins. As he had done in his op-ed, Denson first responded by recounting the testimony of Froboess, the witness that reviewing authorities considered wholly discredited after it was revealed that he had fraudulently posed as a friar. Following up, however, Denson appeared to signal that he, too, was leery of the evidence—a remarkable retreat from the central pillar in the case he had brought against Koch:

> Let me say this, in all sincerity. I did not feel that the skin business, because of the tenuousness of the proof, was of such importance. It merely showed the background of what went on and what took place there. The gravamen of her action was in beating prisoners with her own hand, and causing them to be beaten so that they died. That is the matter that was really the basis for the sentence, I am sure.[90]

Denson's stunning about-face now suggested that the crimes of the woman he had recently dubbed "a sadistic pervert of monumental proportions unmatched in history" lay in the far less sensational charge that she had instigated the beating of prisoners. Even in this, however, Denson appeared to hedge when pushed by Ferguson on the evidence. "Did you have testimony that she personally had either selected or singled out anyone . . . on whom punishment was visited resulting in their death?" While he "couldn't confirm it under oath," Denson explained, as he worried about his memory a year after the case had closed, he indicated, "I think probably there was."[91] Denson assured the committee, however, that while he had elicited the testimony of only ten witnesses at Koch's trial, he had dozens of others he could have called to the stand to provide similar accounts but did not, in the interest of efficiency. Following up with a query about Denson's view of Koch's guilt, Chief Counsel Rogers asked whether the fact that Koch lacked a formal role at the camp may have made her "less culpable than the other defendants." To the contrary, Denson answered,

"I think she was more culpable because this was gratuitous." This response, however, undercut the very basis of her conviction: that she was a participant in a common scheme to commit war crimes at Buchenwald. Koch's guilt, Denson now contended, was *more* acute than that of her codefendants because "there was no reason in the world for her exercising the authority she exercised."[92] Ferguson, unfazed by this contradiction, concluded with a final and fundamental question. Could Denson "think of any reason at all to possibly justify this reduction?" he asked. "No sir," Denson replied, "I cannot."[93]

As the Ferguson committee adjourned to assess the trial record and study various documents and reports generated during the review of Koch's case, US military authorities searched for a way out of the growing controversy. Immediately following his appearance before the committee, Secretary Royall requested that General Clay study the possibility of conducting a second military trial of Ilse Koch "for another offense," recognizing that the principle of double-jeopardy prohibited trying her twice for the same crime.[94] On October 2, Clay replied to Royall that, given the breadth of the original common design charge, it was "doubtful whether any such evidence will be found" as to warrant new and distinct charges.[95] Nevertheless, he informed Royall that he had instructed Harbaugh, Straight, and the War Crimes Review Board to submit reports to account for their original decisions and the appraisals of the evidence that had led them to recommend the commutation of Koch's sentence. Directly addressing suggestions in the press that Koch's commutation had stemmed from nefarious influence, Clay made clear that "no investigation of bribery or connection between Ilse Koch's pregnancy and reduction in sentence is contemplated.... The evidence pertaining to Ilse Koch was reviewed by nine lawyers ... all of whom agreed in the reduction." To pursue such insinuations would be "an unfair reflection on their integrity as officers and members of the bar." The final responsibility was his alone, Clay wrote:

It has been my lot to pass on many death sentences as well as life imprisonment. It is a responsibility which I have taken most seriously and in each case I do make a careful study of the summarized evidence before taking final action. . . . I am sorry to have brought the Army under attack, but decisions of this type cannot be political. They are and cannot be other than decisions of conscience.[96]

As Clay's response to Royall laid bare, the ever-growing controversy surrounding the commutation of Koch's sentence was raising troubling questions that threatened to undermine confidence in American military leadership. As *Time* put it most dramatically, the fallout from the reduction of the sentence of "the sexually psychotic 'Bitch of Buchenwald'" left the US Army to be "boiled in angry oil."[97] By mid-October, the scandal had raised sufficient concern at the White House that President Truman sent Secretary Royall a pointed letter requesting a "complete file on the case," and a comprehensive explanation of the various "unusual circumstances" surrounding the commutation of Koch's sentence and the differing assessments of her guilt.[98] At the news of Truman's intervention, Senator Ferguson, a Republican serving amid a Democratic administration, declared he was "pleased to note the President is now interested in the case," and also happy to "assure him of the complete cooperation of the committee." Apparently keen to place responsibility at Truman's feet, however, Ferguson was quick to point out that, as commander in chief, the president was in a position "to correct any injustice in this woman's sentence if he so desires."[99]

At the end of November 1948, Clay submitted his report to Royall concerning the possibility of conducting a second US Army trial of Ilse Koch, confirming that this potential avenue out of the crisis was not viable. Clay confirmed first that, while the prosecution had indeed amassed evidence against Koch that was not introduced at her trial, it was "of little to no probative value," and was wholly insufficient to support new charges.[100] At a more fundamental level, the common design charge employed at the Buchenwald trial was so expansive as to have already encompassed any offense Koch might have committed against non-German nationals between the war's outbreak and its end. Even if new evidence did exist, new charges by the United States would violate the principle of double jeopardy. Given "the announced mission of the occupation to re-establish the rule of law in Germany," Clay insisted, a new American trial would be counter-productive, and would constitute "persecution and not prosecution."[101] Clay finished his report, however, with a brief exploration of another way to pursue new proceedings against Koch. While he expressed only tepid support for the idea, he noted that a potential solution to the crisis would be a trial before a German court, for violations of German law, committed against German nationals. "Whether or not such a trial will be permitted," Clay concluded, "will depend upon the desires of the German authorities, the proposed charges, and the evidence in support thereof."[102]

Clay's notion of a new trial of Ilse Koch by German judicial authorities likely stemmed from proposals that first emerged from Germany in the autumn of 1948. On October 9 of that year, Buchenwald survivor and chief chronicler Eugen Kogon had published an opinion piece in the *New York Times* that argued for the retrial of Koch in the regular German court system, where judges who could understand the survivor-witnesses in their native tongue would be most likely to render a conviction. In an argument Clay would echo, Kogon pointed out that German courts had the jurisdiction to try Koch for crimes beyond the purview of the US military court at Dachau. Kogan was confident there was ample unheard evidence from survivors to reconvict her, especially as it pertained to crimes committed against German nationals.[103]

The following day, the *New York Times* reported that Dr. Philip Auerbach, a survivor of Auschwitz and the Bavarian commissioner for racial and political persecutees, had requested that all former inmates of Buchenwald submit testimony concerning Ilse Koch in anticipation of new legal proceedings. Auerbach also formally requested that Bavaria's minister of justice, Dr. Josef Müller, hold Koch for trial upon her release from American custody.[104] On October 18, the *Times* quoted Müller as saying that he had "no doubt" that German proceedings against Koch would soon be launched.[105] Anticipation of a German trial of Ilse Koch, however, was predicated on the assumption that Koch would be released from American custody in October 1949 as scheduled. This remained an uncertainty as Ferguson's commission announced its plan to reconvene, in anticipation of making its own recommendations on how the United States government could most effectively "bring Ilse Koch to justice."[106]

The Prospect of a New Trial

Since the adjournment of the Senate investigations subcommittee on September 28, 1948, anticipation of further hearings had grown steadily, especially since Ferguson had announced in early October that all future hearings on the Koch case would be public.[107] By the time the committee reconvened on December 8, however, following study of the Buchenwald trial record, political realities in Germany had forced Ferguson to reconsider. As Cold War tensions had risen dramatically with the Soviet blockade of Berlin and the subsequent Allied airlift, the US government had little appetite for publicly airing grievances with its own military leadership. Ferguson was forced to explain that, despite his earlier promise, there was a fear on the part of the committee that "prolonged public testimony might give the Russians . . . an opportunity for hostile propaganda," and that the committee therefore did not want "to provide a forum for any possible public embarrassment just now to the United States commander in Germany, Gen. Lucius D. Clay, as he confronted the Russians across the crisis of Berlin."[108] That the affair surrounding Koch's commutation had grown to the point of prompting concerns it could undermine US authority during a time of global tension laid bare how high the stakes had risen as Ferguson resumed committee hearings behind closed doors and recommenced the search for an American-made solution to the controversy.

Proceedings reopened with the testimony of three survivors of Buchenwald—Dr. Kurt Sitte, Dr. Paul Heller, and Dr. Peter Zenkl—purportedly "to give the committee some idea of the camp itself and the operation of the camp in a general way."[109] The questioning of these former inmates strayed quickly from this line, however, and instead appeared geared toward eliciting damning sworn accounts of Koch's activities. Ferguson called Dr. Sitte first and asked him to begin by describing for the committee what he had learned while working in the camp's pathology department regarding the demographics and death rate at the camp. Seemingly fascinated by Sitte's firsthand knowledge of the most macabre practices of the camp SS, the committee followed up with no less than sixty questions concerning how human skins were gathered, tanned, stretched, and distributed. As he had testified at Dachau, however, Sitte explained that he could not connect Ilse Koch to these activities. What he could offer the committee concerned only Koch's instigation of beatings, and even that constituted "what might be called hearsay."[110] Apparently realizing the seeming impropriety of eliciting witness testimony against Koch not heard at trial, Chief Counsel Rogers felt compelled to follow Sitte's excusal with a reminder to the committee that the survivor-witnesses "are not here for any purpose of retrying the case."[111] Nonetheless, the questioning of Dr. Heller and Dr. Zenkl that followed appeared remarkably close to this line.

Dr. Heller, who had not appeared as a witness at the Buchenwald trial, answered questions almost exclusively focused on details of incidents he had witnessed involving Ilse Koch. Heller described Koch as having "had not the slightest feminine feeling," as she derived pleasure from watching SS beatings that, he testified, her presence would inspire.[112] The testimony of Dr. Zenkl, the former deputy prime minister of Czechoslovakia, also detailed beatings of concentration camp inmates, and was, Chief Counsel Rogers concluded, "not very direct about Ilse Koch," but was important "to show the type of prisoner they had at Buchenwald."[113] Though the testimony of the three survivors piqued the interest of the committee in the depths of the atrocities that had occurred at Buchenwald, it either repeated what could already be found in the trial record or provided new evidence not heard at Koch's trial that therefore was unhelpful in accounting for the judgment reached by the Dachau court and by judicial authorities upon review.

With testimony of survivors having set the stage, the Ferguson committee called Brigadier General Charles Kiel, president of the Dachau court, to account for the judgment and original sentence handed down to Ilse Koch. The insights that the committee hoped to gain, however, were frustrated from the outset by shortcomings in Kiel's legal training, experience, and recollection. Explaining that the Buchenwald trial was one of only two over which he had ever presided, Kiel exasperated the committee with answers that seemed both vague and uninformed. When asked by Chief Counsel Rogers to explain what crime Koch and her codefendants were charged with, Kiel responded that he "would have to see the charge sheet."[114] Asked about the prosecution case against Koch, Kiel was unable to recall whether the court had heard direct evidence tying Koch to beatings that resulted in the deaths of prisoners.[115] Kiel similarly was unable to shed light on the dynamics of the adjudication of Koch's case, remembering neither whether the guilty verdict or the life sentence had been reached unanimously, nor whether the vote for conviction had required a straight majority or a two-thirds majority from the panel of seven judges he led.[116]

Senator John L. McLellan (D-Arkansas), who now joined the hearings, was incredulous at Kiel's testimony. "What strikes me," he exclaimed, "is that you are a little hazy in your memory about some very important things. . . . Here is the head of the trial court, unable apparently to recollect some very important procedures, as to whether they were followed, how they were followed, or whether they were not followed."[117] Asked what had informed his conduct of the trial, Kiel explained that he could recall no further instruction beyond receiving the US Army's "Manual for the Trial of War Crimes" and a single sheet summarizing trial procedures. When it came to matters of law, Kiel explained that he had generally depended on the advice of the court's sole lawyer. "In other words," Chief Counsel Rogers interjected with unconcealed frustration, "all you know is that you were made presiding officer of the court and you read the charge; and you can't tell us what law the charge violates." He continued: "So as I gather, "the only thing you did was look at the piece of paper that included the charge before you and decide whether or not the testimony you heard proved the defendants guilty under the charge?"

"Right," Kiel responded.[118]

If Kiel's testimony had accomplished anything, it had inadvertently made a case for the US Army's judicial review process and the necessity of having qualified lawyers assess the verdicts and sentences handed down by the inexperienced judges that presided at Dachau. Called to testify next were those responsible for this very process—Harbaugh and Straight. In a tone that betrayed hostility from the outset, Ferguson demanded that the two men provide the rationale that had guided the sentence reduction they had recommended. Neither Harbaugh nor Straight minced words, declaring plainly that, despite everything written in the press, there was no credible evidence to tie Ilse Koch to any crime beyond the instigation of the beating of at least one inmate.[119] This explanation, however, maddened Ferguson as it had done Denson, prompting Ferguson to lead a heated exchange over the jurisdiction of reviewing authorities to assess the credibility of testimony they had read off the page but had not witnessed in court. "Show us the rule," Ferguson demanded, "that allows a reviewing court to pass on the credibility of the evidence." As Harbaugh attempted to explain that the practice of assessing credibility was done "uniformly" and was "a custom right from the beginning," Ferguson interjected twice more with his refrain unchanged: "Show us the rule."[120]

Ferguson grew more agitated as Harbaugh explained that no written regulation existed to account for this common practice, and followed up by asking rhetorically why the US Army bothered to hold trials he described as a mere "formality." He asked, "Would it not have been much better to have disposed of these eight officers and merely had commissioners take the testimony?"[121] Flatly rejecting Ferguson's depiction of the trial as a formality, Harbaugh insisted that the court's verdict was regarded "in a very high manner," but that the reviewing authorities "considered everything that would be sent in to us in the interest of doing justice." Ferguson fired back that a formality "is all it amounted to. You went out and got other evidence and passed on credibility."[122]

Disturbed by the fact that US Army regulations had allowed Koch's defense counsel to petition reviewing authorities after the completion of trial, Ferguson asked whether Harbaugh knew "of any procedure in America, in our administration of justice, that allows the appellate court to consider evidence that was not before the trial court in the reduction of sentence," and whether such a procedure was "in conformity with our ideas of justice." Seizing on Ferguson's ill-fitting comparison, Harbaugh reminded him that "these were different kinds of trials," that review was not synonymous with appeal, and that even while such procedures did not exist in civil courts in the United States, there was no reason to believe them unfair.[123] Rather than an injustice, Straight interjected, the review process that resulted in Koch's sentence reduction and that was carried out by seasoned jurists was a vital form of check and balance given the limited skills of the military men who acted as Dachau court judges. "The American Army officer," Straight argued, "has no unusual ability to judge the credibility of a witness similar to that of a judge on a court who has had experience over 20 years."[124] Conspicuously missing from Ferguson's criticism of judicial procedures at Dachau was any mention of the lax rules of evidence that allowed for the extensive use of hearsay, and by extension, that facilitated the conviction of Ilse Koch by the Dachau court judges in the first place. Ferguson was framing his criticism of the review process in terms of its deviation from American domestic judicial norms, but his exchanges with Harbaugh and Straight betrayed a willingness to pick and choose the specific procedures and principles where divergence should not be tolerated.

After adjourning hearings following a day of combative exchanges, Ferguson reconvened the committee the following morning to push Straight and Harbaugh on a final and pressing question: Could General Clay's decision to grant Ilse Koch clemency be reversed, and if not, could Koch be retried? From the outset, Straight and Harbaugh were doubtful. Straight explained that, while Clay technically had the authority to reach a new verdict, to do so after already announcing his final decision would be without precedent and "would violate all standards and customs thus far followed in military law."[125] He added, as a reminder to Ferguson, that Clay was standing by his decision and had already publicly defended the verdict he had reached. Unsatisfied, Ferguson asked whether President Truman could force Clay to reconsider. Growing incredulous, Straight insisted that, if the President were "to delegate authority to somebody and then jerk it back," that would violate "universally accepted standards of justice."[126] "In other words," Senator McClellan interjected, "it would be a greater mistake to try to correct the mistake than it would be to let the mistake stand since it favors the accused?"[127] Answering in the affirmative, Harbaugh upped the emotional temperature in the room, insisting that he couldn't imagine anything that would be "further afield from democracy" than for Clay to revisit a case and change a sentence, which would essentially be "the same thing the Nazis used to do."[128] In a dig at Ferguson, Harbaugh explained that "in Germany today we are trying to introduce the rule of law, not the rule of men."[129] McClellan indicated his agreement, despite his personal feeling that Koch "should have her neck broken." Ferguson, however, resented the insinuation and pushed back, insisting that if anyone had acted arbitrarily, it was Harbaugh and Straight as they prepared their recommendations.[130]

As the exchange between Harbaugh and Ferguson grew heated, Chief Counsel Rogers attempted to steer the hearings toward a more productive consideration of the central question that remained: If Clay's decision to grant Koch clemency could not be undone, could Koch be retried? As this line of questioning commenced, Straight and Harbaugh again bristled, warning the committee that a second US trial of Ilse Koch would constitute double jeopardy and would therefore violate the universally accepted legal principle that protects a defendant from being tried twice for the same crime. Harbaugh warned the committee that a second US trial would have "the appearance of persecution," and would be counterproductive to the ongoing American efforts to promote core principles of democracy in Germany. Rogers then raised the proposal that Dr. Eugen Kogon had floated in his *New York Times* editorial that October: Could Koch legitimately be brought to trial before a German court, for crimes committed against German nationals? Though Harbaugh was cautious in his assessment of the idea, he confirmed for the committee that any such crimes would have been beyond the jurisdiction of the Dachau court and therefore that such a trial would not constitute double jeopardy. As the prospect of a German trial now appeared to provide a legitimate avenue to resolve the crisis spurred by Koch's clemency, Rogers asked Harbaugh a final question before allowing him to exit: Would such a trial nonetheless be damaging to the image of the United States? "I cannot think of anything that would be harmful," Harbaugh concluded, "provided it was a good sound charge and that competent, credible evidence was available."[131]

With a solution in hand that allowed for the retrial of Koch without violating legal principle or stirring further ire from the US Army's judicial authorities, Ferguson's committee drew its proceedings to a close at day's end and retired for three weeks to draft its recommendations. The committee's subsequent report, released December 27, 1948, roundly criticized the review process that had resulted in Koch's clemency. Clearly unconvinced by the testimony of the military authorities who oversaw the Dachau trial program and by the conclusions of their legal teams that had rejected the most serious allegations against Koch at every stage of the review process, the report's authors characterized Koch as both uniquely monstrous and unambiguously guilty. The clemency granted Koch constituted a grave injustice, they argued, and one that required immediate remedy.

At the heart of the committee's report lay a series of central claims that were in various ways incongruous. First, the committee reiterated Chief Prosecutor Denson's charge that the assessment of the credibility of evidence was the exclusive domain of the court, and that in "usurping" this role, reviewing authorities not present at trial had relied on the "cold printed record" to reach flawed conclusions.[132] Ironically, however, the committee nonetheless used its own review of the same trial transcript to declare that there existed "no persuasive mitigating evidence in the record to justify any reduction in sentence."[133] The committee further argued that reviewing authorities, in basing their recommendations on an assessment of evidence that concerned specific atrocities attributed to Koch, had lost sight of the single charge with which she had been tried: participating in a common design to commit war crimes. Prosecutors could not have foreseen, the report claimed, that reviewers would not sustain Koch's lengthy sentence unless there were clear evidence that her actions had led to the death of specific inmates; if they had known this, prosecutors would have presented their case differently and would have had ample evidence at their disposal to prove a single charge of murder.[134] The committee's own assessment of Koch's guilt, however, appeared to contradict the report's emphasis on the primacy of the common design charge. According to Ferguson and his colleagues, "every act committed by Ilse Koch as shown by the evidence, was that of a volunteer. Such voluntary action, contrary to every decent human instinct, deserves utter contempt and denies mitigation." Further, the report treated her violation of gender norms as central to her guilt and a key factor in determining her punishment. "Being a woman made her participation more unnatural," it stated, "and more deliberate." This insistence, however, that Koch's allegedly devious nature had led her to act out "of her own volition and without provocation" was fundamentally at odds with the legal case against her; its central premise was that she had participated in a common scheme to operate Buchenwald concentration camp.[135]

Before outlining its perceived remedy to "bring Ilse Koch to justice," the committee pointed out other shortfalls it saw in the review process. It stressed the inadequacy of the review and recommendations document prepared by the deputy judge advocate for war crimes, arguing that it provided insufficient justifications for rejecting the credibility of the testimony against Koch. The committee's report did, however, provide some information suggesting that the reviewers' assessments were not ill-founded—noting, for instance, that key prosecution witness Froboess was currently serving time in prison for a fraud conviction. The report also criticized the American judicial authorities' serious error in delaying the announcement of the decision. Noting the public mood, the committee claimed that much of the controversy surrounding the Koch case could have been avoided had military authorities immediately and thoroughly explained the decision to grant clemency. By instead letting months pass until a leak to the press forced an announcement, they had raised suspicions that the news was being deliberately suppressed.

The last part of the report was reserved for consideration of the only solution the subcommittee found to be viable: the retrial of Ilse Koch by the German judiciary. The members of the committee, it assured, "do not disagree with the position taken by the military authorities that it would be unwise to reopen the case at this time," but also wanted to ensure that, if any German process were to emerge, the US military would render assistance. "General Clay has said that the German courts have expressed their intention to try her for crimes committed against Germans," the report observed, and "it would then be the duty of our military authority to give complete cooperation to the German authorities and make available all records, evidence, and witnesses within their control." The closing words of the report suggested that the very integrity of American justice depended on a speedy and fitting resolution of the Koch commutation controversy. It was "highly important that Ilse Koch receive the just punishment she so justly deserves without further doing violence to long-established safeguards of democratic justice. . . . The error in the Koch case is an isolated blemish on the vigilance and certainty of this democratic justice. Its repetition must be prevented."[136]

Throughout the Senate subcommittee hearings, Ilse Koch keenly followed developments from her prison cell in Landsberg. That October, in the midst of the hearings and the controversy that had spurred them, a reporter from the *Washington Post* paid Koch a visit and recorded her impressions. Not surprisingly, the article began with a description of her looks and how they stacked up against her alleged sexual prowess. "Neatly clad in a well-fitting green dress," it began, "her appearance after three years in prison is surprising." Finding Koch "sharp-nosed" and "wearing a pose of injured innocence," the reporter marveled that she now appeared to be "neither the sultry female once depicted as the wife of the Buchenwald commandant nor the blousy creature described during her trial. She looks healthy, extremely well-fed, and considerably younger than her 42 years." As the interview began, Koch revealed herself to be "surprisingly well informed on the latest details of the furor created by the army's drastic commutation of her life sentence," explaining that she received German newspapers and *Stars and Stripes* in prison, and was "following the case" closely. Koch, however, was unwilling to reflect on Americans' reactions to her sentence reduction, charging that any statement she made would be twisted "into lies like everything else that has happened before," and would be "used as propaganda against me throughout the whole world." As Koch repeated her assertion that military authorities had suppressed evidence that could have proven her innocence, the author noted that "she demonstrated a degree of self-possession that bordered on arrogance."[137]

If the press was quick to paint Koch's confidence in her innocence as conceit, her own public comments did little to warm her image. *Stars and Stripes* reported at the end of September that, far from glad for the clemency granted her, Koch was "furious" at her new four-year sentence, and resentful of those "liars with dirty minds" who accused her of crimes at Buchenwald. "Why should I be glad," Koch demanded, "when I have been kept in jail for three years and will be here for another year and I am completely innocent.... What can I do? I have no money, no bed, no home. I have three children, they are supported by the welfare office."[138] With her mandated release scheduled for October 1949, Koch likely felt that she had little need to be contrite. In a telling and rare silence, however, she reportedly only answered "no comment" when a *New York Times* reporter suggested to her that the result of the Senate hearings could well be new charges and a new trial in Germany.[139] Increasingly, Koch's perceptions of her predicament were defined not only by frustration and rage, but a sense of self-pity born of a growing belief that the deck had been hopelessly and unjustly stacked against her. "Mine," she lamented, "is a tragic story."[140]

5   New Charges, New Challenges in a Divided Germany

At the dawn of 1949, Ilse Koch's slated release from prison lay less than a year away. Although the report of the US Senate subcommittee released at the end of December 1948 had shed some light on the grounds for the dramatic reduction of Koch's life sentence, it did little to quell the controversy roused by this act of clemency. Chief Prosecutor William Denson continued his public attack on the military review process that had undone the sentence he had fought so hard to secure, authoring a multipage article in the new year's issue of the popular newsmagazine *Look* to challenge how "any sane, self-respecting human would argue she should go free."[1] The article, which featured a half-page photo of Koch in a bathing suit and well-worn sexual clichés that satisfied the continuing public appetite for salacious details of Koch's alleged activities, made no mention of the Senate subcommittee or its much-anticipated recommendations. Instead, Denson concluded with resignation, lamenting that the "one cold, clear fact" was that "Ilse Koch will soon be free."[2]

Denson's tone of despondency notwithstanding, the Senate subcommittee's musings about future criminal proceedings against Koch had cast real doubt on her impending release. Its conclusion that the legal obstacles hindering an American retrial of Koch would largely evaporate if she were instead brought before a German court, and for crimes committed against German nationals, touched off behind-the-scenes diplomatic activity that would culminate in new charges and a new chapter in Koch's legal odyssey. Yet against the backdrop of increasing Cold War tensions, authorities in the western and eastern zones of occupied Germany came to compete fiercely for an opportunity to prosecute Koch, viewing her case as a litmus test for the respective resolve of western democratic and communist forces in dealing resolutely with the vestiges of the Nazi past. While the United States would fight to ensure that Koch's case remained under the jurisdiction of legal authorities in the western zone, conflict with authorities in the Soviet zone would threaten to undermine Koch's successful prosecution.

Once the idea of instigating a German prosecution of Koch took shape in the recommendations of the Senate subcommittee, editorial pages across the United States helped to fuel the drive for new proceedings. The press response to the subcommittee's conclusions reflected the unabated outrage of the American public, with newspapers advocating Koch's retrial, in some cases by reproducing the same allegations of human-skin lampshades that judicial authorities had testified were spurious. The *Philadelphia Inquirer* hailed the subcommittee's release of a report that "corroborates the sentiments of a majority of Americans on the Army's handling of the case of this 'bestial' woman." New proceedings against Koch were "essential," it continued, because the commutation had given the world "grounds to doubt the certainty of American justice."[3] The *Washington Post* similarly urged that "every effort within the law ought to be made to redeem this atrocious reflection on the competence of military justice," and the *New York Times* likened Koch's looming release from US custody to a "crime against humanity."[4] Within many of the editorials on the subcommittee's recommendations there was also a recognition that, while the Koch affair had left the reputation of American military justice in tatters, the available avenues to its repair were perilous. The *Washington Star* opined that "great care should be taken to avoid any further mistakes in the Koch case," and that further missteps in the pursuit of Koch could cause "the prestige of democratic justice [to] suffer an even greater blow."[5] Although some editorials still advocated retrial by the United States military as the best means of repairing its damaged reputation, there was a general acknowledgment that, unless new evidence were to surface that permitted charging Koch with crimes that had lain outside the purview of the Dachau court, this could not happen. The alternative, it was broadly recognized, lay in a German court.

Still, while the Senate subcommittee had expressed support for Koch's retrial before a German court, it had also made clear that the US Army should first devote "vigorous attention" to exhausting even the most remote possibility of Koch's being "brought to justice in a United States military court."[6] General Lucius Clay, under whose final authority Koch's commutation had been confirmed, found himself under immense pressure to act zealously on the Senate recommendations. Having earlier insisted to Secretary of the Army Kenneth C. Royall that retrial before a US military court was out of the question, Clay now felt compelled to satisfy the demands of the subcommittee by instigating one last, futile examination of this option. Despite his previous assertions, Clay now directed his legal staff to reassess the evidence gathered for Koch's trial at Dachau in the faint hope it would allow for new charges—and some repair of the US military's tarnished reputation.

If the army were to avoid violating the principle of double jeopardy, however, it would need to find evidence either of crimes committed at Buchenwald that fell beyond the expansive "common design" charge for which Koch was tried at Dachau, or of crimes committed outside Buchenwald altogether. Judge Advocate Colonel Harbaugh, tasked with reviewing the evidence, had his doubts from the outset. On

January 12, 1949, his special assistant for war crimes, Colonel Wade M. Fleischer, submitted a ten-page report to him that analyzed the evidence gathered by the prosecution team at Dachau, including unused testimonies that Chief Prosecutor William Denson had told the Senate subcommittee could convict Koch many times over. Fleischer's conclusions were very different. "There is no evidence," Fleischer wrote, "that Ilse Koch committed any offenses except during the period of time she lived at Buchenwald Concentration camp." Even the unused evidence surrounding her activities at Buchenwald, Fleischer continued, "would have little probative value against her."[7]

Harbaugh would not have been surprised by these conclusions, but his willingness to pass them along as the final word on the matter frustrated Clay. On January 25, Harbaugh reported to Fleischer that he had received a phone call from a "considerably upset" General Clay, demanding to know why he was not working on an opinion regarding Koch's retrial by a US military court. Harbaugh reminded Clay that he himself had already signed off on a report to the Secretary of the Army in November 1948 that declared that "the entire question of her re-trial had been carefully analyzed and the conclusion reached that such a trial would violate the principles of double jeopardy." Nevertheless, Clay concluded his dressing-down of Harbaugh with an order that he provide an official report at once on the matter.[8] If Clay hoped, however, that Harbaugh's bottom line might change, he would be disappointed. In his memorandum to Clay dated February 2, 1949, Harbaugh described the evidence against Koch as "of little probative value," and "generally not of such character that it would be admitted in a Court of Justice." Elaborating, Harbaugh wrote, "Some of the statements are utterly bare of details; others . . . conflict with the known facts about Buchenwald; others are in conflict with the evidence produced by the prosecution at the trial and tend to establish that other persons committed many of the criminal acts commonly attributed to Ilse Koch." Harbaugh did not dismiss the unused evidence against

Koch altogether, but saw nothing in it to justify an American retrial; at best, some of it might "be developed to provide credible evidence against Ilse Koch in a German court."[9]

On February 7, 1949, Clay passed on his staff's reports to Secretary of the Army Royall, unequivocally stating that new American charges against Koch were not possible and that no choice remained but to turn to German judicial authorities in the US occupied zone. Although the formal independence of the West German state would not be granted until May, Clay's legal staff had reassured him that there was "no lack of an adequate German judicial system to try Ilse Koch for crimes committed by her, which were not war crimes, but which were violations of German law."[10] As the German legal code, adopted with the formation of the unified German state in 1871, had never been abrogated during the Third Reich, its provisions on murder and abuse remained the law of the land. Working out how, exactly, Koch would be prosecuted on the basis of this legal code would become a task for German authorities. For now, Clay informed Royall that he had "asked [the] Minister President of Bavaria to designate representatives at once to work with our representatives to develop from the evidence her participation in crimes against German nationals with a view to her early trial."[11]

The Koch Case between East and West

General Clay's decision to initiate legal action against Koch through Bavarian authorities was broadly logical, given that the Landsberg prison where Koch was incarcerated lay in Bavaria. Yet the choice to tap Bavarian jurists to prepare the new prosecution of Koch immediately generated controversy and recriminations in an ideologically and politically divided Germany. In the Soviet zone, news of Koch's sentence reduction had been met with condemnation and held up as evidence that western democratic authorities were soft on fascism. The

Tägliche Rundschau had depicted Ilse Koch's imminent release as the kind of ongoing "cooperation between American Imperialists and the old fascists of the Hitler years" that allowed people of her ilk to be "protected by democracy."[12] The *Berliner Zeitung* had seen in the United States' act of clemency "evidence of the process of the revival of fascism going on in the West."[13] Most outraged at news of Koch's reduced sentence had been the Buchenwald Committee, which operated under the umbrella of the Berlin-based Association of Persecutees of the Nazi Regime (Vereinigung der Verfolgten des Naziregimes, or VVN). Made up largely of communist survivors, including Eugen Kogon and other prominent Buchenwald inmates, the Buchenwald Committee, like the VVN as a whole, saw itself as a vanguard against the resurgence of Nazism. Describing news of Koch's clemency as "a punch in the face to anti-fascists the world over," the Buchenwald Committee released a widely publicized resolution, endorsed by the VVN, calling for the immediate transfer of Koch to German custody and her swift punishment for crimes against "German anti-fascists."[14]

The official reaction in the Soviet zone to news of Koch's abbreviated sentence had been to take up the call of the Buchenwald Committee and demand that she be transferred to their custody for trial. In October 1948, the legislature of the province of Thuringia, in which Buchenwald fell, passed a resolution demanding that state judicial authorities take "all steps necessary for the extradition of Ilse Koch in order to make her stand trial at the Weimar Court which has jurisdiction with regard to the locality of her crimes."[15] While Bavaria's minister of justice, Josef Müller, initially had expressed his willingness to see Koch tried under his own jurisdiction, the provincial secretary of state, Dr. Carl Lacherbauer, informed officials in the Soviet zone in a letter dated November 8, 1948, that Thuringia would indeed cede future proceedings against Koch to them and would hand over any evidence already collected by the commissioner for racial and political persecutees, Dr. Philip Auerbach.[16] On November 16, the Weimar district court formally issued a warrant for Koch's arrest on suspicion of having committed "numerous crimes against humanity."[17] Perhaps anticipating future challenges to its jurisdiction, the Thuringian Ministry of Justice declared that "Buchenwald is located in the district of Weimar [regional court], making the chief public prosecutor of that court the appropriate prosecuting authority."[18]

Thuringian authorities had staked a forceful claim to Koch's future trial but, with nearly a year of her sentence in American custody remaining, such legal maneuvers were premature, if possibly preemptive. Once the United States declared its interest in seeing Koch tried by a German court, the initial decision of Bavarian authorities to permit and support Koch's future trial in the Soviet zone created substantial difficulty. For General Clay, such a trial would be unacceptable given that it threatened to further undermine rather than restore the prestige of the United States military. The optics of permitting Koch's prosecution in the Soviet zone would only affirm the accusations of critics who presented Koch's clemency as evidence that western democratic forces were soft on Nazi criminals and could not be trusted to deal forcefully with the remnants of fascism. It was no coincidence, therefore, that in February 1949, when General Clay finally came around to the idea of bringing Koch before a German court, he turned to the Bavarians. For them to wrest her case back from officials in the Soviet zone, the Bavarian state government would have no choice but to break its word.

On March 22, 1949, General Clay announced publicly his request to Bavarian Minister-President Hans Ehard that a prosecutor be recommended for formal appointment by US occupation authorities to examine the evidence in the Koch case and "determine whether or not her trial is warranted in a German court."[19] As Clay had final word in the American zone of occupation, Ehard had little choice but to comply, prompting US judicial authorities to compile the evidence in their possession and place it at the disposal of the Bavarian state. Wary of breaking its agreement with Thuringia, however, the Bavarian Ministry of Justice remained noncommittal on the future location of Koch's trial, leaving open the possibility that she might still be extradited for prosecution in the Soviet zone.[20] Nevertheless, the news that the United States was now cooperating with Bavarian authorities on possible proceedings against Koch infuriated both the Thuringian legal authorities and the VVN, prompting both to renew their demands that the Bavarians follow through on their earlier promise to deliver Koch to the Soviet zone for trial.[21] Under German law, neither jurisdictional claim took precedence over the other, as German courts were empowered to try defendants for crimes committed either in the state where the crimes had occurred (in this case, Thuringia) or in the state where the defendant resided (in this case, Bavaria). By late April, the quarrel over jurisdiction to try Koch had grown sufficiently acrimonious that increasingly alarmed US occupation authorities were prompted to intercede. Fearful that the Bavarians might yield to pressure from Thuringia and hand Koch over unilaterally, Clay signed off on a directive expressly prohibiting her extradition from the American zone.[22]

Clay's letter barring Bavarian authorities from honoring their previous agreement with the Thuringian government effectively guaranteed that any future proceedings against Koch would be launched within the soon-to-be-independent West German state. Breaking the promise, however, would not go without consequences. The Buchenwald Committee, which had continued to press for Koch's extradition, now also demanded that its members submit witness statements "only and directly to the Chief Prosecutor of Weimar."[23] Further discussion among its members led it to declare that any proceedings launched against Koch under Bavarian auspices would not be recognized.[24] The effective boycott of the Buchenwald Committee meant that testimony from the most prominent body of camp survivors would not be forthcoming, significantly reducing the pool of German witnesses available for examination. And so, while Clay's directive spurred Bavarian legal authorities to action, it also guaranteed that the preliminary investigation of Koch would begin with a struggle to secure witnesses.

The Struggle to Indict

If anyone could restore the faith of Buchenwald's leery survivors in the case to be built against Ilse Koch in the West, it was the jurist endorsed by the Bavarian Ministry of Justice to pursue new legal charges. Dr. Johann Ilkow, chief prosecutor of the Superior Court at Bamberg, had unimpeachable antifascist credentials, having himself been persecuted under the Nazis. Born in 1899 in Brno, in what was then the Austro-Hungarian Empire, Ilkow had distinguished himself as a particularly bright student of law during his studies in Prague and Vienna. By the time the Nazis occupied Czechoslovakia in March 1939, Ilkow had established a successful career as a state prosecutor in his home city. Under the Nazis, however, Ilkow was barred entry to the Reich Justice Service, following his refusal to annul his marriage to his Jewish wife, Marianne. Finding himself outside the organization that permitted him to practice law under the occupation, he was both dismissed from his post and denied any further work as a jurist. After his wife's deportation to Theresienstadt ghetto, Ilkow and his son were drafted into forced labor in the Ore mountains in 1944. All of Ilkow's family survived, but they returned to find their home looted of its contents in a liberated Czechoslovakia now hostile to the ethnic German minority to which they belonged. In search of a more stable future, Ilkow relocated his family to Bavaria and resumed his career as a state prosecutor there. By the time he turned his attention to the Ilse Koch case, he already had experience with Nazi crimes,

Fig. 5.1 Chief Prosecutor Johann Ilkow. Courtesy Bavarian Main State Archive, Ministry of Justice.

having prosecuted three men who had caused the death of a Jew in Würzburg during the 1938 Kristallnacht pogrom.[25]

Despite his experience, Ilkow's appointment to the Koch case led him into unfamiliar territory as a German jurist operating under American auspices in a state yet to gain its independence. Not surprisingly, Ilkow initially grappled to understand the parameters of his assignment. Receiving direction from both the Bavarian Ministry of Justice and US occupation authorities, Ilkow used his first meeting with Judge Advocate General Colonel Harbaugh to ask "just what he was supposed to do." Harbaugh read directly from General Clay's directive: Ilkow was to assess the evidence now at his disposal with an eye to bringing charges against Koch as quickly as possible.[26] It was only upon taking up Koch's case, however, that Ilkow discovered to his dismay that he would first have to fight to establish the legitimacy of the investigation he now led among the survivor community on whose assistance he would depend. Previously unaware of the diplomatic maneuvers that had led to his assignment and the Bavarian decision to hold on to Koch, Ilkow met with Buchenwald Committee president Karl Feuerer during an initial official visit to Munich in April 1949. Ilkow was alarmed to learn about not only the earlier agreement to extradite Koch to Weimar but also the subsequent instruction to the Buchenwald Committee members not to participate in his investigation. "Until this moment," Ilkow later recalled, "the prehistory and the background of my official assignment had been unknown to me."[27]

Ilkow was dismissive of the Buchenwald Committee's claim that Koch could be tried legitimately only in the eastern state of Thuringia, where her crimes had occurred, but he conveyed to US judicial authorities that it "should not be taken too lightly" that the group was pressuring former Buchenwald inmates not to assist his effort. "I should never be able to master the situation," Ilkow warned, "if the organizations of political persecutees . . . were to refuse to me their cooperation."[28] The irony that the very organization that had pushed so forcefully for Koch's prosecution was now attempting to hamper the investigative process would not have been lost on Ilkow, who had no choice but to wait and see whether this resistance would soften as the investigation got underway. His impulse in the meantime was to build trust through transparency. "I do not think," he advised the Bavarian Ministry of Justice, "that we as Bavarians lose face if we admit candidly that the Bavarian trial was only instigated by the intervention of the headquarters of the American forces in Europe or, more concretely, by General Clay, who refused to extradite Ilse Koch to Weimar."[29]

Ilkow's review of the evidence provided to him by US authorities was slowed by the fact that he neither spoke nor read English and so required the assistance of translators to assess the voluminous evidentiary materials now in his possession.[30] At the same time, Ilkow began the search for German witnesses willing to participate. By early April, Ilkow reported to US authorities that he had gathered some twenty statements from former inmates in the Munich and Bamberg region, and would expand his search to the French and British zones of occupation after Easter.[31] For the time being, witnesses in the Soviet zone remained off-limits. Ilkow also sought the names of any relevant witnesses that Dachau Chief Prosecutor William Denson could provide; as well as responding to Ilkow's inquiry with a few suggestions, Denson expressed his eagerness to assist in any way he could "to keep [Koch] in jail for at least another ten to twenty years."[32]

With the review and gathering of evidence underway, Ilkow moved to contend with Koch herself, who sat in the same Landsberg prison cell she had occupied since her sentencing by the Dachau court in August 1947. On April 29, Ilkow came face to face with her for the first time, hoping to extract a signed statement. The fifteen-page document summarizing their meeting suggests an encounter that was surprisingly nonconfrontational, given Koch's oft-expressed disdain for the authorities responsible for her Dachau conviction. Perhaps trying not to antagonize Koch to keep the door open for future questioning, Ilkow used his initial encounter to ask only general questions about her life, and avoided interrogating her about the criminal allegations for which she was now famous. For her part, Koch used the session as an opportunity to reminisce at length about her childhood and early years, and to repeat what were by then familiar alibis deflecting moral and criminal responsibility for what had occurred at Buchenwald.

As she had done at Dachau, Koch claimed that, despite her marriage to Karl, she remained entirely in the dark about his activities in the concentration camp system and that he had made clear to her that his work was secret and could not be discussed. Again painting a picture of herself as wholly consumed by her domestic obligations, Koch maintained that at Buchenwald she had "lived a very isolated life, only for my husband and my children."[33] She was, she insisted, barely familiar with the other leading SS men at the camp, and knew their wives only enough to occasionally say hello. Beyond presenting herself to Ilkow as nothing more than a dedicated and apolitical mother and wife, Koch explained at length that she had left the church in 1937 only at her husband's instigation but remained a believer. Koch emphasized her acquittal at the 1944 SS trial that led to her husband's execution and claimed to have been present only to deliver her testimony and then to hear the judgment of the court. At every turn, she distanced herself from potential sources of knowledge that would undermine her claim of ignorance of the crimes that had occurred in her midst. Of any crimes that she herself may have committed, there was no mention.

Ilkow's questioning of Koch betrayed few hints of the legal peril she once again faced. Only two weeks after his meeting with Koch, however, Ilkow was satisfied that the evidence he had reviewed and gathered warranted criminal charges. He reported to US authorities in mid-May of 1949 that he had elicited 110 statements and that the evidence "indicates that Ilse Koch may be guilty of having committed aggravated assaults on 3 or 4 individuals which resulted in their deaths. It also indicates that she participated in 30 or 40 minor assaults. . . . All of these victims were German nationals."[34] As per the instruction Ilkow received from US judicial authorities, these crimes were to be categorized and ultimately prosecuted according to statutes of the regular German legal code. At his first meeting with Judge Advocate General Colonel Harbaugh in March, Ilkow had asked whether US authorities might consider allowing Koch's prosecution under Control Council Law No. 10. This law, which had never been used by domestic German courts in the American zone, empowered occupying authorities to employ the novel legal charges that had been created for the Nuremberg trial, including the charge of crimes against humanity. Harbaugh advised that it would be preferable to charge Koch for violations of preexisting German law, to head off any objection that her prosecution was based on ex post facto law.[35]

Now confident that a case could be built, Ilkow formally applied to open a judicial *Voruntersuchung* (preliminary investigation) of Ilse Koch on May 15, 1949, in accordance with German law.[36] Ilkow submitted the findings of his initial examination to an "investigating judge," who approved his application on May 31. The investigating judge would now head this preliminary investigation in cooperation with Ilkow, acting in a similar fashion to a grand jury in the United States. It would be up to the investigating judge to assess the evidence collected and determine whether the case should go forward. While Ilkow would remain responsible for drafting the formal indictment, his role at this stage was advisory, as all charges had to be certified by the investigating judge at his sole discretion.[37] Knowing this would involve close collaboration to gather evidence, with the shared goal of indicting Koch, Ilkow had proposed to the Bavarian Ministry of Justice that his colleague from the Superior Court at Bamberg, Erich Jagomast, be appointed investigating judge. The ministry agreed, having initially sought to appoint an investigating judge from the court at Augsburg, where Koch's trial was to be held, but not having found a suitable candidate there.[38] Ilkow and Jagomast were now formally assigned to the state prosecutor's office in Augsburg, with recognition that both would continue to work from Bamberg.

Erich Jagomast hailed from East Prussia and, as a speaker of both English and Yiddish, possessed language skills that would prove exceedingly useful for the investigation. Never a member of the Nazi

Party, Jagomast had nonetheless served as a judge in occupied Poland before being transferred to a post in a civil court, ostensibly because he refused to hand down capital sentences. In 1943, after a number of further legal decisions unpopular with Nazi authorities, Jagomast was sent to serve in the Wehrmacht. Following the war, a denazification tribunal deemed Jagomast untainted by his association with National Socialism.[39] Like Ilkow, therefore, Jagomast would be another politically reliable jurist, free of the lingering Nazi sympathies that would prove a potent force in inhibiting the zealous prosecution and punishment of other Nazi crimes in independent West Germany in the fifties and sixties.

It was now up to Jagomast to pursue the legal allegations contained in Ilkow's three-page application, while gathering more evidence with Ilkow's assistance. On the basis of the statements he had taken and the evidence he had reviewed, Ilkow had accused Koch of multiple counts of four distinct crimes. First, Koch was accused of fourteen counts of inflicting bodily harm with a dangerous weapon, based on numerous reports that she had used her riding whip on prisoners as she rode through the camp on horseback. Second, she was accused of twenty-eight counts of incitement of grievous bodily harm, based on various claims that she had reported prisoners to the camp SS knowing that beatings would follow. Third, Koch was accused of four cases of incitement of grievous bodily harm resulting in death, based on similar incidents, but with fatal consequences. Last and most serious, Koch stood accused of acting in conjunction with others to commit murder, on the basis of a single statement that placed her among a detail of SS men on horseback who had chased a group of more than twenty Jews toward the camp quarry and shot them dead. Koch herself, Ilkow alleged, had drawn her own pistol and participated in the killing.[40] This highly unlikely scenario that cast an armed Koch, without official rank or position in the SS, as taking part in mass murder would soon underscore for Ilkow the vexing and illusive nature of the search for hard evidence sufficient to prove the most serious charges he pursued. Notably, and perhaps taking his cue from the US judicial authorities who had reviewed the findings of the Dachau court, Ilkow made no reference to the allegation that had served to make Koch a household name, that she had sought tattooed prisoners for the production of human-skin lampshades and book bindings.

Although at this stage Ilkow's accusations were provisional and designed only to facilitate the opening of Jagomast's formal investigation, these charges eventually would require unimpeachable and corroborating testimony that for many of them was still lacking. This evidentiary deficit was felt acutely in the jurists' pursuit of the murder allegation in the months that followed. The alleged incident involving Koch's participation in the killing of Jews near the camp quarry originated in statements made by witness and former kapo Friedrich Thumm. A remarkably problematic witness, Thumm had a history of petty crime, had previously served a prison sentence for child molestation, and was currently incarcerated in Straubing prison following a 1947 conviction for rape and fraud.[41] It was from behind bars that Thumm recounted for Ilkow the story of twenty-four Jews he said were executed after being driven along the road toward the quarry by SS men on horseback. Thumm insisted that he could "state definitively" that Koch had drawn her own pistol and participated in the shooting.

Thumm, however, had difficulty dating the killing, stating initially that he believed it to have occurred in the spring of either 1940 or 1941.[42] Ilkow appears to have assumed that Thumm was in fact recalling a notorious killing that had occurred in the camp on November 9, 1939. He dated it in his application accordingly. On that date, many former inmates recalled witnessing the selection of twenty-one Jews who were subsequently shot in the camp quarry, ostensibly as a reprisal for an attempt on Hitler's life that had taken place in Munich the day before. Many recalled the names of the SS perpetrators; none, however, had named Koch as a participant. Ilkow nonetheless appears to have found Thumm's account compelling, though in need of corroboration from more reliable witnesses. If it could be proven, Ilkow felt, Koch's conviction for murder would be secured.

Thumm's testimony, it gradually became clear, was a red herring. Ilkow and Jagomast attempted to fortify his account with testimonies of other witnesses who referred to what they assumed was the same incident, but the more energy they devoted to the task, the more their efforts faltered. In dozens of depositions collected in the months that followed, witness after witness was asked for any verification of Thumm's description of events, but none was supplied. Many recalled in great detail the killing in November 1939, but not one recalled even rumors of Koch's participation.[43] Asked if some separate but similar incident of mass-killing of twenty-four Jews might have occurred in the spring of 1940 or 1941, almost all survivor-witnesses were doubtful. Most, like witness Josef Warscher, replied that they had "never heard of anything like that."[44] Jewish survivor and "block elder" Emil Carlebach insisted that, given his prominent position among inmates at Buchenwald, he would certainly have heard about it "had it actually happened."[45]

Some went further, directly challenging the logic or likelihood of Thumm's account. Former inmate Erich Bormann pointed out that, had the shooting occurred in the grassy area before the quarry, it would have sent bullets flying toward the SS guard chain "as well as those farming the fields only a hundred meters away."[46] Leopold Lukasik concurred, adding that the SS would not have carried out a mass killing in such an exposed location.[47] Witness Willi Bleicher explained that "people were liquidated almost every day, and sometimes in numbers as high as twenty-four" in a day, but that "these were always individual killings."[48] Witness Clemens Bukowski added that "at that point in time [the SS] already had better methods of extermination."[49]

While a few believed that such a shooting might have happened, none could testify to its occurrence.

Frustrated, Ilkow reported to US authorities that he and Jagomast were finding it "extremely difficult . . . to prove her direct connection with the deaths of many of the individuals in the Buchenwald concentration camp."[50] In a lengthy report submitted jointly to the Office of the Judge Advocate General the Office of US Military Government in Bavaria, and the Bavarian Ministry of Justice on June 27, 1949, Ilkow informed his superiors that he had been forced to scale back his prosecutorial ambitions and had for the time being dropped the murder charge because "the main witness is a criminal."[51] On the basis of the evidence gathered thus far, Ilkow warned, he could build a case only on the charges related to inflicting or incitement of bodily harm, and only sufficient to sentence Koch to nine or ten years imprisonment.

Well aware that such a conviction would be a disappointment to US authorities and would do little to calm the emotions stirred up by Koch's impending release, Ilkow felt obliged to account for the shortcomings of his case as it stood. "We meet with the largest difficulties in collecting our evidence," his report continued. "Criminal and anti-social elements are to be avoided as witnesses as far as possible," Ilkow emphasized, but finding cooperative witnesses from the preferred categories of political, racial, and religious persecutees was challenging. Most former political prisoners, Ilkow explained, were communists and now aligned with the Buchenwald Committee, which was still actively working to "hinder the Bavarian criminal proceedings by acts of sabotage." Those persecuted on racial grounds were primarily Jews, most of whom had now emigrated from Germany and to the United States. Given that the Koch case would be argued before a jury drawn from the "religious farm-people of Swabia," Ilkow indicated that religious persecutees, especially "clergy of both confessions," would be particularly valuable as witnesses. Here, too, they were experiencing difficulties, however, as "one cannot simply approach these witnesses . . . [because] they do not wish to be reminded of the time which they spent in a concentration camp." To overcome this resistance, Ilkow reported that he and Jagomast had sought the assistance of the secretaries of the Archbishops of Munich, Salzburg, and Cologne, and were beginning to have some success.[52]

Despite Ilkow's less than optimistic assessment of the case he was building, he concluded his report with an urgent proposal: to circumvent the difficulties of gathering evidence in Germany he deemed it essential to embark on an officially sanctioned investigative mission to the United States. There, Ilkow argued, he could gather statements from Jewish survivors who could testify to "the gravest of the suspected crimes," and from key witnesses from the hearings at Dachau and the US Senate such as Dr. Kurt Sitte, Dr. Peter Zenkl, and Dr. Paul Heller. While military authorities had already interviewed dozens of witnesses in the United States, this had "good results in only a few cases," Ilkow explained, and had produced statements not sanctioned by, and therefore not admissible in, a German court of law. The best hope for securing a lengthy sentence for Koch, Ilkow insisted, now lay in a US-sponsored trip to the United States, which would allow investigating judge Jagomast to produce, in the presence of Ilkow and Ilse Koch's chosen defense attorney, court-certified depositions that would, according to his unique authority, be acceptable as evidence in a trial in Germany. Jagomast could then be called as a witness at trial, where he would "reproduce the given testimonies . . . as lively as the witnesses did," and "for the benefit of the jury, paint a colorful picture of occurrences in the camp." Ilkow explained that because he would argue his case "before plain people," Jagomast could convey to the jury "who those witnesses are, what impressions he had of them . . . and why they must be believed."[53]

So "vitally important" was this trip to gather evidence, Ilkow warned, that he could not guarantee the success of his prosecution without it. A murder conviction, he insisted, depended on it. He added further urgency to his proposal with a tacit reference to the public protests over Koch's commutation that continued to flare up across the United States. "If my charge is to lead to a complete success—and it is generally known that such is the desire of a large number of the American people also—I cannot disregard those witnesses who had to suffer the hardest tribulations."[54]

The Office of the Judge Advocate General, apparently swayed by Ilkow's arguments, supported his petition for an investigative mission to the United States and secured the necessary approval of the War Department in Washington, DC. During the twenty days granted for their stay, Jagomast would take witness depositions in the presence of Ilkow and Ilse Koch's recently appointed defense counsel, Dr. Alfred Seidl. Given the political backgrounds of Ilkow and Jagomast, it's hard to imagine warm working relations among the three. Seidl had joined the Nazi Party in 1937 and completed a doctoral dissertation in Munich in 1938 that positively espoused the emphasis on "will" in the National Socialist approach to criminal law. After serving in the Wehrmacht throughout the war, he returned to legal practice in Bavaria in 1945 and soon gained notoriety as a prominent and zealous defender of Nazi war criminals.[55] At the International Military Tribunal at Nuremberg, Seidl served as defense counsel for Hans Frank and Rudolf Hess, and at subsequent Nuremberg proceedings launched unilaterally by the United States he defended other leading Nazis, including chief concentration camp administrator Oswald Pohl and Dr. Karl Brandt, administrator of the Nazis' "euthanasia" program known as T4. Along with Ilkow, Jagomast, and an American official from the Office of Military Government in Munich, Seidl would depart for New York by plane on August 12, 1949.

When the jurists arrived in the United States and set to work, it was in a climate still charged by continuing protests over the commutation of Koch's sentence. In the preceding months, numerous veterans

Fig. 5.2   Koch's defense counsel, Alfred Seidl, during the Trial of the Major War Criminals at Nuremberg, March 1946. Süddeutsche Zeitung Photo.

organizations, as well as the state governments of Ohio and Michigan, had passed resolutions demanding that Koch not be released from US custody; a protest rally held in May by the Allied Veterans Council that featured a speech by William Denson had required a hall for two thousand.[56] In this context, it is not surprising that Ilkow and Jagomast were welcomed by a large number of camp survivors eager to assist in Koch's further prosecution. Aided by the Department of the Army, the lawyers set up in room 606 of the US Army Building on Whitehall Street in Manhattan and invited witnesses to testify. In marked contrast to the obstruction of the Buchenwald Committee, the American Association of Former Inmates of Concentration Camps and its chairman, Dr. Arnold Eisler, considerably assisted the effort to organize camp survivors' participation. In letters cosigned by Jagomast, Eisler personally implored dozens of Buchenwald survivors to appear at specified times for deposition, telling them their participation was "of decisive importance."[57]

As promising as the situation appeared with survivors eager to participate, the depositions gathered in New York tended to reproduce rather than resolve the problems experienced with the gathering of evidence in Germany and Austria. The few witnesses able to provide direct evidence that Koch had perpetrated an act of violence testified to relatively minor assaults they themselves had suffered at her hands. Witness Simon Barsam reported that he had been "hit three times on the back" by Koch's riding whip after she observed him working too slowly, while witness Moritz Schwarzwald recalled being struck by Koch after making the mistake of looking in her direction.[58]

Most commonly, witnesses spoke of Koch writing down the numbers of inmates and reporting them to SS guards, ostensibly for beatings. These accounts, however, involved conjecture, as no witness had the opportunity to see what she wrote and few would state definitively that her alleged report was the cause of a beating. Witness Paul Wallentin said he observed Koch writing down what he assumed were prisoners' numbers, and that the kapo who supervised his work detail drove the men harder and more brutally when she was present.[59] Witnesses Abner Rand and Michael Sprechmann both reported hearing Koch complain to kapos about the pace of prisoner labor near her family residence, resulting in beatings at the hands of kapos.[60] Rand recalled hearing Koch exclaim, "look how slowly these damned Jews move!" Witnesses Karl Press, Siegmund Flamm, Arthur Albers, and Ernst Federn all testified that, while none of them had witnessed Koch perpetrate or instigate violence for himself, "it was generally known in the camp" that she reported prisoners for beating.[61] Witness Bruno Kriss said essentially the same, but added that he had been present on an occasion when Koch's "two children of about 4 or 5 years . . . threw stones at the prisoners and called them 'Jewish pigs' without being reprimanded by the woman."[62]

While these depositions helped to place Koch at various locations throughout the camp, and to name her as an instigator, perpetrator, or observer of violence, this picture was little different from that already painted by the dozens of witnesses interviewed in Germany in the preceding months. Ilkow's primary goal in traveling to the United States had been to "fully substantiate . . . charges of murder" by gathering testimonies from well-placed witnesses who would be believed by the Augsburg court.[63] Yet, just as in Germany, attempts to have witnesses confirm Thumm's account of mass-murder universally failed.[64] Some spoke of incidents not previously mentioned by other witnesses in which they said Koch incited the killing of inmates, but direct evidence of these new allegations also remained elusive. Witness Jacob Werber recalled seeing a group of SS men standing over some twenty badly beaten inmates, a few of whom were dead, and Koch standing nearby. "In opinion of witness," Jagomast recorded, "the order to this action was given by Ilse Koch. Witness could not hear what she said, but it could be gathered from her gestures that she gave orders."[65] Dr. Paul Heller, who had testified before the Senate subcommittee, recalled that it was Koch's presence at a work site that prompted a frantic SS beating of a number of inmates, two of whom died.[66]

These testimonies and dozens of others collected in the United States during the course of the investigation did not provide the basis for a renewed murder charge as hoped. Largely circumstantial in nature, their utility even for the lesser charge of incitement to murder was limited. An additional problem common to all depositions was that the victims of the alleged offenses were of various nationalities, but only crimes committed against German or Austrian nationals were within the purview of the charges. Some witnesses surmised that victims had been Germans or Austrians because the crimes in question had occurred before the outbreak of war in 1939, when few foreigners were present in the camp, but they could not be definitive. Jagomast noted in Jacob Werber's deposition, for instance, that "as far as witness knows, there were German and Austrian Jews among those killed."[67]

Given the circumstantial nature of these allegations, witnesses were often asked whether they recalled incidents referred to in the depositions of the witnesses who had appeared prior to them, in the hopes they could round out the picture. Seldom, however, could subsequent witnesses do more than comment on the likelihood that an event had occurred, or whether or not it matched rumors that circulated in camp. Ludwig Scheinbrunn, who had worked as a "corpse carrier" at Buchenwald, testified that he had seen Koch note down the numbers of tattooed inmates, and later saw their corpses in the mortuary with injection marks in their arms. He also reported seeing some of their skins in the pathology department a year later, and concluded that Koch had ordered the deaths of these inmates for the production of tattooed household objects.[68] Doctors Kurt Sitte and Peter Zenkl, who had worked in Buchenwald's pathology department throughout their incarceration, and had testified at Dachau and before the Senate subcommittee, could offer little support for Scheinbrunn's claim. Sitte testified that during his three years there he had only heard rumors of Koch's predilection for human skins, and that it had been SS Dr. Erich Wagner who had taken a research interest in tattooed inmates. Dr. Zenkl could be no more definitive, leading Jagomast to note that the witness only "knows from hearsay that Ilse Koch owned articles made of human skin."[69] While camp rumor and what was sometimes referred to as the "common knowledge" of inmates may have proved useful in providing Ilkow with clues in his search for evidence of murder, he remained keenly aware that a successful conviction would require substantially more.

In the end, the trip to the United States did little to advance Ilkow's case. Although he initially had hoped that Koch's trial could begin in the autumn of 1949, Ilkow returned to Germany in early September still convinced that the few hundred testimonies gathered to date remained insufficient to successfully prosecute Koch for the most serious charges he had levied. Ilkow was also growing frustrated with what he believed was the waning interest and support of the Bavarian Ministry of Justice. Ilkow and Jagomast continued to work largely alone, and reliant to a significant degree on American authorities for resources, including their $300 per diem while in the United States.[70]

In a scathing report submitted to Colonel Fleischer in the judge advocate's office on September 21, Ilkow revealed his growing anxiety that his case could founder in the recently independent West German state. West German authorities, Ilkow lamented, appeared most invested in sweeping Nazi crimes under the rug as the influence of the Allied powers receded. "Interest in the successful completion of this matter does not exist," he wrote. "I can't count on anybody's support or assistance. My own ministry is just quietly watching, having told the chief prosecutor in Weimar that they are not in the least bit interested in proceedings against Ilse Koch," but had taken the case and assigned him prosecutor only through American pressure. Referring to the Bavarian Ministry of Justice as "two-faced," Ilkow blamed its tepid support of his efforts for the continued attacks on the legitimacy of his investigation by communist survivors both inside and outside the Soviet zone. The participation of communist survivors was vital to a successful prosecution but was still being withheld, or half-heartedly supplied through the submission of "unimportant and untrue statements [made] with the sole aim to sabotage the Bavarian proceedings." Ilkow concluded his report with a plea for reassurance from Fleischer that the United States, which continued to exercise considerable influence in West Germany through its still-functioning Office of Military Government, would continue to provide both moral and material support for his efforts. Ilkow recognized the "extraordinary" support that American authorities had continued to provide even after the formal independence of West Germany on May 23, 1949, but warned that, in the absence of it, his efforts would be "absolutely sure to fail."[71]

Ilse Koch in German Custody

In spite of his growing anxieties and the shortcomings of the evidence he had gathered thus far, Ilkow filed a successful application for Koch's arrest on September 22, 1949, to ensure that she would be transferred directly into pretrial custody following her scheduled release from prison on October 17. Issued by investigating judge Dr. Jagomast, the arrest warrant accused Koch of either perpetrating or inciting bodily harm and murder. While much of the evidence remained circumstantial, Ilkow viewed the witness statements he had gathered as sufficient to label Koch "highly suspected" of having inflicted or incited bodily harm "in a not to be established number of cases which yet exceeds the hundreds by far." Despite the near total failure of his efforts to verify Thumm's account, Ilkow also declared Koch suspected of murder for "having, together with several other persons, jointly, deliberately and with premeditation, killed 24 human beings."[72] In a description almost identical to that presented in his May application, Ilkow summarized Thumm's allegation placing an armed Koch among a group of SS men that shot Jews near the camp quarry, but now changed the stated date of the incident from November 9, 1939, to the spring of 1941. It is instructive that this unsubstantiated incident, recounted by a convicted rapist and fraudster and drawn into question by numerous witnesses, remained the sole basis for a charge of murder against Koch. Despite mounting evidence of her complicity or participation in numerous lesser acts of violence, the now substantial body of testimony that Ilkow had collected did little to support the popular and most diabolical image of Koch as arch Nazi war criminal and mass-murdering "Beast of Buchenwald."

Immediately following the issuance of the warrant for Koch's arrest, her defense lawyer Dr. Seidl lodged a complaint with the Bavarian Constitutional Court on his client's behalf. Seeking not only to challenge the legitimacy of Koch's impending arrest but to void the investigation that justified it, Seidl alleged that the Bavarian Ministry of Justice had appointed Jagomast and Ilkow from the Superior Court at Bamberg solely because of their "political soundness," and had unlawfully passed over the appropriate judge and corresponding prosecutor from the District Court at Augsburg where the trial would occur.[73] What Seidl's complaint did not state explicitly was that, were it upheld, Jagomast's replacement would be an Augsburg jurist who had joined the Nazi Party in 1931 and been a member of the Intelligence Branch of the SS.[74] Given that eighty-five percent of all state prosecutors in Bavaria (as well as eighty-two percent of all judges) were former members of the Nazi Party, Seidl must have calculated further that Ilkow's replacement likewise would have proven more ideologically sympathetic to accused war criminals.[75] Seidl's complaint was dismissed, although only after the Constitutional Court sat to formally rule on the matter in June 1950.[76] Koch's arrest could not be forestalled, and on the morning of October 17, 1949, she was successfully transferred into German pretrial custody.

Koch's arrest, though described by Ilkow as having taken place "without disturbance," was not without its drama. As the day of Koch's official release from Landsberg approached, American military authorities informed Ilkow that her arrest could not take place in the prison courtyard as he requested; instead, Koch would have to be "actually at liberty" outside the prison grounds before she could be taken into German custody.[77] Alarmed, Ilkow warned that he could take no responsibility for the chaos that might ensue if the arrest had to take place outside Landsberg, given the intense public and media interest in her case. Landsberg prison director Colonel Walter R. Graham conceded, agreeing both to allow Koch's arrest in the prison courtyard

Fig. 5.3   Koch walks out of Landsberg prison, moments before her rearrest, October 17, 1949. AKG Images / Ullstein Bild.

and to forbid entry to the anticipated throng of reporters and photographers. To Ilkow's dismay, however, when he arrived at Landsberg accompanied by members of the criminal police and the president of the Bavarian prison department, he found that military authorities had changed their mind at the last minute and had allowed the press into the courtyard.[78]

Koch emerged from the prison administration building at 7:15 AM with a broad smile, wearing a heavy wool coat and oversized green beret, and carrying a large canvas bag. Flanked by American military police, she put her bag down and turned toward the waiting press. As camera bulbs flashed, she reportedly quipped, "children, children, you must be awfully poor if you must take pictures of me to make a living."[79] Consistent with patterns of the past, the journalists she addressed front-loaded their reports with commentary on her looks, but now indulged in descriptions not of her alleged beauty but of the degree to which Koch, at forty-two, was no longer the "sexy beast" she had once been. "A blowzy woman now 165 pounds," *Stars and Stripes* reported, the "fading witch of Buchenwald" now "looked like any dumpy hausfrau."[80] As Koch responded to the questions, her tone vacillated between hopeful and dour. "This is your big day of liberation—how do you feel?" one reporter asked. "This is not a day of liberation," Koch shot back, "it is one of my darkest days."[81] Nonetheless, Koch appeared optimistic at her future prospects, predicting her exoneration before a German court. "I will have plenty to say about Americans and Germans when I get on the stand," she added cryptically, but would not elaborate on what she intended to say. "Wait until I publish my memoirs," she finished, "and you will find out what I think."[82]

Koch's moment before the cameras and the press was short-lived. Soon after she exited the building, Ilkow stepped forward and informed her that a warrant for her arrest had been issued, and that she would be transferred immediately to the women's penitentiary at Aichach in Upper Bavaria. Yet while Koch provided no resistance as she was escorted to a small green patrol wagon and driven away, the sixty-five kilometer trip was interrupted on numerous occasions when the accompanying director of Aichach, Anna Baumann, became car sick. Each time the van was forced to pull over, the press caught up and continued to hammer her with questions. "Go away and stop bothering me," Koch retorted, impatient with the badgering.[83] Despite her admonitions and refusal to offer further comment, reporters and photographers in six vehicles continued their pursuit to the prison gates, where they ultimately were denied access.

When Koch and Ilkow finally reached Aichach, they were ushered in and met by Jagomast, who read to her the full text of the arrest warrant including the details of the various crimes of which she was suspected. Though Jagomast had hoped to question her, their meeting quickly descended into confrontation. According to Ilkow, "she behaved arrogantly and impertinently," claiming that the current proceedings were intended "to finish her politically."[84] Apparently entertaining revenge fantasies, Koch reportedly declared that, while the Third Reich had lasted only a few years, the current "regime" would not last even that long, and that those taking steps against her "will see what will happen to them." Koch insisted that all those who had provided evidence against her were "perjurers and liars," and that her counsel told her that Jagomast and Ilkow had done nothing in the United States but "listen to Polish Jews and Jews of other nationalities" testify against her.[85] Ilkow later recalled that Jagomast, taken aback, upbraided her, saying she would never dare speak to a judge in such a manner if the Third Reich were still in existence. Koch reportedly responded by accusing Jagomast of trying to threaten her. With Koch growing increasingly agitated and combative, Ilkow and Jagomast departed, leaving her to be escorted into the prisoner compound and eventually to her solitary cell. She would remain uncooperative for the duration of the investigation.

As Koch adjusted to her new life in German confinement, Dr. Seidl again lodged an unsuccessful complaint on his client's behalf, now alleging that her incarceration in Aichach was unlawful. According to Seidl, established procedure dictated that Koch should have been transferred to the responsible remand prison in Augsburg, rather than to Aichach penitentiary twenty-five kilometers away. Seidl argued that, while her transfer to Aichach had been justified as a security measure, Koch had not shown herself to be "a particularly violent or dangerous person."[86] The Augsburg Superior Court, however, denied Seidl's complaint and sided with Ilkow, who had argued for the importance of additional security. Apparently influenced by rumors of Koch's wild sexual licentiousness, Ilkow reported to US authorities that Koch's incarceration in a women's penitentiary was necessary because Koch "above all should be kept apart from men."[87]

Through the autumn of 1949, Ilkow and Jagomast continued to struggle to gather evidence they deemed sufficient to convict Koch for murder or its incitement. Central to their predicament was the ongoing obstruction of the Buchenwald Committee and the VVN, as well as East German state authorities. With Koch's rearrest, however, a series of events helped to alter this resistance, eventually allowing for the successful gathering of testimonies from the eastern zone and from communist survivors aligned with the VVN. The initial response of authorities in the newly founded East German state to news of Koch's arrest had been to reiterate their demand that she be extradited into their custody for trial "at the place of her criminal offenses."[88] With that order again rebuffed, however, it appears that reality began to settle in for legal authorities in Weimar. In mid-November, a representative of Thuringian chief prosecutor Dr. Hermann Rodewald paid an unannounced visit to Ilkow and Jagomast, and carried with him an unusual proposal. Through this emissary, Rodewald offered to turn over all the evidence he had gathered in preparation for an East German trial of Koch if the Bavarian Ministry of Justice appointed him co-prosecutor for Koch's trial at Augsburg. Rodewald, a well-connected member of the East German communist party, also promised to rally the support of the VVN for the Bavarian proceedings and secure the long-sought participation of witnesses from the East.[89]

Without providing any comment on the spot, Ilkow agreed to relay Rodewald's proposal to Hans Walther, director of the criminal law division at the Bavarian Ministry of Justice. Not surprisingly, Walther responded that, even setting aside the problematic political dimensions of this proposed arrangement, "a non-Bavarian prosecutor pleading beside a Bavarian prosecutor before a Bavarian court in a Bavarian trial as counsel for the prosecution [would be] juridically unacceptable and inadmissible."[90] The official rejection of this unlikely proposal in December 1949 did not, however, spell an end to the possibility that the participation and goodwill of witnesses in the East could be secured. Instead, it appears that the leadership of the Buchenwald Committee began to accept that East German proceedings against Koch were not in the offing, and that continuing to seek leverage by withholding their participation could threaten the prospect of Koch's successful conviction in Augsburg. Ever distrustful of the West German and American authorities' resolve to punish former Nazis, Buchenwald Committee leaders further worried that a less-than-watertight case might provide an excuse to drop the charges against Koch altogether. At the end of January 1950, they therefore officially resolved to change course and began imploring their membership to cooperate with Ilkow's efforts and to provide depositions and appear in court if required. The VVN, and eventually the relevant organs of the East German state, followed suit, putting aside their resistance to—if not their public skepticism of—the Augsburg prosecution to assist in providing witnesses as necessary.[91] This hard-won cooperation of the Buchenwald Committee represented a major boon for Ilkow, who could now work alongside Jagomast to take depositions from dozens of additional and well-placed witnesses over the months that followed.

While the Buchenwald Committee had reversed course in its obstruction of the investigation, the same could not be said of Koch herself, who still refused to cooperate or to provide any comment on the growing list of crimes of which she was accused. Leery of Koch's hostility and ostensibly concerned for her mental state, investigating judge Jagomast decided to compensate for the absence of her direct input in his investigation by subjecting her to a psychiatric evaluation. Chosen for the task was Dr. Werner Leibbrand, who had worked for the United States providing similar psychiatric evaluations of the defendants at the 1947 Doctors Trial at Nuremberg. Leibbrand could confirm Koch's fitness for trial and perhaps also, it was hoped, provide insight into her worldview and her perceptions of her guilt or innocence. Leibbrand first visited Koch at Aichach only a week after her arrival. According to the observations of prison staff, her behavior had been relatively normal as she adjusted to life in her solitary cell. Despite a tendency to complain about prison conditions, she reportedly spent her days relatively quietly, reading Germanic myth and poetry borrowed from the prison library, attempting to learn English, and writing what she referred to as her "memoires." When Leibbrand appeared, however, she was as defiant and combative as ever, refusing cooperation and insisting that he would only arrive at foregone conclusions he carried with him.[92]

After two unsuccessful attempts to engage Koch, Leibbrand applied to the Augsburg court to have her sent to the Erlangen psychiatric institution for a substantial period of observation, during which he hoped to build her trust. Koch's defense attorney Dr. Seidl immediately lodged a complaint to the court, arguing that Leibbrand's work at Nuremberg made him "hopelessly biased" and also that psychiatry was "a science in its infancy" that provided doctors "wide latitude and discretion" in reaching conclusions—in this case, undoubtedly, ones that would aid Koch's prosecution. Further, Seidl demanded to know why Koch would be transferred to Leibbrand's home institution at Erlangen when it lay outside the Augsburg court district.[93] On January 25,

1950, the Augsburg court ruled on the matter, deciding that the nature of the accusations leveled against Koch did warrant an examination of her mental state, but also striking a compromise: Koch would be transferred to a psychiatric institution for up to six weeks of observation as desired by Jagomast and Ilkow, but rather than Erlangen she would go to the more local psychiatric institution at Günzburg, under the directorship of Dr. Albert Sighart.[94] Then, both Dr. Sighart and Dr. Leibbrand would submit separate assessments, the latter now required to visit Koch at Günzburg to complete his work.

The psychiatric assessments submitted to Jagomast in early April 1950 stressed Koch's fitness for trial. Leibbrand's assessment, substantially hampered by Koch's refusal to cooperate, was mainly based on his observations of Koch's interactions with others, her confrontations with him, and interviews he conducted with her mother and brother. Cautious of drawing wide-ranging conclusions, given his inability to converse with Koch, Leibbrand was confident in reporting merely that she was not mentally ill, had a good grasp of her circumstances, maintained control over her emotions, and had an intellect that was perhaps above average.[95] In contrast, Dr. Sighart's assessment was much bolder, replete with Freudian assertions and steeped in misogyny. Drawing not only on his conversations with a somewhat more cooperative Koch, but also on witness statements supplied by Jagomast, Sighart concluded that Koch displayed a "psychopathic disposition" with a tendency toward "sadistic sexual cruelty."[96]

While Sighart saw no evidence of mental illness in Koch, he believed that she had unconsciously channeled resentments born of an unhappy marriage, the alleged "sexual dependency" of her husband, and the boredom of life at Buchenwald into sexual deviance and a "level of cruelty alien to female nature."[97] Dismissing Koch's denials, Sighart argued confidently that her alleged taunting of prisoners amounted to "verbal sadism," her reporting of inmates for punishment "had an erotic aspect," her assaulting of prisoners with her riding whip satisfied her "sexual lust," and her alleged predilection for the tattooed skins of inmates resulted from her "sexual inclination to cruelty." Sighart, however, had reached these condemnatory conclusions by consulting the written affidavits of witnesses whom he never examined and whose testimony remained untested in court, rendering his observations fundamentally flawed. Still, the shared conclusion of Leibbrand's and Sighart's assessments was that, as Jagomast hoped and as Seidl feared, Koch was in full control of her faculties and ready to stand trial.

With the psychiatric evaluations complete, and dozens of long-sought statements from East German witnesses submitted, Jagomast paid Koch a visit at Aichach on April 4, 1950 to provide her with a final opportunity to respond to the allegations against her before he formally concluded the preliminary investigation. Her subsequent refusal brought the investigation to a close and signaled an end to Jagomast's official role in Koch's prosecution.[98] Ilkow was now expected to submit a formal indictment of Koch in short order. Yet the flow of witness testimonies from East Germany continued, sometimes providing allegations of previously unknown crimes. On April 15, therefore, Ilkow requested that the Bavarian Ministry of Justice authorize new investigations to pursue additional charges against Koch that Jagomast had not considered. The Ministry balked, declaring that there was already more than enough material to move forward with an indictment and that Ilkow needed to ensure, given the international interest in Koch's case, that trial proceedings began as soon as possible.[99] Ilkow objected, however, that even without new investigations, he was overwhelmed and physically exhausted by the sheer volume of material he had collected, and he needed more time to draw up a "usable" indictment. "Despite my hardest efforts," Ilkow explained, "I am working until all hours of the night." While the materials gathered thus far were "heavily incriminating," he continued, "the volume is so large, and the legal questions are far from easy to solve." Ilkow warned that, unless he were given more time to work, the result could be another insufficiently prepared indictment reminiscent of those that formed the basis of Koch's SS and American military trials.[100] The Ministry of Justice would not back down. Ilkow would have to indict without further delay.

6 The Augsburg Trial of Ilse Koch

In the German judiciary, the drafting of an indictment is chief among the tasks of the prosecution. In striking contrast to the brief enumeration of criminal charges that constitutes the bulk of a typical indictment in the American legal system, an indictment prepared for criminal proceedings before a German court is an exhaustive document that lays out the prosecution case in its entirely *before* trial proceedings begin.[1] On the basis of this indictment, the court's judges decide whether the prosecution has put together a case sufficiently compelling to warrant an official order to convene for trial. Once proceedings commence, it is the indictment that will guide the court's judges, who in the German system lead the examination of witnesses as neutral inquisitors. Because of the inquisitorial rather than adversarial nature of this system, a judge's primary duty is, in principle, to "find the truth of the matter at hand," rather than adjudicating between two opposing parties.[2] To this end, once the indictment has been submitted, the prosecution plays a relatively modest role at trial itself, relegated primarily to asking supplementary questions of witnesses while the court's judges conduct proceedings. Though the prosecution is granted an opportunity to deliver closing arguments, the indictment remains the most crucial component of the prosecution's case and the means by which it "shapes and directs the course of the trial."[3] Moreover, because no transcript is kept of German trial proceedings, and because even the notes of the court's judges are destroyed at trial's end, the indictment provides the best indication of how any given case was presented and supported in the courtroom.

Working under immense pressure and denied the additional time he had sought from the Bavarian Ministry of Justice, Chief Prosecutor Johann Ilkow submitted his 151-page indictment of Ilse Koch on May 10, 1950. To influence the course of future court proceedings to the best advantage of the prosecution, Ilkow had needed to carefully consider how to present the results of the preliminary investigation and the evidence it contained.[4] Unlike prosecutors in the American system, however, Ilkow was not permitted to act in a strictly partisan fashion, seeking above all to present his case in the most advantageous manner possible. Instead, as a civil servant of the state, he was formally obliged to aid in establishing the legal "truth" in a given case and to assist the court as it strove to determine the details of the crime in question and the proper application of the law.[5] This somewhat ambivalent position therefore required Ilkow to present the most compelling case against Koch that the evidence allowed, while nonetheless adhering, at least in theory, to an official duty to assist the court in establishing a factually accurate picture of her alleged crimes.

Ilkow's indictment charged that at Buchenwald between 1937 and 1943, Ilse Koch had committed twenty-five misdemeanor counts of grievous bodily harm, incitement (*Anstiftung*) to grievous bodily harm in a number of cases "no longer determinable," sixty-five felony counts of incitement to attempted murder, and twenty-five felony counts of incitement to murder.[6] To enlighten the court on the context of Koch's alleged crimes, Ilkow followed his enumeration of the charges with an expansive history of the concentration camp system as a whole, and of Buchenwald in particular. This history, which consumed twenty-six pages of the indictment, detailed everything from the geography of the camp and the organization of its SS and prisoner populations to the conditions and punishments that accounted for how "every fifth man who entered the camp of Buchenwald lost his life."[7]

Next, Ilkow presented a "Curriculum Vitae of the Defendant," ostensibly to provide the court with Koch's personal history, but also to indicate that her actions had stemmed from the motives that German law stipulated must be present to prove a charge of murder (or its incitement). In striking contrast to North American law, where a murder charge requires only evidence of a "specific intent to kill," German law requires proof that the killer acted "out of bloodlust, in order to satisfy their sexual desire, [or] out of greed or other base motives." The law defines base motives as those "which according to healthy sensibilities are ethically particularly despicable," and defines bloodlust as "an unnatural joy at the destruction of human life."[8] In seeking to provide insight into Koch's motives and perceived psychological disposition, however, Ilkow at times drew upon misogynistic stereotypes and inflammatory gossip, sometimes only loosely related to the crimes for which she was charged.

Koch, Ilkow wrote, was "avaricious, possessed with boundless arrogance and cruel in a manner which is rarely found in women." Ilkow underscored the "inner pleasure" she had derived from the acts of violence and killing she stood accused of inciting. Ilkow also sought to attack Koch's moral character more broadly. Drawing upon statements provided by Koch's stepsister, Erna Raible, and her former landlady, Maria Klaus, Ilkow claimed that Koch "was not even a good mother. . . . When the defendant was entertaining she was seen to drink a good deal of alcoholic beverages. She started to have intercourse with other men. . . . She was always running around with married men. . . . She did not behave . . . as was to be expected of a lady."[9] Rather than assisting the court's judges in establishing "truth," Ilkow's persistent resorts to sexist stereotypes to impugn Koch's character only fortified rather than dispelled the popular legend of the diabolical and sexually depraved "witch" who had terrorized Buchenwald's inmates. Ilkow's indictment made clear the central role that Koch's allegedly deficient moral disposition would play in how he would argue his case.

After detailing Koch's Dachau and SS trials and addressing several jurisdictional issues, Ilkow sought to characterize her position and place at Buchenwald for the court. Above all, he portrayed Koch as the all-powerful "commandeuse" of Buchenwald, despite the fact that this contention had been vehemently rejected by SS witnesses during Koch's trial at Dachau, and ultimately by American judicial authorities. Largely on the basis of the hearsay testimony of former inmates, Ilkow claimed that Koch, despite lacking official title or position at the camp, gave orders "to leaders, sub-leaders, guards, kapos, foremen, and prisoners." Hence, she was "one of the most feared persons in the camp, and was practically one of its commanders."[10] Karl Koch, Ilkow continued, may have been commandant, but "[was] her devoted slave in everything" and "yield[ed] to her in everything."[11] Ilse Koch, meanwhile, "showed the liveliest interest in camp-institutions and in all occurrences in the camp," and had a perverse fascination with the corporal punishment of prisoners.[12] Koch seldom missed an opportunity to observe the flogging of inmates, Ilkow asserted, and she took particular pleasure in watching naked prisoners inspected for lice or whipped on the *bock* (saw horse). In particular, Ilkow continued, "the defendant did not want to miss a performance of the inhuman punishment of tree-hanging. . . . She was tickled by the terrible sight."[13]

The final and most significant portion of the indictment consisted of paraphrased excerpts of testimonies from 201 witnesses, collectively supporting every count of the crimes of which Koch now stood charged. Typical of the twenty-five alleged incidents of inflicting grievous bodily harm was the beating reported by Austrian witness Franz Schneeweiss, who managed a Salzburg hospital at the time his deposition was taken. In March 1939, Schneeweiss purportedly was approached by the defendant on horseback while he was carrying stones for road construction. As the indictment would summarize the encounter, "With the words 'why do you look at me?' she beat him with her riding crop violently over his right eye, his nose and mouth. Schneeweiss started at once to bleed [and] his eye . . . got inflamed and he could not see with it for a long time."[14] Representative of allegations that Koch had incited others to inflict grievous bodily harm was an incident from the winter of 1939, reconstructed from the depositions of seven separate witnesses: as a work column marched through thick slush and passed before Ilse and Karl Koch, Ilse had reportedly turned to her husband and complained, "Must I suffer to be stared out by these dirty pigs, do you not notice it?" In response, Karl ordered that the column of at least five hundred prisoners be made to drill in the bitter conditions, and to lie in the slush. "Their clothes were soaked," Ilkow wrote, adding that "the men were perspiring in spite of the wintry cold and there must have been disastrous consequences for some of the prisoners."[15]

The sixty-five counts of incitement to attempted murder largely concerned Koch's alleged habit of reporting prisoners for punishment. A typical incident was recounted in the summarized testimony of the witness and former political prisoner Philipp Hermann Hausmann. Hausmann recalled Koch verbally abusing him while he worked in her home to install some fixtures in the autumn of 1938. "In the evening, after roll call," Ilkow wrote, "Hausmann . . . received 25 blows with a heavy whip. As a reason for the punishment, they [told him] 'slow working in the commander's house.' The defendant had reported [him]. The whipping gave Hausmann blood-suffused streaks on his buttocks which brought on boils and necessitated several operations."[16] These incidents amounted to incitement to attempted murder rather than to grievous bodily harm because, Ilkow argued, Koch was well aware that reporting prisoners to SS guards could easily, and sometimes did, result in death:

Since the defendant in her reports has never decided the manner
and measure of punishment and since it was left to the discretion
of camp-leaders to pronounce any punishment according to their
mood, and since the defendant knew all these facts as well as any
SS-man, it was as clear as daylight that she has, with each report
given by her personally . . . acknowledged the prisoner's possible
death and has committed her deed, regardless.[17]

The majority of the twenty-five counts of incitement to murder
concerned incidents that were similar to those above, except that the
prisoners who were reported for punishment allegedly died of their
injuries. While the most common allegation concerned flogging on the
bock, some involved killings that allegedly took place directly in front
of Koch and as an immediate result of her complaint. Based on depositions given by witnesses Siegl, Rieser, and Spendlingwimmer, Ilkow
described a particularly brutal incident that had allegedly occurred in
the autumn of 1939 just a few meters from the camp's main gate. Koch,
who was reportedly standing with a group of SS men observing a
column of men hauling rock, "pointed to one of the prisoners . . . who
was tottering considerably under the load of his stone."

> She spoke a few words to a red-headed *Scharfürer* (troop leader) who
> was standing beside her. Then this *Scharfürer* jumped on the pris-
> oner . . . [and] kicked this man a few times in the abdomen until
> he was falling down and lost the stone. . . . Then the *Scharfürer* lifted
> the stone and beat it with great force down on the prisoner's
> head. There was one short scream, blood was gushing all over
> the prisoner on the ground and he did not move anymore. . . . If
> the defendant had not drawn attention to this prisoner he would
> have returned to the camp, unmolested. She was well aware of the
> consequences of [her] instigation.[18]

As Ilkow understood, successfully convicting Koch for incitement to murder required convincing the court not only that such incidents had occurred, but that the final sentence in this passage was true: that Koch understood that death was a possible, and even likely, outcome of the reports she made. Whether Ilkow had sufficient evidence to meet this challenge was yet to be seen.

Ilkow concluded his indictment with the most notorious crime of which Koch had been accused: the selection and killing of tattooed prisoners for the production of household objects. Because of the involvement of SS doctors and staff in this alleged practice, Ilkow explained that the genesis of the scheme to kill inmates for their tattooed skins "cannot be established anymore . . . [but] it is certain that the defendant played a large part in materializing this idea."[19] The specific incidents Ilkow constructed from witness depositions were largely circumstantial in nature and reliant on hearsay. "When it was generally known in the camp that the defendant evinced an extraordinary interest in tattooed prisoners," Ilkow explained, "[inmate] camp-leaders warned all tattooed inmates not to be seen by her, unless completely dressed."[20] One incident presented by Ilkow drew upon the statements of witnesses Marian Zgoda and Willi Klug, and began with Koch allegedly spotting four tattooed inmates among a work gang. "The defendant seemed to search painstakingly for the numbers of these prisoners. . . . Since the prisoners' trousers were covered with loam so that the defendant was unable to read their numbers, she chased them to get their jackets and took the numbers therefrom; then she rode away toward the stone quarry."[21] That ill later befell these prisoners was left for the court to assume. Direct evidence of Koch's role in the presumed killings of tattooed inmates had to be inferred from her actions or distilled from camp rumor.

In total, Ilkow dropped 121 charges against Koch, excluding some from the indictment because the alleged victims were not German, others because the nationality of the victims could not be determined, and the remainder because of insufficient evidence.[22] Most notably absent from the indictment was the charge of murder and account of the incident described by the witness Friedrich Thumm, which Ilkow had struggled in vain to corroborate. In a letter to the Bavarian Ministry of Justice, Ilkow felt it necessary to explain that he had had no choice but to withdraw the long-sought charge because "the personality of this only witness is so dubious that a conviction on the basis of his testimony is unlikely."[23] Thus, while the Augsburg court judged Ilkow's indictment sufficient to warrant the convening of trial proceedings, the monstrous and omnipotent "commandeuse" that Ilkow had depicted would stand charged only as an indirect perpetrator of killings meted out by the camp's SS and not as a murderer in her own right.

Despite the pressure Ilkow had faced to launch court proceedings by indicting Koch quickly, the much-anticipated trial of Ilse Koch would not begin until November, following a series of unexpected delays. First, complications arose following the discovery and subsequent arrest of former Buchenwald prison bunker chief Martin Sommer at the end of February 1950. Known as the "Hangman of Buchenwald," Sommer had been a codefendant in the 1944 SS trial of Ilse and Karl Koch. Apparently seeking "economy of proceedings," Ilkow's superiors at the Bavarian Ministry of Justice proposed holding a joint trial of Koch and Sommer, once the preliminary investigation and subsequent indictment of the latter had been submitted.[24] The assumption was that the testimonies of the survivor-witnesses called to the stand at such a trial would be relevant to, and fortifying of, both cases. Ilkow, however, wrote the ministry on May 15 to "speak out against this idea forcefully," concerned that preparations for such a trial would cause extensive delays, while Sommer's ill health would likely mean frequent interruptions to court proceedings once they were underway. Beyond practical considerations, Ilkow warned that the optics of such a trial could be confusing to an expectant public. "The guilt of Ilse Koch as mere inciter," Ilkow wrote, "will pale in comparison to the doubtlessly immense guilt of Sommer and the thousands of murders he committed, and would seem to be of secondary importance, while the true essence of the trial would not be grasped."[25] In light of Ilkow's depiction of Koch in the indictment as the brutal "commandeuse" of Buchenwald, this was a striking evaluation of her guilt relative to that of one of the camp's lesser-known but far more murderous SS staff.

Ultimately, Sommer's ongoing health problems brought an end to the idea of a joint trial, but not before significant time had been lost fruitlessly awaiting his indictment.[26] Delaying proceedings further was Ilkow's own declining health, resulting from the immense strain under which he worked. At the end of July 1950, a Bamberg doctor declared Ilkow "unfit for service." Just fifty-one years old, he was in a "state of severe mental and physical exhaustion," suffering from a variety of maladies including kidney stones, chronic gastroenteritis, and heart disease. He was forced in mid-August to suspend trial preparations for nearly two months.[27] It was therefore only after significant delay, and more than a year after Ilse Koch had been taken into custody, that proceedings commenced on November 27, 1950.

Proceedings at Augsburg

Because of the extensive bombing damage that Augsburg had suffered during the Second World War, no intact and sufficiently spacious court building was available to host Ilse Koch's trial and the expected throng of journalists, photographers, and members of the public the proceedings would attract. Instead, the Augsburg Kolpinghaus, a community center located near the city's thousand-year-old cathedral, was selected for a trial that one local newspaper anticipated would likely be "the largest that Augsburg has ever seen."[28] Ilkow had complained to the Ministry of Justice about the choice of venue, believing that the hall, surrounded by narrow streets and heaps of rubble, was too sparse, dark, and generally lacking in stature to lend trial proceedings the requisite sense of dignity and authority.[29] With his objections overruled, however, Ilkow had to make do, in part by supplementing the large crucifix that hung in the makeshift courtroom with other adornments designed to communicate the gravity of the crimes with which Koch had been charged. From the Hamburg chapter of the VVN, Ilkow borrowed a bullwhip and the corresponding wooden bock on which prisoners were flogged, and placed them immediately in front of the bench at which the judges and jury would sit. A large map of the Buchenwald camp complex was placed on a stand to the right and immediately behind where Koch and her counsel would sit.

The three-judge panel that would hear the Koch case was led by the presiding judge, Georg Maginot, with the assistance of judges Karl Bauernfeind and Fritz Wiesenthal. To the right of the judges would sit a six-member jury empowered by the German judicial system to decide matters of both fact and law and to vote alongside the court's three judges to arrive at a verdict and commensurate sentence. Selected to serve on the Koch trial jury were two farmers, one merchant, one craftsman, a factory worker, and a clerk. Yet if Koch's defense counsel, Dr. Alfred Seidl, expressed concerns about the preconceptions held by such a citizen jury, he could scarcely complain about the presumed political leanings of the court's presiding judge. Born in 1898 in the Palatinate region of Germany, Maginot had joined the SS in 1934 and the Nazi Party in 1937. In light of his past political associations, a postwar denazification panel had judged him a "follower," a category of complicity that shielded him from sanction following the so-called Christmas Amnesty of 1947.[30] Maginot's relationship with National Socialist authorities appears not to have been particularly cozy, however. Prior to the seizure of power, Maginot had presided over the prosecution of Nazi supporters involved in political riots, a fact that the local party faithful would not allow him to forget after 1933.

Indeed as a judge in Würzburg during the early years of the Third Reich, Maginot came into repeated conflict with the local Gestapo, resulting in his eventual transfer to Augsburg. In 1939, Maginot was drafted into the Wehrmacht and served as a soldier until 1945.[31] By the time Maginot was selected to preside over the Koch trial in 1950, he typified the membership of a German postwar judiciary dominated by former Nazis.

When Maginot officially opened proceedings in the packed Kolpinghaus courtroom amidst the ticking of rolling cameras and incessant flashbulbs, all eyes were on Ilse Koch, who entered wearing a dark green plaid dress with a white starched collar and matching white handkerchief in her front pocket. In the absence of a transcript of court proceedings, what transpired once the trial was underway must be gleaned from the regular but often brief reports that appeared in the press. The *Schwäbische Landeszeitung*, a local Augsburg newspaper that covered the trial frequently, presented a particularly vivid description of Koch's reaction to the five-and-a-half hour reading of the indictment that opened proceedings, and to the questioning by Judge Maginot that immediately followed. The report underscored the prominent place Koch's gender and alleged sexual deviance would play at trial, and the sense of incredulity that would greet her blanket denials.

> There is no doubt that this woman, who now stands before the jury court in Augsburg in a simple housedress, is clever in some way. To a certain extent, she knows how to present her behavior, her appearance, and her personality with conscious confidence, yet sometimes a little carelessly and informally. She sits in the glaring light of the cameramen's lamps, now and then looking almost bored ... [as she] studies the wood paneling on the ceiling of the Augsburg Kolpinghaus. . . . But when the presiding judge calls her for questioning, this 44-year-old, red-blond woman jerks up and

her slightly freckled, reddish face becomes pale. Everything about her is now aggressive. After she has overcome a certain timidity, her answers come fast, certain, like a gun. She seems to sense every question beforehand, and her answer is ready before the question is even finished. She's certain, quite incredibly certain—too certain perhaps. . . . She denies everything, absolutely everything, even things that she could easily admit without in any way incriminating herself. "I never saw anything—any offense against humanity . . ." That she did not know what was going on in the concentration camp, although she was able to watch the inmates almost every hour, seems absolutely implausible. "I have not hit or mistreated anyone!," she continues. . . . Accounts of tattooed human skins, the lampshades, the gloves, the book covers made from prepared human skin, she rejects brusquely as "completely nonsensical." When the chairman delves into the more delicate problem of her notorious sexual deviance, she emphasizes again and again, "I am a normal woman. What is being said here is the greatest fantasy you can imagine. I'm here as the result of a prisoner conspiracy. I haven't done anything, not the slightest thing . . . !" One has the impression that she absolutely believes everything she says. . . . "I have never owned a riding whip. I never went into the camp. So I couldn't hit anyone either," she concludes. "I am glad that the trial has now started. Hopefully what I have to say about these things will also get into the press one day, and not always just the statements of the public prosecutor . . . ," she concludes, now much less controlled and more angry than at the beginning of the day's proceedings.[32]

With the indictment read and Koch's emphatic rejection of the charges registered, the court spent the six weeks that followed hearing from a total of 241 witnesses the prosecution and defense counsel had invited to testify. Koch's trial at Augsburg was therefore of an entirely

Fig. 6.1 Presiding Judge Georg Maginot addresses Ilse Koch in the Kolpinghaus courtroom at Augsburg, November 1950. Alfred Stroble / Süddeutsche Zeitung Photo.

different magnitude than her previous trial at Dachau, where the US military court had heard less than twenty witnesses attest to her alleged crimes.[33] First to testify at Augsburg were three prominent and well-educated survivors of Buchenwald Ilkow had chosen as "expert witnesses" to enlighten the court on the general conditions that existed at Buchenwald, as well as on any knowledge they had of Koch's activities. Dr. Benedikt Kautsky, a lecturer at the University of Graz, had published a memoir in 1948 titled *Devils and the Damned: A True and Damning Expose of Nazi Concentration Camps*. In a calm and objective fashion, Kautsky described the horrors of life at Buchenwald and the various methods of murder employed by the SS, and draped his body over the bock at the center of the courtroom to demonstrate how flog-gings were carried out. As Ilkow had hoped, Kautsky's serious de-meanor and detailed testimony made a deep impression, prompting the *Süddeutsche Zeitung* to opine that while "Kautsky describes little that is not already known . . . one wishes that millions could hear these pro-ceedings . . ."[34] As this report suggested, however, Kautsky shed little light on Koch's specific crimes, testifying that he personally had not seen her abuse prisoners, but had been told that she was "the most dangerous commander in the camp," and that she had had friends of his whipped.[35]

Rounding out the testimony of the expert witnesses called to paint a broad picture of conditions at Buchenwald was VVN national of-fice head Alfred Knieper and Josef Ackermann, a Bavarian state sen-ator and head of the Bavarian Association of Journalists. While Ack-ermann, like Knieper, built on Kautsky's testimony to further illuminate for the court the nature and unique terrors that informed prisoner life at Buchenwald, it was his testimony concerning the pro-duction of objects made of tattooed human skin that was reported most widely in the press and that brought this notorious crime back into the spotlight. Taking the stand on the trial's third day, Acker-mann testified that during the five years that he had worked in the camp's pathology department, he had learned of an order that the tat-tooed skins of dead inmates had to be removed and tanned. While he could not implicate Ilse Koch directly, he recounted how SS lab director Dr. Heinz Muller had told him of a lamp being prepared as "a very special present" for Karl Koch's birthday. The final product, Ackermann testified, was a lamp made of human bones that "was switched on by pressure against the little toe on one of the three human feet which formed the stand."[36] In a response to a query from judge Maginot, Ackermann explained he had seen the lamp and knew that the corresponding shade was made of tattooed human skin "because you could see the nipples."[37]

According to Ackermann, the lamp had been delivered to the Koch home, but was removed a few weeks later after higher SS authorities caught wind of the lamp and thought it in bad taste. To fortify Ackermann's testimony, Ilkow introduced as evidence three samples of tattooed human skin borrowed from US authorities that had been found at Buchenwald at liberation. Like Ackermann's testimony, however, the evidence presented did not directly implicate Koch, who had left the camp in 1943—a fact often omitted from the corresponding press coverage. For her part, Koch responded with incredulity, declaring that the lampshades in her home "weren't of human skin but of customary parchment."[38] In a line of argument that she would repeat frequently throughout her trial, Koch insisted all such testimony was purely the product of the wild fantasies of former inmates out for revenge. When Judge Maginot asked Koch whether she ever had owned "a pornographic book bound in human skin" as Ackermann further testified, she snapped back angrily, "never!"[39]

Ackermann's testimony provided the court's judges with an early indication of the challenges they would face in assessing both the credibility of the evidence before them and its relevance to questions of Koch's guilt or innocence. Under German law, judges are much less constricted by rules of evidence than their American counterparts and instead possess wide latitude in the nature of the testimony they choose to hear. Guiding Maginot and his colleagues on the bench was the principle of "free evidentiary evaluation," according to which it is a judge's right and obligation "to evaluate any and all evidence relevant to the final verdict according to his free conscience."[40] It was therefore Maginot's prerogative to permit hearsay testimony in the Augsburg court, or evidence not directly related to the defendant's alleged crimes, if he felt it assisted the court in arriving at the truth of the matter at hand. At the same time, however, the evidentiary value of the testimonies of many of the witnesses who would take the stand was often diminished because they drew largely upon the so-called "common knowledge" of Buchenwald's inmate population. While such testimony may have helped to paint a picture of how Koch was perceived, the fact that Koch was on trial only for crimes committed against German and Austrian prisoners meant that even eyewitness testimony would have to be discounted if the nationality of the victim was unknown.[41] Complicating matters further was the fact that the survivor-witnesses called upon to testify at Augsburg recounted events and sometimes conversations that had occurred between nine and thirteen years earlier. As a result, they often had trouble pinpointing where and when an incident had taken place—a common problem that Seidl, Koch's defense counsel, frequently used to attack a witness's credibility.

Nevertheless, the testimony of the prosecution witnesses called to the stand over the course of the first few weeks of the trial was, for the most part, devastating to Koch's rather ill-conceived strategy of total and absolute denial. The first witness to directly implicate Koch in a crime and undermine her primary alibi was her sister-in-law, Erna Raible. Appearing on the fourth day of trial, Raible disputed Koch's self-presentation as a loving and dedicated mother and wife wholly ignorant of camp affairs. Although Raible previously had testified at Dachau that she had never seen Koch abuse anyone, she now recounted a stay at the Koch villa during which she witnessed Koch's dogs attack a prisoner upon her command. "Once I said to her," Raible testified, "why must you sic the dogs on the prisoners? She answered, 'But you have a compassionate heart—shame on you!'"[42] Raible testified further that, contrary to Koch's denials, she did indeed own a riding whip, though Raible had never seen her use it.

Fortifying Raible's testimony was Koch's old nemesis Konrad Morgen, whose SS investigation had led to her arrest and her husband's execution. Appearing on the same day as Raible, Morgen further undermined Koch's claims to dutiful motherhood, describing her as "the most hated woman" at Buchenwald for "the slinky clothing she wore," her affairs with other SS men, and her complicity in her husband's corruption. So salacious was Morgen's testimony concerning Koch's adulterous sex life that Maginot felt compelled to temporarily shut out the public and the press, and proceed behind closed doors.[43] Morgen's testimony, though helpful in illuminating how Buchenwald functioned, provided little hard evidence of Ilse's activities and instead presented secondhand information gleaned from the inmates and camp personnel he had interviewed while conducting his SS investigation eight years earlier.

As witness followed witness to implicate Koch in beatings and in the reporting of prisoners for punishment, her blanket denials appeared progressively more implausible and drew her into conflict with an increasingly frustrated panel of judges. Particularly damning for the court was the testimony of two clergymen, Father Andreas Rieser and Father Alfred Berchtold, chosen by Ilkow in part because of the moral authority he hoped the judges and jury would attribute to them. Recounting the same incident he had provided to Ilkow for the indictment, Rieser testified that he had witnessed an SS man smash a prisoner's head with a heavy stone after Koch had singled him out from his work column and reported him for punishment.[44] Berchtold, who was now rector of the Social Institute of the Catholic Workers Union in Kochel, testified that he had seen Koch single out a prisoner from a column of inmates carrying stones from the camp quarry and report the man to an SS guard. By his account, the prisoner did not return, and Berchtold soon after learned that the man had been murdered in the bunker.

For the court, as for the press, the sworn testimony of Rieser and Berchtold was particularly weighty, and prompted Maginot to push Koch to respond to it. "Do you still claim that you have never seen ill-treatment? Have all the witnesses who testified here committed perjury?" he asked. "Yes," Koch replied. When Maginot asked her specifically if Berchtold, as a Catholic clergyman, had therefore committed perjury, Koch again replied in the affirmative, drawing loud protests from the audience in the courtroom. Now visibly distraught, Koch reportedly declared with tear-filled eyes, "I have an excellent memory and a clear conscience."[45] Koch remained insistent that she neither saw nor participated in the abuse of Buchenwald's inmates, but it appears that the testimonies of Rieser and Berchtold significantly eroded the credibility of this claim. Commenting on the impact of their words on top of what was said by witnesses before them, the *Schwäbische Landeszeitung* concluded that "when Catholic clergy, government counselors, and journalists testify under oath and their statements are confirmed by other witnesses, the last doubts shrink."[46]

Yet, despite the momentum Ilkow was building through the testimony of his carefully-chosen witnesses, the prosecution case suffered some notable hiccups. On the fourth day of trial, a witness named Ludwig Tobias testified that Koch had kicked out thirteen of his teeth after she watched him bend down to pick up a scrap of bread on the road near the Koch villa. The following day, however, Seidl presented two former inmates who testified that Tobias had told them his teeth had been knocked out by the Gestapo during an interrogation.[47] Similar inconsistencies appeared in the testimony of a witness named Friedrich Widder, who described an SS football game in which Koch had participated that involved kicking the heads of prisoners buried up to their necks in sand. Maginot, however, struck Widder's testimony when the defense introduced a deposition Widder had previously submitted that directly contradicted what he said in court.[48]

Some witnesses were reprimanded by Maginot for outbursts of passion or unruly behavior. Witness Jacob Ihr turned his back to Koch while he described seeing her demand the punishment of a prisoner who was subsequently beaten senseless. When Ihr referred to Koch as "this sow" and "this real pig," Maginot demanded that Ihr refrain from insulting the defendant.[49] More dramatically, witness Otto Axmann had to be brought to order when he grabbed the bullwhip on

Fig. 6.2   Koch confers with defense counsel Alfred Seidl in the Augsburg court. Süddeutsche Zeitung Photo.

display and stood in front of Koch shouting "I was beaten in camp because of this woman!" Witness Alexander Karoly, who had come to Buchenwald at age sixteen and suffered a brain injury there, collapsed on the stand after testifying that prisoners from a snow-clearing detail had died after Koch had reported them for punishment. Suffering a seizure and then screaming uncontrollably, Karoly was carried from the court by police.[50]

As the press observed, Koch's confidence seemed to waver in the face of Karoly's testimony and the incriminating evidence that mounted with each witness who took the stand. Her deteriorating composure raised questions about her mental health:

During the testimony on Thursday, the defendant trembled all over, she often put her head in her hands, and repeatedly pulled out her handkerchief. She also cried during the break. Her answers are tormented. Questions had to be repeated three or four times. She claimed her memory was intermittent. Apparently she couldn't remember what year the war broke out.[51]

Contributing further to Koch's mounting stress was a devastating blow Ilkow delivered to her credibility when he proved that she had lied under oath by presenting to the court irrefutable documentary evidence of her oft-denied Nazi Party membership. By the end of the trial's second week, Koch appeared to crack under the strain and suffered an apparent nervous breakdown in her prison cell. According to press reports, Koch smashed the window of her cell in a state of frenzy, and proceeded to shout "obscene sentences from the window in high-pitched tones." Prison officials feared a suicide attempt and had her hospitalized. During Koch's transfer, they reported that she quoted from Dante's *Inferno* and spoke incessantly about heavenly purgatory and the need to atone for her sins; upon arrival, she yelled, "I am guilty! I am a sinner!"[52]

When the Augsburg court reconvened on Monday, December 11, Koch's chair was empty. Maginot questioned the two doctors who had attended to Koch and assessed her psychiatric state and her fitness for trial. Dr. Rudolf Englert testified that "she behaved like a child, danced around in her cell, called the day the most beautiful day of her life, and directed me, the doctor, out of her cell." Her behavior, he concluded, was "entirely theatrical and artificial," and designed purely to "sabotage or at least delay her trial," now that her strategy of total denial had collapsed. Dr. Sighart, who had previously conducted one of Koch's psychiatric assessments, concurred, referring to Koch's behavior as a calculated "escape into illness."[53] As a result, Maginot ordered proceedings to continue without Koch, declaring that her illness was of her own making and that "her shot missed the mark."[54]

Maginot's frustration boiled over when Koch reappeared on Tuesday but collapsed on the sidewalk outside the courthouse and had to be carried in by two policemen. Meeting Koch at the door of the courtroom, Maginot demanded, "What is happening here? Sick again? Enough! Straight back to prison. I can't proceed with a woman like this." In response, Koch reportedly stood up suddenly, wiped her hand over her eyes, and said to Maginot, "oh it was only a dream!"[55] She then took her usual place in the courtroom and sat down with trembling hands and feet while sucking on a candy. The following day she collapsed again, this time lying face down on the defense table while sobbing loudly. Reporting on this final breakdown, the *Schwäbische Landeszeitung* concluded that "you could almost believe that she was finished." On Thursday, December 14, Maginot declared that proceedings could continue without Koch, after a panel of three doctors examined her and declared that she was at least temporarily "unfit for trial."[56]

In Koch's absence, the number of spectators diminished significantly, though witnesses continued to appear. As the judges prepared for the Christmas recess, there emerged a growing consensus that the testimony of the 162 witnesses already heard by December 21 was adequate to prove a number of counts of the most serious charges brought against Koch, and likely sufficient to send her to prison for life. In the interests of economy and expediency, the court therefore accepted a motion by the prosecution to drop 104 of the charges outlined in its indictment, and moved to cut from the trial roster the sixty-two witnesses originally selected in part to assist in proving those charges.[57] Among the witnesses dropped were all but one of the Americans whose testimonies (to be read to the court) had been gathered at such effort the previous year. Others dropped included a number of those from East Germany, whose promised appearance grew increasingly unlikely as ever-suspicious state authorities denied permission to travel. Some from the East feared appearing after spurious rumors

Fig. 6.3   "Listless and disarrayed," Ilse Koch enters the Augsburg court. Walter Sanders / LIFE Picture Collection / Shutterstock.

circulated of suspicious deaths of would-be witnesses, or the arrests of easterners to be used as hostages by West German authorities.[58] In the whittling down of the charges, Koch won a symbolic victory when the prosecution indicated that it would not pursue further crimes related to the murder of inmates for their tattooed skins. Given the testimony heard thus far, the prosecution recognized that the evidence was circumstantial at best, and that more straightforward cases of incitement to murder provided a less fraught route to conviction.

Following a week's recess for Christmas and the paring down of the case it was hearing, the court now turned to the questioning of witnesses that Seidl had selected in defense of his client. Apparently eager to hear their testimony, Koch again appeared in court, now looking disheveled and noticeably unwell. She had, it turned out, refused food since Christmas, having undertaken a somewhat half-hearted hunger strike that she would abandon a few days into the new year.[59] Taking the stand on December 29 were nine former SS guards who had served at Buchenwald and who were all now incarcerated at Landsberg prison. Unanimously they testified that Koch had never entered the camp compound, had never owned a whip, and had generally been polite and gracious.

Some, drawing on overtly misogynistic gender stereotypes, argued for Koch's innocence on the grounds that the authority she was being accused of wielding would never have been tolerated of her as a woman in the otherwise entirely masculine domain of Buchenwald. "Karl Koch," one explained, "was a man who was not influenced by anyone, especially not a woman."[60] This sentiment was also expressed by former Higher SS and Police Leader Prince Josias of Waldeck, whose investigation had led to the Kochs' 1943 arrest. Waldeck testified that the idea of Ilse Koch issuing orders to the camp SS was absurd and that, had he heard of such a thing, he would have "punished every corporal [who obeyed such an order] and given any such woman a couple of smacks around the ears."[61] These witnesses appeared keen to insist that, had Koch exercised authority and perpetrated violence in the manner alleged in the indictment, they would have been no less outraged than the members of the court, or the public at large, at her perceived violation of conservative (or National Socialist) gender norms.

Undercutting the value of the testimony of all SS witnesses was their personal interest in the trial's outcome: each recognized clearly that, if Koch could be brought before a German court after serving out her US-imposed sentence, then he could, too. Like Koch, therefore, most engaged in implausible blanket denials, sometimes provoking substantial disturbances in the courtroom. When Werner Berger, currently serving a life sentence for his role carrying out mass executions at Buchenwald, testified he knew nothing of any mistreatment that had occurred at the camp, the court struggled to retain order as two outraged former inmates stood up and engaged Berger in a yelling match. Sharing the incredulity of the survivor witnesses, judge Maginot asked repeatedly whether these SS witnesses truly understood the nature of the oath they had taken. "Yes I am happy to take the oath," one replied. "I am a Christian and I know what the oath means."[62]

That a mass murderer like Berger would benefit from a popular clemency program that would see him freed from prison by 1954 underscored the peculiar nature of the popular crusade to see Koch imprisoned for life for lesser crimes. That Koch's trial was more a moral crusade than an attempt to reckon with the crimes of the concentration camp system was thrown into stark relief by the fact that witness Waldeck, under whose administrative authority Buchenwald fell, was set for release from Landsberg prison the same day that he appeared at Koch's trial.[63] His release raised few eyebrows, even though he had organized the murderous evacuation of prisoners from Buchenwald in anticipation of the camp's liberation.

Not limited to reliance on SS witnesses to testify on Koch's behalf, Seidl's defense strategy largely centered on a challenge to the legitimacy of the legal charges based on the assertion that Koch's current prosecution constituted double jeopardy. To preempt this challenge, Ilkow had already called to the stand Dachau trial assistant prosecutor Robert Kunzig. Yet while Kunzig testified that jurisdictional limitations had meant that Koch had never been tried for crimes committed against German nationals, Seidl prompted Kunzig to concede that the "common design" charge employed at Dachau revolved around the concept of collective liability.[64] As such, the prosecution had never had to prove that the accused had committed any particular crime against any specific individual—of any specific nationality. Seidl used Kunzig's explanation to fortify his argument that the common design charge had been all-inclusive and proven in part by the testimony of German witnesses such as Eugen Kogon, Herbert Froboess, and Josef Ackermann and the abuse they and their countrymen had suffered.

To strengthen his assertion that crimes against German nationals had already been prosecuted at Koch's US military trial, Seidl called to the stand Dachau defense counsel Richard Wacker and Emil Aheimer. Wacker described Koch's trial at Dachau as "opaque," and Aheimer characterized it as part of a program of "mass justice" in which judges provided no explanation for the verdicts they handed down.[65] Wacker directly challenged the prosecution's contention that, while the Dachau court may have heard evidence of crimes against German nationals, it did so only to illuminate what occurred at Buchenwald but never as the basis of conviction.[66] Wacker pointed out that, in the absence of a written judgment or any accompanying explanation from the court's judges, the claim that crimes against German prisoners were excluded from the court's deliberations was purely a matter of faith. "The judge pounded his gavel on the table and announced, 'death by hanging.' That was it," Wacker testified.[67] Further buttressing Seidl's argument, Wacker claimed without evidence that the Dachau court had falsely considered German-Jewish victims to have been either stateless or "members of the United Nations," and that crimes committed against them therefore had been considered within the court's jurisdiction.[68] Seidl contended that, because it was "practically impossible to prove whether the military tribunal tried criminal offenses against Germans" and because the Dachau court had allegedly convicted Koch in part for crimes committed against German Jews, Koch's prosecution at Augsburg was legally invalid.[69]

Before Judge Maginot invited Ilkow and Seidl to present their closing arguments, he called to the stand the trial's most anticipated, and ultimately disappointing, witness. Dr. Eugen Kogon, who at the time of his appearance was not only editor of the Catholic left-wing *Frankfurter Hefte* but also president of the Union of European Federalists and chairman of the Executive Committee of the German Council of the European Movement, had initially been slated to appear at the beginning of December. Kogon's testimony, Ilkow hoped, would be particularly weighty, not only because he was a noted public figure but also because he had penned what was at the time the most authoritative and popular history of the Nazi apparatus of terror, *The SS-State: The System of the German Concentration Camps* (later published as *The Theory and Practice of Hell*). Kogon, however, had misgivings about taking the witness stand and requested that his summons to court be delayed a month, arguing that his work obligations made his appearance difficult.[70] Then, at the beginning of January, as the date of his rescheduled appearance approached, Kogon again petitioned the court, this time asking to be excused because he had nothing of use to add to the prosecution case, was in poor health, did not want to relive the past, and was still too consumed by important work.[71]

Ilkow, however, was determined not to lose a man he had hoped would be a star witness, and threatened Kogon with legal sanction if he failed to appear.[72] Yet while Ilkow succeeded in pressuring him to take the stand, Kogon soon revealed that his testimony indeed could contribute little to Koch's conviction. As he had previously testified at Dachau, Kogon explained that he had seen Koch only twice during his six years at Buchenwald, and at a considerable distance. As to her crimes, he could speak only to rumors he had heard, or assumptions he deemed reasonable. Kogon came closest to implicating Koch in a crime when he testified that, as a prisoner clerk, he had once removed the name of an inmate from a personnel list after he was taken to the bunker, allegedly at Koch's instigation. While Kogon couldn't speak directly to the prisoner's ultimate fate, he believed "it would have been a miracle if this prisoner left the bunker with his life."[73] The most surprising moment in Kogon's testimony came in response to a query from Seidl concerning his popular book *The SS-State.* Kogon explained that, if he had it all to do over again, he wouldn't write the book at all, as he had no desire to dwell on the horrors of the past. His intent now was to look only to the future and think about more beautiful things.[74] Kogon, it seemed, wished to be anywhere else in the world but on the witness stand.

In the wake of Kogon's rather anticlimactic testimony, Maginot signaled that he would call no further witnesses, and instead summoned Ilkow to deliver his closing argument to the court on January 11, 1951. Termed a *Plädoyer* in German, the closing argument is literally a "plea" in which the prosecution presents a summation of its arguments regarding questions of both fact and law, and its recommendations for sentencing. Koch, however, would not be present to hear the chief prosecutor's plea. As Ilkow rose to speak, Koch again collapsed, prompting an ever-more frustrated Maginot to intervene and have her removed from the court. "Do you want to play theater again? You can't achieve anything with that," Maginot exclaimed. Two police officers then carried Koch out of the courtroom in her chair, to the cheers of the two hundred onlookers crammed into the gallery.[75]

When Ilkow finally was able to begin, he commented first on the role of the proceedings in deepening understanding of the Nazi period and shedding light on the heroism of the "thousands of resistance fighters" who died at Buchenwald and elsewhere. "This trial," Ilkow began, "is an essential contribution to the history of those years 1933–1945. . . . The German revolution against National Socialism was one of the bloodiest in history. That it failed to succeed is not the fault of those who were imprisoned in concentration camps."[76] Beyond reciting the crimes of which Koch had been accused and the witness testimony that proved her guilt, Ilkow argued that her actions at Buchenwald were particularly egregious because she occupied no official position in the Nazi state. Instead, "chased by the demon of brutality and unrestrained instincts," she had acted on her own volition to commit "unimaginable crimes with cold-blooded composure."[77] To emphasize that Koch had acted out of the base motives necessary to prove the charge of incitement to murder, Ilkow recalled the psychiatric assessments of doctors Sighart and Leibbrand that had been read out in court, and how they emphasized her emotional coldness and "sexual inclination to cruelty." Koch, Ilkow declared, had been driven by greed, arrogance, and animalistic impulses, and had "surrendered to her sexual instincts without shame."[78] That she had shown no remorse in court, Ilkow argued, only revealed further her moral depravity and need for punishment. In conclusion, Ilkow argued that justice could only be served if the court imposed on Koch a life sentence and permanent loss of her civil rights.

As a counterbalance to Ilkow's plea, the court next asked Seidl to present his final arguments in defense of his client. Seidl demanded first that Koch be acquitted of all charges relating to crimes that had occurred either after September 1, 1939—the point in time from which the Dachau court claimed general jurisdiction—or involving "the Jewish cases," contending that these crimes had already been tried by the United States.[79] Seidl further argued that his client's prosecution had been driven primarily by a fanatical public obsession sparked by rumors of human skin lampshades, despite the fact that, after the testimony of more than two hundred witnesses, this charge could not be proven.[80] Seidl therefore sought to portray Koch's prosecution as a witch hunt. He pointed in particular to the fourteen hundred other Dachau trial convicts, and insisted that unless they, too, were brought before German courts upon their release from US custody and charged with crimes against German citizens, any conviction handed down by the Augsburg court would be appealed as a violation of the constitutional principle of "equality before the law."[81] Recognizing that the total acquittal of his client was not in the offing and that some period of incarceration was a given, Seidl concluded his plea with a request that the court credit Koch for the sixteen months she had already spent behind bars awaiting trial.

As the court reconvened the next morning to provide Koch with an opportunity to have the last word before the judges and jury began their deliberations, a group of two hundred protesters gathered outside the Augsburg Kolpinghaus holding placards demanding swift and stern punishment. Inside the court, Koch was observed having a lively conversation with her lawyer. Yet, when Maginot turned to ask her if she had anything she would like to say before the trial concluded, she remained motionless and refused to answer each of the four times the question was repeated.[82] Before Maginot formally brought proceedings to an end, Koch again had to be carried from the hall still sitting in her chair. At Aichach prison that Friday evening, she reportedly began to rage in her cell and again smashed her furniture. Through a broken window, she shouted, "Hey, look up here, I'm Ilse Koch!" This state of frenzy was treated with tranquilizers and she was placed in a padded cell.[83]

When Maginot reconvened the court on what turned out to be the particularly rainy morning of Monday, January 15, 1951, Koch's chair was empty. Many among the crowd of two hundred spectators who had braved the elements to gather outside the Kolpinghaus in the hopes of getting a glimpse of Koch would be disappointed. Inside the courtroom, some had brought binoculars in the hopes of watching Koch's face in detail as her sentence was announced. Instead, Maginot handed down the court's judgment in Koch's absence, illuminated by stage lights and the incessant flashing of camera bulbs. The court, Maginot announced, found Koch guilty of one felony count of incitement to murder, one felony count of incitement to attempted murder, five independent misdemeanor counts of inciting grievous bodily harm, and two further misdemeanor counts of inciting grievous bodily harm that stemmed from a single criminal offense. The court acquitted Koch of the remaining five counts of incitement to either murder or grievous bodily harm that were still on the roster. Siding with the recommendation of the prosecution, the court sentenced Koch to the most severe punishment permitted in the Federal Republic of Germany: life imprisonment and the permanent loss of her civil rights.[84]

Accounting for the court's verdict and sentence, Maginot explained that the court had very carefully weighed the testimony it had heard, and that, while evidence presented by some witnesses had been discounted, most was astonishing in its objectivity. Countering Koch's central line of defense, Maginot pointed out in particular that the court's meticulous study of the testimonies heard over the preceding six weeks revealed no "conspiracy of witnesses" who had coordinated and fabricated stories in the interest of revenge.[85] Instead, Maginot argued, the evidence illustrated beyond a doubt that "this ruthless, hard-headed woman" had been entirely aware of the beatings, whippings, and hangings that Buchenwald's prisoners fell victim to on a regular basis. It was through the unusual influence she wielded over her husband and other SS men at the camp, Maginot explained, that Koch "had done everything in her power to worsen the condition of those poor tortured men."[86] "Without any remorse," Maginot concluded, "she was insatiable in her hunger for power and devoid of all feminine feelings. She stood before the court without any regrets and behaved in an unprecedented fashion. The court sees no reason to offset her sentence with her pre-trial detention."[87]

While newspaper reports provided only snippets of Maginot's closing comments, the court provided a more elaborate accounting of the verdict and sentence in the 137-page written judgment it subsequently submitted. The judgment explained first that the court had wholly rejected the argument pursued by the defense that Koch's prosecution constituted double jeopardy. The judges reasoned that the Dachau court had had no jurisdiction to try crimes against German nationals and had clearly stated as much; if the American court had acted counter to its jurisdiction, the defense had provided no concrete evidence of this, and had, the court felt, engaged in conjecture. In a similar fashion, the court found no evidence in the Dachau trial record that any special category had been created to allow German Jewish victims to be regarded as stateless or "members of the United Nations" despite the suppositions of the German jurists that Seidl had called to testify on Koch's behalf.[88]

The insights provided in the written judgment of the Augsburg court are limited by the fact that the names of the witnesses are concealed, at times making it impossible to identify whose testimony the court found compelling and whose testimony it rejected. Beyond the extensive summaries of the testimonies of anonymized witnesses, however, the judgment does elucidate the way the court deliberated and how it perceived Koch's moral and criminal guilt. In striking contrast to the findings of the American military court at Dachau, the written judgment of the Augsburg court reveals fastidious deliberations, rooted in a cautious and thorough reading of both German law and witness testimony.

According to the judgment, Koch's conviction for incitement to murder concerned the inmate whose head was crushed with a stone at her instigation, as recounted by Father Rieser and the witness Siegel (referred to as "Pastor Ri." and witness "Sie."). These witnesses had made "the best impression," the court found, and had recounted this incident in a mutually reinforcing and objective fashion deeply convincing to the judges and jury.[89] Rieser's status as clergyman added to his credibility, as Ilkow had intended. With the killing accepted as fact, the court then deliberated at length on whether Koch could have known, and indeed whether she desired, that death would result from her reporting of this prisoner to the SS guard who stood nearby. The court reached the conclusion that, because overwhelming evidence showed Koch to have been well aware of camp conditions and the punishments and killings of inmates, "she knew that, according to the basic attitude [among the camp SS] at the time, an act with a possible fatal outcome was very likely." Further, the court concluded that Koch had incited the killing out of a perverse desire for the "inner satisfaction" that observing such violence gave her. "Incidents of this kind satisfied her," the judges wrote, adding that. "Due to her physical condition as a woman and since she did not belong to the supervisory organs [at Buchenwald], she had to limit her own crimes to beating with her riding whip. Since this did not satisfy her, she used to observe the . . . violence of the supervisory organs and intervened at times with hints, suggestions, and orders." In this case, "the court was convinced that Koch had imagined the death of the detainee as a possible consequence of her hint," leading to her conviction.[90]

The court's caution in arriving at its verdict is illustrated both by the charge of incitement to attempted murder of which Koch was convicted, and by the various charges of which Koch was acquitted. Similar to the incident recounted by Rieser and Siegl, the incitement to attempted murder conviction stemmed from a brutal beating meted out by an SS guard after Koch had singled out an inmate and reported him. The witness Scha., whose account was confirmed by the written deposition of the deceased witness Eid., had "dispassionately and objectively" described how Koch had caught a German inmate looking at her as she passed by on horseback. After striking the prisoner with her riding crop, the prisoner had grabbed her weapon in defense, prompting Koch to call to the nearby SS guards. She then "watched with inner satisfaction as the SS-men trampled the prisoner without restraint" until he lay motionless and was rolled into a nearby ditch.[91] Yet while Scha.'s assumption that the inmate had died led the prosecution to charge Koch with incitement to murder, the court was unconvinced, ruling that the evidence was conclusive only in so far as it proved incitement to attempted murder. "Even if some of the facts, such as the intensity of the violent act and the prisoner lying motionless for several hours, speak indeed to the likelihood death occurred," the judges wrote, "it could not be entirely ruled out that it was only a severe concussion."[92]

The court's sober deliberation was most evident in its acquittals. One count of incitement to murder derived from the testimony of the witness "Klu.," who said that Koch had confronted a laboring prisoner taking a forbidden smoking break and grabbed him by the collar. Startled, the inmate struggled to break free, then suddenly ran into a cordon of SS guards, who shot him dead. The court explained that it "could not follow" the arguments of the prosecution, and ruled that, rather than homicide, the death was a suicide, and one that Koch could not have anticipated.[93] Another acquittal concerned a beating Koch allegedly administered with her riding crop while on horseback, after which the victim was reported to the SS and subsequently flogged to death. In this case, the court dismissed the testimony of chief witness "Schn.," because he also had testified that he himself had been beaten by Koch on March 16, 1939, some six weeks before the birth of her daughter Gisela. The court sought professional medical advice to conclude that it was highly unlikely that Koch would have ridden on horseback and administered beatings at this stage of pregnancy. Its assessment of Schn.'s credibility diminished further when he suddenly mentioned Koch's pregnancy after it was brought to his attention, despite never having included the detail in previous depositions or testimony.[94]

In the case of alleged incitement to murder recounted by the witness "Gr.," the court acquitted Koch after researching a key claim Gr. had made. According to Gr., Koch had beaten a column of at least six Austrian Jews with her riding crop before they were taken to the bunker by SS guards and killed. Yet when the court attempted to confirm the nationality of the victims, the witness declared that he could say with certainty only that one was "the Berlin Jew Paul Friedländer." Troubled by this contradiction, the court turned to the records of the International Tracing Service and confirmed that, while three Friedländers had died at Buchenwald, none was named Paul or wore the black triangle for "asocial" inmates, as Gr. had testified Paul did.[95]

If the court's deliberations reveal an approach to the evidence that was cautious and critical, sentencing was skewed by misogynistic stereotypes and a drive to punish Koch harshly not only for her crimes but for her violation of gender norms. Having handed down to Koch the stiffest penalty the law would allow, the court accounted for its decision by presenting her actions as particularly egregious because she "consciously suppressed any feeling of compassion and pity she had as a woman." By virtue of her gender, the judges implied, Koch should be held to a higher standard of ethical and benevolent behavior in the concentration camps than was expected of her male counterparts. At Buchenwald, the court explained, Koch had given "free rein to her pursuit of power and prestige, her arrogance and her selfishness." The court reasoned that "the conditions reigning in Buchenwald— that Mrs. Koch was well aware of—should have evoked in her, being a woman, compassion and pity." Yet, while other SS wives "did good to the extent that it was possible in light of their weak power, only Mrs. Koch refused a human emotion of this kind."

Koch, the court continued, had derived "inner satisfaction when she contributed to the strictest implementation of the system reigning in the camp. By her personal appearance and her clothes, she provoked the prisoners to look at her, an act she considered, against her better judgment, worthy of punishment." The judges concluded that "Mrs. Koch willfully closed herself to any better insight and to adjusting her behavior accordingly, whereas feelings of pity and empathy would have been especially obvious for every woman." Disturbed in particular by Koch's lack of remorse and "stubborn and irresponsible denial," they considered a life sentence only fitting for someone who could not be moved "to the slightest admission of guilt."[96] The court explained finally that it had denied a request from the prosecution that she serve her sentence in strict "preventative detention" only because Koch "would not have an opportunity for similar offenses in her lifetime" and therefore "poses no danger of committing further crimes."[97]

The German public greeted news of Koch's life sentence enthusiastically and in a manner that went against the grain of the otherwise skeptical views taken toward the postwar prosecution of Nazi crimes. In January 1951, thousands of Germans had taken part in protests outside Landsberg prison to voice the popular demand that clemency or pardons be extended to war criminals the United States had incarcerated there. This sentiment, broadly supported in the press, did not extend to Koch.[98] Instead, the *Frankfurter Allgemeine Zeitung* commented on how rare it was that "a judgment has been received with such satisfaction in Germany as this one, which imposed the highest sentence on Ilse Koch that is possible in the Federal Republic." It celebrated the judgment as evidence that "German law is completely sufficient for German criminals" and that, free of Allied interference, the West German state had shown that it would "lead the real war criminals to their deserved fate." That the paper viewed Koch as just such a "real war criminal" and "one of the most disgusting phenomena of the

Third Reich" is instructive, given that the handful of cases of incitement of which Koch was ultimately convicted pale in comparison to the crimes of the hundreds of Nazi bigwigs and common SS personnel whose ongoing incarceration was the focus of public protest. Koch's crimes were viewed as particularly egregious and worthy of punishment not because they typified those of the concentration camp system, but because they went above and beyond the routinized barbarities that others had perpetrated in the course of "doing their jobs."

Inadvertently, Koch's Augsburg trial therefore served to shift focus away from those who dutifully implemented the genocidal policies of the Nazi state, and onto a unique but unrepresentative personal cruelty that could account for little of the horror that occurred during the Third Reich.[99] Ilse Koch, then, described in *Die Zeit* as that "perverted, nymphomaniac, hysterical, power-obsessed woman," proved to be a useful target for those who sought to condemn the Nazi past without having to reflect on more complicated questions concerning the complicity of those who brought the Third Reich to power and supported or helped to enforce its policies.[100]

7 The Long Years After

Four days passed before Ilse Koch received official notification of the verdict of the Augsburg court after its much-anticipated announcement on January 15, 1951. Locked in her Aichach prison cell since the psychiatric collapse that had led to her ouster from the trial a week earlier, Koch had had access neither to newspapers nor to her lawyer. On learning of the life sentence the judges and jurors had handed down to her, she responded not with the sort of unhinged outburst seen from her in the courtroom and in her cell on numerous occasions over the preceding weeks, but instead with a shrug of the shoulders.[1] Koch viewed the trial as little more than a conspiratorial revenge exercise by a cabal of former inmates in collusion with state authorities; it is unlikely she expected a sentence any less severe. Yet in the coming months and years, her hostility, defiance, and refusal to acknowledge any criminal or moral guilt whatsoever would not serve her well. As she filed again and again for clemency, those charged with reviewing her applications consistently invoked her lack of contrition as grounds to declare her release wholly inappropriate. The long and solitary years that followed led Koch not to self-reflection and moral reckoning, but to deeper resentments and, as prospects of her eventual release dimmed, to an untethered descent into madness, and finally death.

Appeals and Poetry

Six months after the conclusion of Augsburg trial proceedings, Koch's lawyer Alfred Seidl challenged the verdict and sentence of the court in a thirty-six-page appeal submitted June 23, 1951.[2] To a large extent, Seidl restated the objections he already had raised in court. First, he argued, Koch's prosecution constituted double jeopardy, not only because of the expansive nature of the common design charge used by the US military court to convict her but because, Seidl alleged, the American tribunal had already prosecuted her for crimes committed against German nationals. Second, he contended that the Bavarian Ministry of Justice had deprived Koch of her "lawful judge" when it had passed over the designated jurist from the Augsburg court in favor of having Bamberg court judge Dr. Erich Jagomast lead the preliminary investigation. As a result, Seidl argued, Koch had been convicted in part on the basis of testimonies Jagomast had collected unlawfully and that should not have been heard in court. With regard to the specific offenses for which Koch was convicted, Seidl argued that the court had insufficient grounds to conclude what outcome Koch had intended when reporting prisoners for punishment, or whether the unnamed SS men incited by her had acted in a manner that fulfilled the requirements of German law in deeming a killing attempted, or actual, murder. Seidl further alleged that in the wake of Koch's psychiatric breakdowns, the Augsburg court had violated the law by conducting proceedings in her absence. Most broadly, he reiterated his charge that, as the sole Dachau trial convict retried by a German court, Koch had been unfairly singled out and deprived of her constitutional right to "equality before the law."

On April 22, 1952, a panel of seven judges from the Criminal Division of the Federal Court of Germany officially rejected the appeal, bringing the life sentence handed down by the Augsburg court into full legal effect. In a twenty-two-page decision, the panel concurred with the original findings of the trial court and reiterated the arguments the trial court had made. To Seidl's claim that Koch had been the victim of double jeopardy, the panel provided an extensive discussion of her trial at Dachau and argued that, while some crimes involving German citizens had been discussed in the course of those proceedings, they lay outside the jurisdiction of the US military court and were therefore introduced only to illuminate the criminal character of Buchenwald concentration camp in general and "never as the basis of a guilty verdict."[3] That Koch had not been deprived of her "lawful judge" had already been settled, the panel stated, in the ruling of the constitutional court that Seidl had first petitioned in October 1949. As to Seidl's claim that Koch had been deprived of her constitutional right to "equality before the law," the panel declared that, in any criminal proceeding, the question before the court is whether the accused is guilty or innocent; whether "another person one considers guilty is being prosecuted for similar offenses has no influence [on the current case] and does not concern it."[4] Though the panel recognized Koch's right to be present during trial proceedings, the nature of Koch's allegedly self-induced psychological breakdowns did not deprive her of her free will in the manner that genuine psychosis would, resulting in an absence that was "voluntary and culpable."[5] Finally, to Seidl's contention that the court had erred in its evaluation of the specific charges for which Koch was convicted, the panel sided wholly with the Augsburg court and declared its judgments both thorough and legally sound.

With her appeal rejected, Koch had little choice but to contemplate future petitions for clemency while adjusting to life in her solitary cell as Aichach inmate #596. Prison records show that her first years passed largely without incident, save for the odd outburst and a general tendency to be standoffish to prison staff and somewhat hostile to her fellow prisoners.[6] Her contacts with the world outside the prison—and even outside her cell—were few. Prison ledgers show that she seldom received visitors and kept in regular written contact only with her children Artwin and Gisela, and, prior to her death in 1959, her mother Anna.[7] Even these relationships appear to have been somewhat distant and occasionally strained. Gisela recalled finding it difficult to connect to her mother in such an alien environment and confessed to having visited infrequently. "There was always someone there listening to us," she remembered of her first visit as a teenager. "I was so taken aback when I saw my mother. I think I just sat there and hardly talked." She remembered her mother steadfastly professing her innocence, and declaring that she "didn't want anything to do with the murderers" amongst whom she was incarcerated.[8] Koch's prison records confirm that she tended to avoid contact with fellow inmates, often choosing not to visit the prison yard even when permitted, and refusing assignments that offered chances to work with others.[9] Instead, Koch accepted a job as a prison seamstress, repairing garments and producing decorative needlework alone in her cell. A frequent borrower of books from the prison library, she wrote to her mother in 1952 that she had become "obsessed with learning."[10] According to her lawyer, she busied herself in particular with attempting to learn English, in the hope that she could one day emigrate to Australia, where she believed she had distant relatives.[11]

Hints of Koch's self-perception and outlook on her future behind bars can be found in the dozens of letters that were held back by Aichach's rather zealous censors. Because anything deemed to contain inappropriate political or personal sentiments was blocked, these were retained in her prison files. In general, Koch's letters are steeped in self-pity, sentimentality, and hopes for vindication. Occasionally there are fantasies of revenge; expressions of guilt or contrition are wholly absent. A frequent source of consternation for Koch was the clemency granted other Nazi war criminals—whom she pointedly referred to as the "war condemned"—while her life sentence remained unaltered. "I am furious," she wrote to Gisela in 1956, "when I see how many of my co-sufferers have been released for years now, while I go to bed day after day behind bars with the lullaby, 'another day, innocently behind bars, so help me God.'"[12] The following year, she appeared heartened by the recent return of the last German POWs held in the Soviet Union, and believed the tide might be turning in her favor. In 1957, she wrote Artwin that "even the much-maligned East has released all their war condemned," and continued optimistically, "So, my son, it shall only be months, not years, before we see each other again."[13] These hopes, however, were soon dashed, and gave way to an increasingly desperate need to have at least her children accept her professed innocence while she dreamed of release. In a 1962 letter to Gisela, written more than ten years after her trial had ended, she continued to plead her case, even as Artwin's faith in her innocence apparently had wavered:

I lived isolated in our house and garden [at Buchenwald] thinking only of your happiness. Believe me, I was awake early to late caring for you. . . . What a wonderful time. I didn't see anything evil or hear about any crimes, so help me God! Thank you from the bottom of my heart for believing in my innocence; Artwin has gone crazy listening to what others say, but I'll be able to convince him one day.[14]

Some of Koch's letters included her own poetry—poorly composed verses for which she nevertheless developed outsized ambitions. The sentiments conveyed by these poems speak to Koch's state of mind and the depth of her belief in her innocence, despite all the delusion it entailed. While some are merely trite celebrations of the natural world, many of her poems, which rhyme in the original German, combine complaints of her suffering with enduring faith in divine judgment and punishment for those responsible for her incarceration. A 1952 poem dedicated to her children is typical:

A lot of years have passed / since I have seen my child last
I am still kept prisoner / In contravention of all justice.
When they can't get hold of the guilty / Others have to ascend
    the scaffold.
However they twist in pain / They will only be mocked
Then at some point fate will turn / And those who have been
    ostracized will be honored
The pain of hell will be over / And everything will be turned
    around.[15]

The following two poems, included in a 1962 letter to Gisela, express similar sentiments:

For years, wherever I look, bars / I hardly see the blue of
    the sky
The window is too small to see / How could this ever happen?
They called God as a witness / but he hid his face
But it is not the time for Him / to judge and to exalt
Woe! How could this have happened?

A human being fights in this earthly domain / for truth and for
    justice
And calls out for God, in his highest suffering / condemned to
    powerlessness
And like an echo, it is said to him / hold on, you don't know my
    plan
I don't stand idly by / because injustice was done to thee

Those who have gone astray in blind hatred / those who called
   upon me with perjury
I will judge them, according to my wisdom / Time doesn't count
   in eternity.[16]

In letters to her mother and to Artwin, Koch expressed pride in
her poetry and even a confidence that her "gift" might allow her to
achieve both fortune and a more positive basis for fame. "Not everyone
can do this," she wrote to her mother in 1952. "Talent cannot be acquired by industry alone. It requires higher power. That I am finding
in myself more and more."[17] In 1957, she wrote to Artwin that if Germany's sentimental *Schlager* singers could earn so much money with
their pop ballads, "then I should be able to find a publisher that would
be interested in my poems—perhaps a publisher who senses a good
business opportunity who would set me up with a couple of thousand marks, that would at least help us to build a new home." To be
published, she continued boastfully, "you do not only have to have
the capability, but you also need a name, and I, without any doubt,
have both. Even my enemies would read me out of curiosity. From
the outset, my book [of poems] promises to be a best-seller on the
market."[18] Although Koch's dreams of literary renown grew more
muted over time, she continued to compose and to send out poetry
until her death, suggesting an undiminished confidence in the quality
of her prose and its ability to communicate her innocence and faith
in the divine punishment that her enemies would receive.

   While Koch's poetry describes those responsible for her incarceration in vague and often supernatural terms, her letters reveal a deep-
seated antisemitism. What she had avoided expressing under interrogation or in court, she now drew upon to account for her fate. "A
new hate propaganda was orchestrated against me mainly by Jews,"
she wrote to Artwin in 1955. Dispensing advice to her son, she further
developed her fantasies of Jewish victimization:

> Be careful not to end up in a Jewish company like your sister
> Gisela, because it is impossible to work for Jews, buy from Jews,
> and to have connection to Jews in any way, especially when you
> have a mother who has now suffered under a heavy prison sen-
> tence for ten years mainly because of Jews that villainized me, de-
> famed me, maligned me in the most evil way in all the newspa-
> pers, and accused me and gave false oaths at court.[19]

That Koch believed that Jews, who in reality were a small minority
of those who had testified against her, were chiefly responsible for her
imprisonment is made still more clear by a list she created in her address book of the names of nearly a hundred witnesses who had given
evidence against her. Koch carefully underlined all those whom she
believed to be Jews.[20] In a letter to Gisela, her antisemitism took on
spiritual dimensions as she presented herself as a victim of mystical
Jewish forces. "I have no luck at all," she wrote. "The curse of the Jews
is upon me."[21]

Koch's belief that she faced insurmountable forces determined to
see her die behind bars only grew as her various petitions for clemency were rejected. In 1955, Koch's first plea for early release was submitted not by her lawyer Alfred Seidl, but by Stille Hilfe für Kriegs-
gefangene und Internierte (Silent Aid for Prisoners of War and the
Interned). This somewhat secretive right-wing organization was
established in 1951 by Bavarian Catholic aristocrat Helene Elisabeth
Princess von Isenburg to lobby for the release of condemned Nazi war
criminals and to provide them and their families with legal, financial, and moral support.[22] Isenburg, whose followers referred to her
as "Mother Elisabeth" for her purported maternal dedication to the
condemned Nazis at Landsberg prison, became an ardent supporter
of Koch and the only person beyond her immediate family to whom
Koch began to send letters (and sometimes poems) on a semi-regular
basis. Isenburg's support for Koch was such that she came to employ

Koch's daughter Gisela in the Stille Hilfe office and housed her for a period of more than two years.[23]

Isenburg's 1955 petition, addressed directly to West German chancellor Konrad Adenauer, asserted that the ten years Koch had spent behind bars since her arrest by US authorities in 1945 was sufficient penance for any possible crime she may have committed. Seeking mercy for the sake of Koch's children, Isenburg wrote that Gisela and Artwin were suffering terribly as a result of the "defamation of their mother." She concluded her petition with an offer that Koch would frequently restate in the future petitions she would submit: Isenburg was "prepared to personally care for Ilse Koch" upon release.[24] Included within Isenburg's application was also a letter from Koch's mother who, like her daughter, attacked the witnesses who had testified in court and hinted at the same antisemitic conspiracy that Ilse drew upon to explain her incarceration. "They are unbelievable, they contradict themselves, and any unbiased human being would see that," she wrote. The witnesses "have become the victims of an evil polemic and of their own hatred." Referring to Koch's absence at trial, her mother argued that it had been easy to convict Koch because she was not present to defend herself. "Injustice," she wrote in a full-throated rejection of her daughter's guilt, "is not erased by letting the innocent suffer."[25]

State judicial authorities quickly rejected the petition and concurred with an accompanying report provided by Aichach prison officials that recommended against clemency, on the basis that Koch wholly lacked any understanding of her guilt and continued to insist that she had nothing to atone for.[26] Unbowed, Koch turned to her lawyer to prepare a lengthy and more formal challenge to her incarceration, but indicated she had no intention of displaying contrition to help her case. In a letter to Seidl in November 1955, she wrote that she fundamentally opposed the term "clemency plea," insisting that it implied a guilt that she wholly rejected.[27] Not surprisingly, therefore, the nineteen-page petition subsequently submitted by Seidl in June 1957 presented Koch as an innocent victim of state-sanctioned injustice. This combative and unapologetic plea, though rejected out of hand by the Bavarian Ministry of Justice, would form the basis of the near-annual appeals for clemency that Koch would file for the next decade.

Seidl's 1957 petition argued first that Koch's prosecution had been driven by a public obsession with her case derived from spurious rumors of tattooed skins and lampshades that originated with the US Army and were spread by "a certain section of the press." Seidl drew considerably upon such thinly veiled antisemitic tropes concerning pervasive Jewish influence behind the scenes. "Certain string-pullers" and "masterminds," Seidl contended, had "artificially steered public opinion," while "influential circles in the American Senate" and the "followers of the former [Jewish American] finance minister Morgenthau" had pressured the German government to rearrest and prosecute Koch.[28] Seidl pointed to the "unconvincing" nature of the evidence against Koch to contend that, even two years after the formal independence of the West German state in 1949, the Augsburg court had "acted for the occupation." Even the federal court that had rejected her 1952 appeal, Seidl insisted, was "far from being . . . truly independent."[29]

Seidl's unsubstantiated arguments, which scarcely could have won him much sympathy from the senior German jurists tasked with considering his application, were rounded out with familiar contentions he had made in court. He maintained that Koch's prosecution constituted double jeopardy, and that she had been deprived both of her "rightful judge" and of her constitutional guarantee of "equality before the law." Seidl underscored the undeniable incongruence of the fact that Koch remained in prison while only three of the major war criminals sentenced by the International Military Tribunal at Nuremberg were still incarcerated at Landsberg; of the more than sixteen hundred war crimes suspects tried by the US military courts at Dachau, Seidl pointed out, Koch was now the only one still behind bars. Even if Koch had committed crimes, Seidl concluded, thirteen years imprisonment, especially when compared to the terms ultimately served by other "war condemned," was more than sufficient for her to atone for her sins.[30]

The subsequent rejection of Seidl's 1957 appeal for clemency was recommended in the requisite accompanying report submitted by officials at Aichach prison. Describing Koch as "cold, egocentric, and craving attention," they noted that she "lacks any insight, remorse, or empathy for the [concentration camp] prisoners who were tortured or killed," and viewed herself instead as a guiltless "political prisoner."[31] Koch reacted to the refusal of her clemency plea with deep frustration, complaining to the Bavarian Ministry of Justice that she deserved a retrial because her absence in court had prevented her from sufficiently defending herself and from unmasking the alleged perjury she insisted was at the heart of the testimonies given against her.[32] Even nineteen-year-old Artwin protested the rejection of his mother's clemency, pleading with federal judicial authorities to either release his mother or explain why she remained behind bars. "It's terrible," he wrote in rather childlike terms, "that a person can't have a mommy, even when she still lives. Please, please, finally do something . . . ! Can one really condemn an innocent person? Who has that right? Don't look away any longer. Do something please!"[33]

Though Seidl's chosen approach to winning Koch's clemency did not appear to serve his client well, it was the basis for subsequent (and unsuccessful) appeals filed by Koch in 1960, 1961, and 1962. In her rather hostile 1960 application, she declared, "I don't need a pardon, I need justice." After calling out those "who confront hatred with hatred," she demanded that the Bavarian Ministry of Justice reconsider the 1957 application.[34] In 1961, she similarly requested reconsideration of Seidl's original plea, this time pointing out with urgency that she had reached the age of fifty-five, and it would become increasingly hard for her to reintegrate into society and find work with each year that passed; she added that her post-imprisonment life would still be difficult enough "because of people's hatred toward me."[35] In March 1962, with these clemency pleas summarily rejected and with little evidence of gaining traction with Bavarian judicial authorities, Koch attempted a new tack: appealing her case to the European Commission on Human Rights. That Koch viewed herself as a victim rather than a perpetrator of human rights abuses underscores her unaltered and deeply skewed self-perception. Yet laying out Seidl's central legal concerns regarding double jeopardy, equality before the law, and court proceedings that occurred in Koch's absence was a futile exercise. The commission declared her application "inadmissible" on the grounds that Koch had not sufficiently shown violations of the human rights protected by the commission's charter, and also because the trial itself had concluded two years before the West German government had joined the European Commission in 1953. As a result, alleged legal abuses that occurred before that date lay beyond the commission's mandated jurisdiction.[36]

"Confinement Psychosis"

Koch's steady accumulation of defeats in her quest for clemency coincided with, and perhaps contributed to, a deterioration in her mental health. Immediately following the rejection of her 1961 clemency petition prison authorities noted that, on the night of December 4, she had torn up the contents of her cell and had refused to get dressed after taking off all her clothes. In the state of delusion that followed, Koch interspersed nonsensical ranting with biblical references and an insistence that she had been released two years earlier. As had been concluded following her outbursts at trial, prison staff categorized her behavior as nothing more than an artificial performance designed to help secure early release on compassionate grounds linked to the state of her health.[37] Yet as Koch's psychiatric state deteriorated further, this refrain, though continuously proffered by prison staff, grew increasingly implausible. By 1963, Koch's delusions had grown progressively more bizarre, paranoid, and all-encompassing. She was tormented by voices and began to write nonsensical letters to her children and to her dead mother and brother explaining that she was engaged to a fictional fiancé named "Erich Prinz von Brenhoff," whom she asked Artwin and Gisela to refer to as "daddy." She signed his name beside hers on letters and prison documents, and at times referred to herself as "Kunterbunt" (literally "motley"), the imaginary and colorful pen name of the published author that she had come to believe she was. Further indicating Koch's state of psychiatric decline was her increasingly frequent refusal to eat or to wash, as well as newfound compulsions to urinate and defecate on her bed and sometimes on her food, to expose herself to prison staff, and to masturbate in common areas in view of other inmates.[38]

That Koch's descent into mental illness was not merely a farfetched strategy for clemency is evidenced by the increasingly disturbing nature of her delusions that would have reinforced, rather than challenged, the worst perceptions of her crimes and alleged sexual perversion. Koch became fixated in particular on an antisemitic sexual conspiracy involving her rape at the hands of vengeful Jews whom she believed state authorities allowed into her cell on a nightly basis. In July 1963, she penned an unhinged petition to the European Commission on Human Rights that typified the delusions that began to fill her letters to family members, to state authorities, and to "Mother Elisabeth" during this period. Referring to herself and to her imaginary fiancé, Brenhoff, she declared:

We have been subjected to a trial by a robotic sexual system, without consideration of the danger to our lives, the hygienic conditions, the danger of opium vapours, and transmissions from sexually diseased people, [and have been] helplessly subjected to a criminal gang of . . . rippers and lust-murderers that belong to a private anarchist enterprise. . . . We are tangled in a criminal system that is daily deforming our limbs and we are injected with external semen via unlawful sex; our urination is not our own.[39]

In a letter to Gisela that October, Koch insisted that Jews were using radio devices and tapes to transmit demeaning messages to her brain. "Out of fear that such a Jewish pig could contaminate me sexually with his lustful, dirty semen," Koch wrote, "I am continuously working with a spoon handle in my vagina." (This practice was indeed confirmed by prison staff, leading to the confiscation of her cutlery.) "Since my imprisonment," Koch continued, "every Jew and former concentration camp inmate has the right to enter my cell and get off on me sexually. This is allowed by the German government!! If, in this struggle for justice and truth, I hadn't met and come to love Dr. Brenhoff, you would today be crying about a dead mommy."[40] Expressing similarly vulgar and paranoid sentiments in a letter to her son Artwin in November 1963, Koch counseled him to "renounce having children, because they would be contaminated with stinking Jewish semen and horrible spawn would be born."[41]

It is perhaps tempting to conclude that Koch's psychiatric delusions and warped compulsions reveal elements of her deeper nature and help to confirm the popular image of the allegedly sexually obsessed nymphomaniac who terrorized concentration camp prisoners in pursuit of perverse gratification. It is impossible, however, to determine the relationship between Koch's "authentic" self and the nature of the delusions and compulsions she developed during psychosis. While, based on her earlier letters, her antisemitism is beyond dispute, it is plausible that the manifestations of her psychosis may also reflect the internalization of the myriad, disturbing, and sometimes demonstrably false accusations that fueled her prosecution and that she spent nearly two decades denying. Koch's perverse delusions might, too, involve some channeling of the broader visual vocabulary associated with the Nazi gutter press; antisemitic publications such as *Der Stürmer* frequently and graphically depicted the alleged Jewish sexual "defilement" of Aryan women.[42]

Koch's madness, whatever its content reveals, appears to have peaked in 1964 and overlapped with news of her son's death. On January 23, Gisela wrote prison staff asking that they inform her mother that Artwin had committed suicide.[43] Though Gisela later remembered Artwin as having long struggled with depression and as having spoken of ending his life even as a child, prison officials believed it was "crystal clear that his suicide had resulted from the pressures of being his mother's son."[44] It appears that Koch's purported reaction to the news, recorded by Aichach staff, may have helped to spur a change of direction in the approach to her psychiatric state. On hearing of Artwin's suicide, resident physician Dr. J. S. Weilscher noted that, rather than expressing grief, "Koch appears happy." Though he continued to doubt the authenticity of her psychiatric delusions on the grounds that her behavior "could be interrupted" and because she knew "the time and place," Weilscher nonetheless now advised that it would be prudent to have Koch receive expert assessment.[45]

On April 24, 1964, Koch was transferred to the Psychiatric Hospital for Upper Bavaria. Reportedly aggressive and uncooperative upon arrival, Koch spent the first week force-fed and in restraints while staff administered injections that eventually made her more compliant. Koch emerged "silent and distrustful" at first, but gradually opened up to doctors' questions. She described the voices that tormented her and the paranoid sexual delusions previously expressed in her letters. Once medicated, Koch's doctors noted that she began to act more "po-

Fig. 7.1   A typical cell in Aichach women's prison. Alfred Haase / Süddeutsche Zeitung Photo.

litely," appeared free of delusion, and was reading regularly. Still arrogant in her behavior, Koch's self-understanding was described as stunted and "preadolescent," but her mental illness as authentic. The final diagnosis was "confinement psychosis," described not as "an organic psychosis, but one created by circumstance." Contrary to the conclusions previously drawn by prison staff, Koch's doctors insisted that her psychosis had "nothing to do with conscious and controlled simulation," but was instead "an abnormal psychological development ... and constitutes a real illness." Following three months of "intensive therapy," and with a new medication regime, Koch was deemed "completely recovered" and discharged back to Aichach at the end of July.[46]

Final Years

Following Koch's emergence from psychosis, her final few years were defined by a growing sense of hopelessness and depression, spurred in part by a chain of bitter disappointments. Less than a month following her discharge from psychiatric hospital, Koch filed another plea for clemency with the Bavarian Ministry of Justice. Striking a somewhat different tone than in petitions past, Koch appealed for release on compassionate grounds related to her health. "I am a person with mental illness," she wrote. "I will never lose my persecution complex because I am marked, and stand as evil in the eyes of the world."[47] Only two days later, Koch purportedly attempted suicide for the first time with a rudimentary noose she attached to her sewing machine. "I can't suffer this life behind bars," she wrote in a note to Gisela. "May God forgive me. I have been imprisoned innocently for twenty-one years.... In eternity we will see each other again."[48] How serious Koch was in her attempt is not clear, but she did not succeed. In the recommendation Aichach officials prepared for the Ministry of Justice in response to Koch's clemency plea, her attempt was categorized as an attention grab. Her lack of remorse and "tendency to blame the public and the press," the report concluded, made her petition unacceptable, no matter what the state of her health. "The time is not right to release the world-famous Ilse Koch."[49]

By the mid-1960s, it was growing increasingly clear that for all Koch's lack of contrition, the global notoriety of her case was an equally important obstacle standing in the way of her release—even at a time when almost all of the hundreds of war criminals condemned by Allied courts had since walked free. Particularly revealing was the official response to a 1965 petition for Koch's release filed by Princess von Isenburg and endorsed by federal prosecutor and member of parliament Dr. Max Güde. Güde's position at the time as Chairman of the Special Parliamentary Committee for Criminal Justice Reform lent weight to Isenburg's application. Moreover, Güde was thoroughly familiar with Koch's case, having previously acted as a member of the panel of judges that had rejected her 1951 appeal. Yet, now that Koch had spent more than twenty years in prison, Güde wrote in his appendage to Isenburg's application that "an impartial look at the evidence" in Koch's case would likely provide grounds for clemency, especially as the most "legendary" crimes attributed to her went unproven. "If you place her among the ranks of Nazi war criminals, many of whom were guilty but got off lightly," Güde argued, "one can conclude that she has atoned for her guilt."[50] Unconvinced, the Bavarian minister of justice, Hans Ehard, responded to Güde on July 22, 1965, declaring that he could not back clemency "neither now nor in the foreseeable future." While he agreed that Koch had indeed been convicted of a small fraction of the charges leveled against her, the life sentence handed down by the Augsburg court, he believed, remained appropriate. In an explicit reference to the pressures exerted on him to keep Koch behind bars, Ehard concluded that "public opinion wouldn't have any understanding that such an exponent of National Socialism's violent rule—who even today shows no trace of any insight or regret—should be released by an act of mercy."[51]

By 1966, Koch was increasingly convinced that state authorities had no intention of ever allowing her to leave Aichach alive. Yet her growing despondency at the prospect of living out the remainder of her life behind bars briefly abated with an unexpected occurrence that lifted Koch's spirits and redoubled her determination to join her fellow war crimes convicts in state-granted freedom. On December 15, 1966, Koch's estranged son, Uwe Köhler, born during her incarceration at Landsberg and immediately taken into foster care, reached out to his mother at Aichach after piecing together his true identity. As a child, Uwe later explained, he had managed to glimpse his birth certificate and had remembered the name "Koch." While studying in Ansbach many years later, he had stumbled across an article in a local paper

titled "No Pardon for Ilse Koch," that mentioned the birth of an il-
legitimate son that seemed to coincide with his birth in October 1947.[52]
In his introductory letter to his "dear mother," he explained that his
foster parents had confirmed his suspicions and informed him that
she was "still alive and in prison." Uwe limited his enthusiastic three-
page letter to providing the broad details of his life—the various places
he had lived in orphanages, that he was now nineteen and living alone
in a sublet, and that he was working as a technician for the realloca-
tion of agricultural land. His letter contained numerous questions, and
asked that his mother send him "an extended letter as soon as possible" that would fill in key details of his life including the identity of
his father, and any sisters or brothers he had. "I hope we will see each
other soon," he finished.[53]

Initially, Koch expressed uncharacteristic joy at her reconnection
with Uwe, whom she viewed as a sympathetic ear for her tales of guilt-
lessness and victimization. "I have been waiting for this for a long
time," she wrote in response to his letter. "My fate must have been
shocking to you," she continued, "but I can comfort you by telling
you that I am innocently imprisoned." To account for her predicament, she leaned on vague metaphor, reproducing for Uwe the same
poem originally sent to Gisela four years earlier, concerning the
"human being [who] fights in this earthly domain for truth and for
justice," and whom God vindicates in the end. Koch advised Uwe to
contact his half-sister, Gisela, informed him of his half-brother's recent suicide, and provided an unflattering and rather vague account
of his (unnamed) father, who had "pretended to be someone else" and
whom she had not seen since before Uwe's birth.[54]

Shortly before Christmas, Uwe, described by prison officials as "a
fresh and alert young man," paid his mother the first of a series of
visits.[55] Uwe quickly resolved to avoid discussions of his mother's past.
"She always denied her guilt and said she was the victim of libels, lies
and perjury," Uwe recalled of their conversations. "I didn't discuss it

with her because it was painful for her. I wanted that my mother would have the hope of getting out, and secondly, after two decades in prison, that she have other thoughts."[56] In an apologetic 1971 *New York Times* interview he hoped would help to rehabilitate his mother's name, he confessed that he "was not even sure she was guiltless." "But," he continued, "I have the feeling that she just slithered into the concentration camp world without being able to do anything about it."[57] For her part, Koch's experience of the "joyous reunion" with her son led to disappointment, with prison staff noting that she was "crestfallen" when he wrote her asking for money.[58] Nonetheless, he would continue to visit his mother regularly and correspond with her lawyers in the hopes of securing her release.

Last Appeal and Suicide

In April 1967, Munich lawyer Hans-Günther Pfitzner, recently retained by Koch to plead her case anew, submitted a final comprehensive clemency petition to the Bavarian Ministry of Justice. Fundamentally different in approach and tone than the combative and unrepentant appeals previously drawn up by Alfred Seidl, Pfitzner's application sought to win Koch parole by presenting her as a victim of circumstance. In reaching out to Pfitzner, Koch had presented herself as the blameless target of overzealous state authorities spurred to action by insidious and deceitful "propaganda."[59] Pfitzner's application, however, made no claim to innocence and conceded instead that, at Buchenwald, Koch "became a living part of the officially-sanctioned madness and the disregard for human life to the fullest extent." Falling back on misogynist stereotypes, now turned to Koch's advantage, Pfitzner sought to mitigate Koch's guilt by arguing that she had been naively swept up into a man's world that she was unequipped to navigate. "Lacking the calm guiding hand of her husband," he wrote of the period following Karl's 1941 transfer from Buchenwald, "she was fired up by her surroundings and her milieu." According to Pfitzner's narrative, a woman's purported natural instinct for maternal love existed alongside "tendencies to [violent] excess"—evidenced, he claimed improbably, by the fact that "soldiers during the Spanish Civil War pleaded not to fall into the hands of brigades of Amazon women." In possession of such violent tendencies and with few boundaries provided for her, Pfitzner concluded, "Koch, as a woman, was no doubt unable to cope with this situation." Accordingly, Pfitzner maintained, "the verdict today would have considered her female sex as a mitigating factor." Koch was now seeking only "to live out her final years in peace and quiet," and "will do everything in her power to show she is deserving of this mercy."[60]

Although Pfitzner's application faced long odds from the outset, it was Koch herself who ensured its failure. Koch complained bitterly to Pfitzner when she read the petition he had submitted on her behalf, insisting that it implicated her more than it exonerated her. "I want to tell them again and again," she demanded, "that I am innocent and perjury was committed!"[61] Determined to disavow the application, Koch wrote directly to the Ministry of Justice on May 19, asking that her release be considered not on the basis of what Pfitzner had written, but according to a reevaluation of the plea that Alfred Seidl had submitted in 1957. Erasing any hints of the contrition Pfitzner had implied on her behalf, she declared that those who had testified against her "will have to deal with their conscience and stand trial before heavenly God." Still wholly insisting on her innocence and victimhood, she contended that for her, "the death penalty would have been merciful," given the suffering endured over the course of the decades she had spent behind bars. "The fact that I have not put an end to my valueless life," she finished, "is only because my religious conviction prevents it."[62]

Despite Koch's criticism of Pfitzner, Bavarian Chief Public Prosecutor August Oechsner proceeded with an initial review of the application before recommending its rejection on June 21, 1967. Not surprisingly, Oechsner referred to what Koch herself had expressed to the Ministry of Justice, noting that, contrary to what Pfitzner had argued, Koch "does not see herself as guilty, but instead as a martyr to her circumstances."[63] Oechsner's recommendation was consistent with a strikingly forthright legal opinion he had provided that March regarding the potential for Koch's eventual release. According to Oechsner, whatever the virtues of the arguments submitted in support of clemency for Koch, setting her free "would send an unmistakable political signal with international consequences." The infeasibility of clemency, Oechsner explained, stemmed from the fact that "in the eyes of the world, the name of the commandeuse Ilse Koch is closely associated with the concentration camp system." Therefore, Oechsner concluded, "there is not a 'personal' Koch case, only a 'political' Koch case . . . but such is the fate of this woman."[64]

Oechsner clearly acknowledged what Bavarian judicial authorities had previously only implied: that Koch's continued incarceration following nearly twenty-four years behind bars was increasingly a political act more than a judicial one. Nonetheless, Oechsner believed that public opinion demanded it. Koch continued to be viewed as a woman who had acted outside the formal structures of Nazi power and who had deviated from "good, womanly sentiments" to inflict particularly perverse forms of violence.[65] As a result, Koch existed in a different category from other Nazi perpetrators whom the German public largely forgave for having "followed orders" in the course of their official duties. In the public eye, therefore, there was little irony or injustice in the fact that Koch remained in prison long after West Germany's popular clemency campaign had seen the release of almost all convicted Nazi war criminals by the mid-1950s.

The final decision on Pfitzner's still-pending plea for clemency lay with Bavarian Minister of Justice Philipp Held, who would consider Oechsner's recommendation, advice of the Augsburg court, and submissions from officials at Aichach concerning Koch's behavior and outlook. On August 7, Held invited Pfitzner to discuss Koch's case in person. Any optimism Pfitzner may have had that the invitation suggested a breakthrough in winning Koch's release, however, was quickly dashed as the meeting unfolded. Reporting to Koch a few days later, Pfitzner explained that during "detailed discussions" the minister made it known that the central obstacle to her release was the content of the letter she had addressed to the ministry on May 19. Pfitzner apprised Koch of the fact that, according to standing judicial practice, "insight into one's guilt and a readiness for atonement are preconditions for any clemency." With this in mind, Pfitzner advised Koch that the best way forward was to ask the minister to halt any further consideration of their current applications, and to reformulate a more coherent and unified petition that would contain the expressions of contrition that judicial authorities wished to see. In the meantime, Pfitzner implored Koch to fundamentally change the way she spoke of her past crimes and questions of her guilt, if she was serious about winning future release from prison.[66]

Only a week before her death, Koch penned Pfitzner an indignant response consistent with her prior proclamations of innocence and wholly deaf to strategic considerations. "Don't you think that this is a crime against humanity," she wrote, "to keep a German innocently imprisoned for twenty-four years, despite all legal and factual reasons that speak against this verdict? Do you think this is humane treatment?" Koch again insisted that she had neither inflicted nor ever been aware of cruelties at Buchenwald, and that her only guilt was that she failed "to stand up for the inmates." Drawing a parallel between her suffering and that of Buchenwald's prisoners, she continued: "But no one in this prison has ever expressed a word of empathy to me." In a particularly pointed expression of disdain for Buchenwald's survivors, she blamed her son Artwin's suicide on the alleged "constant heckling" he experienced from former inmates.[67]

Koch's letter, partly illegible, appears not to directly address whether she planned to pursue her lawyer's recommended strategy. If her intentions are only implied in it, however, a final letter written to her son Uwe on September 1, 1967, seems to confirm that she refused to court the idea of expressing contrition or relinquishing the vehement claims of innocence she had made for more than two decades. Death, she now implied, was the only alternative:

> My lawyer wrote that without an acknowledgement of guilt and a willingness to atone, I cannot be released. It's all madness, I'm innocent, I'm not to blame, it's all slander and perjury. Oh my boy, I'm tired of life, I want to die so that there will be peace at last. I don't want to write any more today.
>
> Your miserable mother.[68]

Sometime after eight o'clock the same evening, once prison staff had locked her in her cell for the night, Koch covered the peephole of her door with paper. Picking up her pencil once again, she scrawled out a brief note to Uwe: *Ich kann nicht anders. Der Tod ist für mich eine Erlösung.* (There is no other way. Death for me is a release.)[69] After climbing atop a stack of mattresses used to barricade the entryway, she fastened a noose constructed from a torn strip of bedsheet to a heating pipe eight feet from the floor and hanged herself.[70] It appears that, for all of the defeats that she had weathered in her quest for release over the preceding decades, it was Pfitzner's news that finally brought Koch to her breaking point. She could neither tolerate the prospect of living out the remainder of her years behind bars, nor conceive of pursuing release by confessing to a guilt she stubbornly refused to acknowledge.

Koch's body was discovered at 7:30 the following morning. As rigor mortis had already set in, no attempt to resuscitate her was made.[71] When Aichach officials announced her death that Saturday,

September 2, they were pressed to explain how her suicide could have occurred under prison supervision and why materials were so freely at her disposal. "Even in a penitentiary cell," Aichach chief administrator Schober explained, "there is still enough textile to fashion a noose, and hang oneself with it."[72] Officials insisted that, on the day of her death, Koch had worked her usual shift at her most current job in the prison library and had provided no indication that she was at risk of taking her own life. Despite her 1964 suicide attempt and the suicidal thoughts expressed in various letters that censors had intercepted over the years, Koch's death allegedly had come as a "complete surprise" to prison staff.[73] A more honest response to her death, perhaps, was provided by an unnamed Aichach guard quoted in *Newsweek*. Encapsulating what the article contended were the sentiments of the German public at large, the guard bid Koch good riddance and exclaimed that "it was a wonder that [Koch] had waited so long" to take her own life.[74]

Prison authorities informed Koch's children, Gisela and Uwe, of their mother's death in a curt telegram the morning her body was discovered: "IK dead; please inform us by Sunday at the latest if you intend to conduct a funeral."[75] Because nineteen-year-old Uwe presumably lacked the resources, and twenty-eight-year-old Gisela resolved not to return from vacation with her husband out of fear of confronting a press circus, prison authorities buried Koch in an unmarked grave in Aichach's cemetery on September 5, 1967.[76] Present were Uwe, two policeman, the mayor of the town of Aichach, the prison's two pastors, the graveyard manager and his wife, and a gravedigger. Despite Gisela's fears, the press was barred entry and prevented from photographing the funeral by a tall hedge that surrounded the small cemetery. According to *Newsweek*, Aichach Evangelical Lutheran Pastor Nauschütz offered a brief prayer over the grave. "We plead for mercy," he intoned. Struck by the moment, an unnamed onlooker reportedly remarked, "What else could he say?"[77]

Epilogue

Across Germany, newspapers presented Koch's suicide as the final act of the archetypical "excess" perpetrator, whose alleged sadism and depravity encapsulated Nazi barbarism. In terms both sensational and by then familiar, Koch was remembered variously as a "perverse, power-obsessed nymphomaniac demon," a "sadistic monster," a "tormenter and killer," and the architect of a "reign of terror" at Buchenwald of a "perverse and sadistic nature."[1] The fact that Koch had died while serving a life sentence for the lesser crimes of common assault and inciting others to violence and murder still had not completely registered in a country where reckoning with the Nazi past remained painful and slow. Koch's zealous prosecution had long been touted as evidence that the West German state was not "coddling fascists," but was instead dealing forcefully with the vestiges of Nazism. Yet as news reports on her suicide helped to illuminate, Koch also continued to provide an easy target of popular condemnation for a generation of Germans eager to distance themselves from the Nazi period and disinclined to acknowledge the broad complicity that brought the Third Reich to power.

Journalist and judicial specialist Gerhard Mauz, writing in *Der Spiegel* the week after Koch's suicide, provided a rare and prescient reflection on the role that her case played in Germany's ongoing struggle to come to terms with its past. Mauz underscored the degree to which Koch's popular denunciation was indicative of an everyday tendency of Germans to place responsibility for the crimes of the Third Reich at the feet of those "true culprits" accused of perverse and shocking atrocities during the Nazi period. To be sure, Mauz pointed out, Koch was no innocent victim, but this inclination served to inhibit reflection on how millions of ordinary citizens supported, enabled, and carried out Nazi policies without personally engaging in aberrant and monstrous acts of violence:

> In a world like the one under Hitler, Koch could . . . follow her predispositions. What made a world like the one under Hitler possible—by silence, by willful ignorance, and by following orders—is not discussed anymore. No one dares talk about collective guilt anymore. But it is not only the murderers who are guilty. The world in which an Ilse Koch could mistreat innocent people had a lot of authors. But Ilse Koch was surely not one of those authors. She did what was made possible for her, according to her predispositions. Ilse Koch hanged herself in Aichach a victim of her own guilt, but even more a victim of our collective will to pardon ourselves.[2]

Yet if Mauz recognized that Koch was more a symptom than a symbol of the institutionalized terror that defined the Third Reich, he provided little indication of the misogyny that helped to account for the potency and longevity of Koch's popular image as monster and deviant. Koch's crimes were depicted by jurists and observers alike as particularly worthy of condemnation expressly because they were committed by a woman. This fact helps to explain why Ilse Koch remained a household name in Germany and around the world, while her husband, Karl, and hundreds of other male perpetrators who had orchestrated or carried out mass murder at Buchenwald were largely forgotten. Ever since SS judge Konrad Morgen first charged Koch with a crime in 1943, legal authorities had implied that she bore a dual guilt as not only a perpetrator of violence and a violator of statutory law, but a strident and grotesque violator of established gender norms. At her SS, Dachau, and Augsburg trials, prosecutors had depicted Koch in court as an adulterous and sexually perverse miscreant who had failed in her prescribed role as mother and wife, rendering her, as US Chief Prosecutor William Denson argued, "no woman in the usual sense."[3]

And so, even as sensational charges concerning Koch's alleged collection of tattooed human skins went unproven, lesser crimes of violence were judged as egregious in part because they exposed an allegedly deviant femininity that drove Koch to enter a field of action broadly viewed as exclusive to men. The absence of any explicit reference to the gender of Koch's thirty male codefendants at the 1947 Buchenwald trial suggests that jurists viewed the connection between atrocity and masculinity either as irrelevant or as natural and self-evident.[4] Koch's violence, by contrast, was perceived to be particularly abhorrent because it revealed what her 1950 psychiatric assessment termed "a level of cruelty alien to female nature."[5] If male violence in the concentration camps could be rationalized as both natural and stemming from the obligations imposed on duty-bound men by the state, Koch was judged guilty in part because she was accused of having acted autonomously to commit atrocities in service of allegedly perverse and unwomanly impulses. As the US Senate Subcommittee that had investigated the commutation of Koch's first life sentence had declared in 1948, in light of her "being a woman" and acting independently, her perpetration of violence at Buchenwald had been "more unnatural and more deliberate."[6] That Koch was held to a standard of moral conduct not expected of men was made explicit in the 1951 judgment rendered by the Augsburg court. "The conditions reigning in

Buchenwald," the judges wrote, "should have evoked in her, being a woman, compassion and pity." Instead, Koch was "devoid of all feminine feeling," and deserving of the life sentence she had received.[7]

If the political and social function of Koch's prosecution and popular demonization was most evident in Germany, the cultural reverberations of the Koch case were most pronounced in the United States. Since US military authorities had first displayed human-skin objects to the press following the liberation of Buchenwald in 1945, the image of Koch's notorious lampshade permeated American popular culture. Even among the most senior Nazi war criminals, few received as much coverage in American newspapers as Koch, whose alleged crimes featured in no less than ninety-two stories in the *New York Times* alone between 1947 and 1952.[8] The tendency of such press reportage to focus on unproven claims, including the allegation that Koch had had inmates killed so that lampshades could be fashioned from their skins, took on a life of its own in American popular culture in the course of the two decades that followed Koch's arrest: Woody Guthrie lamented the commutation of Koch's initial life sentence in his 1948 protest song "Ilsa Koch," in part by referring to "lampshades made from skin"; one of the characters in *Exodus*, Leon Uris's 1958 best-selling novel, is traumatized by stories of Ilse Koch, "who won infamy by making lampshades out of tattooed human skins"; Sylvia Plath's heralded 1962 poem "Lady Lazarus" provides a meditation on the poet's suicidal thoughts that describes her skin as "bright as a Nazi lampshade" and her face as "a featureless, fine Jew linen."[9]

Even as they reported on Koch's death in 1967, long after courts of law had concluded that the lampshade charge was without merit, major American newspapers described her as having arranged the deaths of tattooed prisoners to collect their skins for the production of such objects. While Germany's national newspapers indicated that these allegations had never been proven in court, the *New York Times* remembered Koch as "one of the most notorious Nazi war criminals," and a woman who "had a collection of lampshades made from tattooed human skin." The *Washington Post* similarly passed off this spurious claim as fact, referring to Koch as the "Bitch of Buchenwald, who made lampshades from human skin."[10] In perpetuating this most diabolical and ultimately ahistorical depiction of Koch, such newspapers provided readers with an image of concentration camp crimes that required no reckoning with the reality that, rather than monstrous caricatures, most Nazi perpetrators had been "ordinary" human beings who were nonetheless capable of perpetrating genocide. By focusing on crimes unrepresentative of the systematic and bureaucratized mass murder that defined the Third Reich, the extensive American reportage on Koch therefore fundamentally distorted popular perceptions of Nazi criminality.

Beyond simply skewing historical understanding, American newspapers also helped to spawn a voyeuristic fascination with the lurid sexual behavior that many of them attributed to Koch—and did not hesitate to describe in detail. Since Koch's first appearance on the stand at Dachau in 1947, the American press in particular had coupled descriptions of her alleged crimes with expressly sexual descriptions of her looks. In contrast to comparatively conservative reporting in Germany, American papers described Koch as a "blousy creature" with a "voluptuous body" and "bare legs," a "too-prominent derriere" and a "conspicuous bust."[11] Even as it reported Koch's death in 1967, the *New York Times* summoned the image of "a plump woman with vivid green eyes and flaming red hair." As it had done in the past, the paper presented Koch's crimes as explicitly sexual in nature, and reported erroneously that she had required "prisoners to participate in orgies involving sadism and degeneracy."[12] In a similar fashion, the *Washington Post* reached beyond the evidentiary record produced by Koch's three trials to remember her speciously as having "sexually excited inmates" by "striding through the camp in tight riding breeches" and then "removing her blouse."[13] Though she had been tried neither for sexual crimes nor for murder, *Newsweek* eulogized Koch as a "nymphomaniac" and "mass murderess."[14]

In Germany, allegations of sexual deviance had functioned to demonize Koch as reprobate female while serving to reinforce conservative norms of 'good womanly behavior.' In the United States, however, an emphasis on the alleged sexual nature of Koch's crimes served also to fuel a disturbing and popular interest in Koch as a figure of eroticism and sexual domination. In 1971, Ophelia Press, noted as the first publisher of controversial works including William S. Burrough's *Naked Lunch* and Henry Miller's *The Rosy Crucifixion*, published Joseph Como's *Bitch of Buchenwald: The Sex Life of Ilse Koch*. This fictional account of Koch's allegedly violent sexual exploits drew directly upon the content of American newspaper reports and expressly utilized the language they contained. Designed to stimulate readers with explicit sexual content and images of diabolical torture and murder, the book begins:

> Ilse Koch was, first and foremost, a nymphomaniac.... She has been called *The Witch*, but her physical appearance was anything but ugly. With the sensational looks of a German cinema star, she had flaming red hair, emerald-green eyes, and a schoolgirl complexion. Her derriere was prominent and her over-large bust was conspicuous. She was the Nazi glamour girl, the symbol of Teutonic sex appeal. Whatever is said about her—her sexual excesses, her striving for evil power, her barbaric treatment of the prisoners at Buchenwald—she was female.... Ilse Koch solved life's problems by first titillating and then emptying male seminal ducts.[15]

In the wake of Como's book came the 1975 pornographic cult film *Ilsa, She Wolf of the SS*. Shot on the abandoned set of *Hogan's Heroes* and starring the often-nude Dyanne Thorne, the film also directly drew upon popular reportage of the most perverse crimes attributed to Ilse

Fig. 8.1   US theatrical release poster for *Ilsa, She Wolf of the SS*, 1975. Wikipedia.

Koch, and started with a preamble that claimed that the film was "based upon documented fact."[16] Combining graphic images of sadism, sexual bondage and murder, the film portrays Ilsa attempting to satisfy her supposedly insatiable sexual appetites with camp inmates whom she subsequently tortures and kills. Though the film was designed to shock and arouse its audience in the service of a quick profit, it became a surprise success at the box office, pulling in more than ten million dollars and earning a spot on *Variety's* list of the top-grossing fifty films.[17] Although banned in Germany, *Ilsa, She Wolf of the SS* ultimately screened in seventeen countries and spawned three equally lurid sequels.[18]

As the success of *Ilsa, She Wolf of the SS* helps to demonstrate, the predominance and persistence of the popular image of the demonic and highly sexualized "Bitch of Buchenwald" must be viewed as the product not only of a desire to condemn a woman frequently depicted as having committed some of history's most shocking crimes, but as indicative of a popular fascination with the sadistic violence and sexual domination that Koch was alleged to have practiced. That newspaper readers first consumed the sensationalized coverage of Koch's trials in a prudish and sexually repressed postwar America served to make the oft-described sexual dimensions of Koch's violent crimes appear not only more revolting, but for some readers, more rousing and more intriguing.

In the twenty-first century, this cultural phenomenon persists, as does the exploitation of Koch's most shocking alleged crimes for their apparent entertainment value. The 2001 television documentary series *The Most Evil Men and Women in History* summoned the apocryphal claims of sadomasochism and human-skin lampshades to place Ilse Koch in the company of Genghis Kahn, Attila the Hun, Caligula, Count Dracula, Joseph Stalin, and Adolf Hitler.[19] When ninety-five-year-old former Stutthof concentration camp secretary Irmgard Furchner was arrested in February 2021 and charged with "aiding and abetting murder in more than 10,000 cases," Ilse Koch's alleged lampshades again made headlines seventy years after the Augsburg court had dismissed this charge.[20] Capitalizing on interest in Furchner's case, British tabloid *The Sun* published an (a)historical exposé on female concentration camp perpetrators the week following her arrest titled "War 'Witches,'" featuring Ilse Koch, "who made lampshades out of human skin" and who allegedly forced prisoners "to have sex with her."[21] In a similar fashion, the *Daily Star* published an equally lurid and spurious report on Koch the following day, titled "Inside life of female Nazi prison camp guard who made lampshades out of human skin."[22]

In the end, Ilse Koch's story does not permit tidy conclusions. The degree to which her misdeeds have been misrepresented and mythologized over time reveals the limitations of court judgments in establishing dominant narratives of historically significant crimes. The still-pervasive myth of Koch's human-skin lampshades illustrates that the judgment of the public and the press were as formative as the judgment of the courts in generating the enduring image of the "Bitch of Buchenwald." Ilse Koch's legal odyssey and its reception, therefore, tell us as much about postwar perceptions of Nazi criminality and complicity as they do about the individual atrocities for which Koch stood accused.

The wealth of evidence and survivor testimony compiled by both American and German jurists firmly establishes that Koch was not only morally and ideologically complicit in the crimes that occurred at Buchenwald, but an active instigator and perpetrator of violence. While sympathy for Koch would be misplaced, her trials nonetheless betray the extent to which her particularly zealous prosecution and disproportionality lengthy incarceration resulted from social and political pressures that inhibited the dispensation of an impartial justice. The outrage and intrigue generated by reports of Koch's alleged predilection for tattooed human skins and perverse sexual behaviors ironically transformed a woman without rank in the Nazi state into the personification of its most violent excesses. In turn, American and German authorities alike came to view Koch's punishment as an effective shorthand for the communication of an alleged resoluteness to hold Nazi war criminals to account. As Bavarian Chief Prosecutor August Oechsner had conceded in 1967, "there is not a 'personal' Koch case, only a 'political' Koch case . . . but such is the fate of this woman."[23]

Abbreviations

BayHStA   Bayerisches Hauptstaatsarchiv (Bavarian Main State Archive), Munich

BwA   Buchenwald Archive

Denson Papers   William Dowdell Denson Papers, Manuscript Group 1382, Manuscripts and Archives, Yale University Library

IFZ   Institut für Zeitgeschichte, (Institute for Contemporary History), Munich

NARA   National Archives and Records Administration, College Park, MD

StAA   Staatsarchiv Augsburg (Augsburg State Archive)

StAM   Staatsarchiv München (Munich State Archive)

USHMM   Archives of the United States Holocaust Memorial Museum, Washington, DC.

Notes

Introduction

1. Ilse Koch, note to son Uwe, September 1, 1967, StAM, Justizvollzug-sanstalten 13948 / 2.

2. "Best Years of Her Life," *Newsweek*, September 18, 1967, 51.

3. On the question of Allied and popular perceptions of German women as perpetrators of atrocity, see Christina Herkommer, "Women under National Socialism: Women's Scope for Action and the Issue of Gender," in *Ordinary People as Mass Murderers: Perpetrators in Comparative Perspective*, ed. Olaf Jensen and Claus-Christian W. Szejnmann (New York: Palgrave MacMillan, 2008); Susannah Heschel, "Does Atrocity Have a Gender?" in *Lessons and Legacies*, vol. 6: *New Currents in Holocaust Research*, ed. Jeffry M. Diefendorf (Evanston, IL: Northwestern University Press, 2004); Wendy Lower, *Hitler's Furies: German Women in the Nazi Killing Fields* (New York: Houghton Mifflin Harcourt, 2013); Alette Smeulers, "Female Perpetrators: Ordinary or Extra-Ordinary Women?" *International Criminal Law Review* 15, no. 2 (2015): 207–253.

4. No women were tried by the International Military Tribunal at Nuremberg; of the 185 defendants the United States tried during the subsequent Nuremberg proceedings, two were women; of the 1,672 war crimes defendants tried by American military commission courts, fourteen were women. The largest single group of female defendants appeared at the Belsen trial, conducted as part of the British Royal Warrant trial program. Smaller groups of female defendants also appeared at a series of British trials of Ravensbrück concentration camp personnel. For statistics on the US military trial program, see Lisa

Yavnai, "Military Justice: The U.S. Army War Crimes Trials in Germany, 1944–1947" (PhD diss., London School of Economics and Political Science, 2007); for the British Royal Warrant Trials, see Beth A. Healey, "Nazi Crimes, British Justice: The Royal Warrant War Crimes Trials in British-Occupied Germany, 1945–1949" (PhD diss., Northwestern University, 2017).

5. For an exploration of the role of women in Nazi crimes, see, for instance, Irmtraud Heike, "Female Concentration Camp Guards as Perpetrators: Three Cases Studies," in *Ordinary People as Mass Murderers: Perpetrators in Comparative Perspective*, ed. Olaf Jensen and Claus-Christian W. Szejnmann (New York: Palgrave MacMillan, 2008); Herkommer, "Women under National Socialism"; Heschel, "Does Atrocity Have a Gender?"; Lower, *Hitler's Furies*.

6. Lower, *Hitler's Furies*, 166; Gudrun Schwarz, *Eine Frau an seiner Seite: Ehefrauen in der "SS- Sippengemeinschaft"* (Berlin: Aufbau Taschenbuch, 1997).

7. William D. Denson, "Frau Ilse Koch a Sadist from Some Other Tortured World, Prosecutor Says; Assails Cut in Her Sentence," *St. Louis Post-Dispatch*, September 26, 1948.

8. Herkommer, "Women under National Socialism," 114; Heschel, "Does Atrocity Have a Gender?" 304.

9. See Alexandra Przyrembel, "Transfixed by an Image: Ilse Koch, the 'Kommandeuse of Buchenwald,'" *German History* 19, no. 3 (2001): 369–399, for a discussion of Koch's representation as a sexualized "robot of cruelty."

10. Heschel, "Does Atrocity Have a Gender?" 310–311.

11. Dr. Ehard, Bayer, Staatsminister der Justiz, an Herrn Bundestagsabgeordneten Dr. Max Güde, July 22, 1965, StAM, Justizvollzugsanstalten 13948 / 5.

1. Ilse Koch and the World of the Concentration Camps

1. Interrogation of Ilse Koch, Ludwigsburg, June 16, 1945, NARA, RG 549, War Crimes Case Files, Cases Tried, box 440, p. 1; Konrad Morgen, *Wesentliches Ermittlungsergebnis, Buchenwald, 11. April 1944*, StAM, Justizvollzugsanstalten 13948 / 2, 36–40.

2. Urteil des Landgerichts Augsburg im Fall Ilse Koch, January 15, 1951, in *Justiz und NS-Verbrechen: Sammlung Deutscher Strafurteile wegen Nationalsozialistischer Tötungsverbrechen 1945–1966*, 16 vols. (Amsterdam: University Press Amsterdam, 1972), vol. 8, 40.

3. During the period 1925–1932, only 7.8% of NSDAP members were women. See Alexandra Przyrembel, "Transfixed by an Image: Ilse Koch, the 'Kommandeuse' of Buchenwald," *German History* 19, no. 3 (2001): 369–399, 377.

4. SS Fragebogen, StAA, Staatsanwaltschaft Augsburg, KS 22 / 50, box 1; Arthur L. Smith, Jr., *Die Hexe von Buchenwald* (Weimar: Böhlau, 1995), 7–8.

5. Personal photographs of Frau Ilse Koch, 1912–1941, NARA, RG 153-IK, Records of the Judge Advocate General (Army), box 1; Smith, *Die Hexe von Buchenwald*, 9.

6. Tom Segev, "The Commanders of the Nazi Concentration Camps" (PhD diss., Boston University, 1977), 180.

7. Karl Otto Koch, *Mein Tagebüch ab 9. Januar 1917*, collection of the author. A copy is in the United States Holocaust Memorial Museum, Washington, DC, accession no. 2014.561.1.

8. Morgen, *Wesentliches Ermittlungsergebnis*, 2–3.

9. Morgen, *Wesentliches Ermittlungsergebnis*, 3; Insa Eschebach, "Der KZ-Kommandant Karl Otto Koch (1897–1945)," in Günter Morsch, ed., *Von der Sachsenburg nach Sachsenhausen: Bilder aus dem Fotoalbum eines KZ-Kommandanten* (Berlin: Metropol, 2007), 51. The latter is available in English. See Günter Morsch, ed., *From Sachsenburg to Sachsenhausen: Pictures from the Photograph Album of a Concentration Camp Commandant*, trans. Catherine Hales and Sorcha O'Hagen (Berlin: Metropol, 2007).

10. Morgen, *Wesentliches Ermittlungsergebnis*, 3.

11. Karl Otto Koch, Personal-Bericht und Beurteilung, August 4, 1934, StAA, Staatsanwaltschaft Augsburg, KS 22 / 50, box 7; Smith, *Die Hexe von Buchenwald*, 9.

12. Dienstlaufbahn des Karl Otto Koch, NARA, Holdings of the Berlin Document Center, SS Officer Personnel Files, Roll Number A3343 SSO-190A.

13. For brief histories of the camps at which Karl Koch was posted, see Morsch, *Von der Sachsenburg nach Sachsenhausen*.

14. Eschebach, "Der KZ-Kommandant Karl Otto Koch," 52.

15. Nikolaus Wachsmann, *KL: A History of the Nazi Concentration Camps* (New York: Farrar, Straus and Giroux, 2015), 628.

16. Reichsführer SS, SS Command–A–No. 65, "Marriage and Engagement Order," December 31, 1931, German History in Documents and Images, vol. 7: Nazi Germany, 1933–1945, http://www.germanhistorydocs.ghi-dc.org/pdf/eng /English14.pdf. See also Gudrun Schwarz on the SS-Sippengemeinschaft or kinship community. Gudrun Schwarz, *Eine Frau an seiner Seite—Ehefrauen in der "SS-Sippengemeinschaft"* (Hamburg: Hamburg Edition, 1997).

17. Smith, *Die Hexe von Buchenwald*, 7.

18. Vernehmungsniederschrift von Ilse Koch, Landsberg, April 29, 1949, StAA, Staatsanwaltschaft Augsburg, KS 22 / 50, 7.

19. Personal photographs of Frau Ilse Koch.

20. "Lady Mit Lampenschirm," *Der Spiegel*, February 16, 1950, 12.

21. See, for instance, Mark Jacobson, *The Lampshade: A Holocaust Detective Story from Buchenwald to New Orleans* (New York: Simon and Schuster, 2010), 15; Katharina von Kellenbach, *The Mark of Cain: Guilt and Denial in the Post-War Lives of Nazi Perpetrators* (New York: Oxford University Press, 2013); Mark Drumbl and Solange Mouthaan, "'A Hussy Who Rode on Horseback in Sexy Underwear in Front of the Prisoners': The Trials of Buchenwald's Ilse Koch," *International Criminal Law Review* 21, no. 2 (2021): 280–312, 283.

22. Anklageschrift im Mordverfahren gegen Koch, Ilse, 1950, in English translation, NARA, Record Group 549, War Crimes Case Files,—Cases Tried, box 436, 62.

23. Karl Otto Koch, Personal-Nachwies für Führer der Waffen-SS, NARA, Holdings of the Berlin Document Center, SS Officer Personnel Files, Roll Number A3343 SSO-190A.

24. Christian Herkommer, "Women under National Socialism: Women's Scope for Action and the Issue of Gender," in *Ordinary People as Mass Murderers*, ed. Olaf Jensen and Claus-Christian W. Szejnmann (New York: Palgrave Macmillan, 2008), 99.

25. See, for instance, Schwarz, *Eine Frau an seiner Seite;* Claudia Koonz, *Mothers in the Fatherland* (New York: St. Martin's, 1987).

26. See Wendy Lower, *Hitler's Furies: German Women in the Nazi Killing Fields* (New York: Houghton Mifflin Harcourt, 2013); also Schwarz, *Eine Frau an seiner Seite.*

27. Paul Jaskot, *Architecture of Oppression: SS Forced Labor and Nazi Monumental Building Economy* (London: Routledge, 1999), 11.

28. Jaskot, *Architecture of Oppression*, 20; Evelyn Zegenhagen, "Buchenwald Main Camp," trans. Stephen Pallavicini, *Encyclopedia of Camps and Ghettos, 1933–1945*, vol. 1, ed. Geoffrey P. Megargee (Indianapolis: Indiana University Press, 2009), 290.

29. For a detailed study of the relationship between Nazi extermination and economic / slave labor policies, see Wachsmann, *KL*, 392–427.

30. Zegenhagen, "Buchenwald Main Camp," 290.

31. *Buchenwald Concentration Camp, 1937–1945*, ed. Gedenkstätte Buchenwald, compiled by Harry Stein, trans. Judith Rosenthal (Göttingen: Wallstein, 2004), 35.

32. *Buchenwald Concentration Camp, 1937–1945*, 35.

33. Zegenhagen, "Buchenwald Main Camp," 291.

34. *Buchenwald Concentration Camp, 1937–1945*, 176–179.

35. See Benjamin Carter Hett, *Burning the Reichstag* (Oxford: Oxford University Press, 2014).

36. Jaskot, *Architecture of Oppression*, 20.

37. *Buchenwald Concentration Camp, 1937–1945,* 30–31.

38. *The Buchenwald Report,* trans., ed., and intro. by David A. Hackett (Boulder, CO: Westview Press, 1995), 109.

39. Reichsführer-SS Heinrich Himmler to the Surgeon-General of the SS and Police, Subject: Testing of a Typhus Vaccine, Oranienburg, February 14, 1944, NARA RG 549, War Crimes Case Files,—Cases Tried, box 437; Reichsführer-SS Heinrich Himmler to SS-Major Dr. Varnet, Subject: Hormone Research, Berlin, July 15, 1944, NARA RG 549, War Crimes Case Files, Cases Tried, box 437.

40. Zegenhagen, "Buchenwald Main Camp," 293.

41. Aussage von Martin Sommer, 1967, IFZ, Akz. 4118 / 68, 5.

42. Franz Eichhorn, "Barber to the Commandant," in *Buchenwald Report,* 123.

43. Eugen Kogon, *The Theory and Practice of Hell,* rev. ed. (New York: Farrar, Straus and Giroux, 2006), 102.

44. Morgen, *Wesentliches Ermittlungsergebnis,* 51; Wachsmann, *KL,* 220.

45. Morgen, *Wesentliches Ermittlungsergebnis,* 50.

46. Kogon, *Theory and Practice of Hell,* 101–102.

47. *Buchenwald Report,* 40–41; Gisela Koch, interview with author, May 24, 2015. To protect her identity, I have agreed to use Gisela's maiden name.

48. Morgen, *Wesentliches Ermittlungsergebnis,* 20–22.

49. *Buchenwald Report,* 62.

50. Eichhorn, "Barber to the Commandant," 122.

51. For a full exploration of Koch's collusion with Meiners, see Morgen, *Wesentliches Ermittlungsergebnis,* 26–30.

52. Morgen, *Wesentliches Ermittlungsergebnis,* 10; Eichhorn, "Barber to the Commandant," 123–124.

53. Wachsmann, *KL,* 197.

54. Wachsmann, *KL,* 197.

55. Eichhorn, "Barber to the Commandant," 122.

56. *Buchenwald Report,* 44.

57. For numerous photographs of the exterior and interior of the Koch villa, see Ilse Koch's Personal Album # 2, NARA RG 153-IK, Records of the Judge Advocate General (Army), box 1.

58. Ilse Koch's Personal Album # 2.

59. See, for instance, the testimony of Kurt Titz, in *The United States v. Josias Prince zu Waldeck, et al.*, Case no. 000-50-9, Denson Papers, Series II—Trials, 1945–2001, boxes 17–22 (5718 pages), 1235–1274.

60. Kogon, *Theory and Practice of Hell*, 42.

61. Vernehmungsniederschrift von Ilse Koch, April 29, 1949, 12; Przyrembel, "Transfixed by an Image," 378.

62. Emil E. Carlebach, Witness Statement, StAA, Staatsanwaltschaft Augsburg, KS 22 / 50, box 1, folder 1.

63. Anklageschrift im Mordverfahren gegen Koch, Ilse, 88.

64. Smith, *Die Hexe von Buchenwald*, 58.

65. *US v. Waldeck et al.*, 1384.

66. Morgen, *Wesentliches Ermittlungsergebnis*, 43.

67. *US v. Waldeck et al.*, 2971–2975.

68. For more on the dynamics of Nazi family life in genocidal contexts, see Lower, *Hitler's Furies*, 162–165.

69. Vernehmungsniederschrift von Erna Raible, May 3, 1949, StAA, Staatsanwaltschaft Augsburg, KS 22 / 50, 2.

2. Corruption, Murder, and the SS Trial of Ilse and Karl Koch

1. *The United States v. Josias Prince zu Waldeck, et al.*, Case no. 000-50-9, Denson Papers, Series II: Trials, 1945–2001, boxes 17–22 (5718 pages), 5286.

2. Jonathan Petropoulos, *Royals and the Reich* (New York: Oxford University Press, 2008), 120.

3. Petropoulos, *Royals*, 262–263.

4. *US v. Waldeck et al.*, 5297, 2748; Eugen Kogon, *The Theory and Practice of Hell* (New York: Farrar, Straus, and Giroux, 1950), 289.

5. *US v. Waldeck et al.*, 5220.

6. *US v. Waldeck et al.*, 5296.

7. *US v. Waldeck et al.*, 5296.

8. *US v. Waldeck et al.*, 5296.

9. *US v. Waldeck et al.*, 2831.

10. *US v. Waldeck et al.*, 2831.

11. *US v. Waldeck et al.*, 3738–3739.

12. Konrad Morgen, *Wesentliches Ermittlungsergebnis, Buchenwald, 11. April 1944*, StAM, Justizvollzugsanstalten 13948 / 2, 39–42.

13. Morgen, *Wesentliches Ermittlungsergebnis*, 39–42.

14. Morgen, *Wesentliches Ermittlungsergebnis*, 39, 44; Anklageschrift im Mordver-fahren gegen Koch, Ilse, 1950, in English translation, NARA, RG 549, War Crimes Case Files, Cases Tried, box 436.

15. Karl Otto Koch, Personal Bericht, NARA, Holdings of the Berlin Docu-ment Center, SS Officer Personnel Files, roll number A3343 SSO-190A.

16. *US v. Waldeck et al.*, 2744; Dr. Werner Paulmann, Affidavit SS-64, July 11, 1946, *The Trial of the Major War Criminals before the International Military Tribunal at Nuremberg*, vol. 42, 543–550.

17. *US v. Waldeck et al.*, 2865.

18. Arthur L. Smith, Jr., *Die Hexe von Buchenwald* (Weimar: Böhlau, 1995), 71.

19. Dienstlaufbahn des Karl Otto Koch, NARA, Holdings of the Berlin Doc-ument Center, SS Officer Personnel Files, roll number A3343 SSO-190A.

20. *US v. Waldeck et al.*, 2745; see also the Nuremberg testimony of Günther Reinecke, Chief Judge of the Supreme SS and Police Court, *The Trial of the Major War Criminals before the International Military Tribunal at Nuremberg*, vol. 20, 439.

21. Elizabeth White, "Lublin Main Camp (aka Majdanek)," in *Encyclopedia of Camps and Ghettos 1933–1945*, ed. Geoffrey P. Megargee, vol. 1 (Bloomington: In-diana University Press, 2009), vol. 1, 876.

22. White, "Lublin Main Camp (aka Majdanek)," *Encyclopedia of Camps and Ghettos*, 1: 879.

23. SS-Hauptsturmführer Hackmann, an das SS-Wirtschafts-Verwaltung-shauptamt, Amtsgruppe D—Konzentrationslager, 15. July 1942, Betr. Massenaus-bruch sowjetischer Kriegsgefangener, 15. July 1942, Betr. Massenausbruch sowjetischer Kriegsgefangener, NARA, Holdings of the Berlin Document Center, SS Officer Personnel Files, roll number A3343 SSO-190A.

24. SS-und Polizei Gericht Berlin III, Einstellungsverfügung—Das Ermitt-lungsverfahren gegen Den SS-Standartenführer Karl Koch, 17. February 1943, NARA, Holdings of the Berlin Document Center, SS Officer Personnel Files, roll number A3343 SSO-190A; SS-und Polizei Gericht Berlin III, Telefongespräch mit SS-Stormbannführer Schmidt-Klevenow, betr. Ermittlungsverfahren gegen Den SS-Standartenführer Koch wegen fahrlässiger Gefangenenbefreiung und evtl. fahrl. Dienstpflichtverletzung, 22.10.1942, NARA, Holdings of the Berlin Document Center, SS Officer Personnel Files, roll number A3343 SSO-190A.

25. Der Reichsführer-SS, Persönlicher Stab, an den Chef des SS-Personal-hauptamtes, Berlin, den 25.7.1942, StAA, Staatsanwaltschaft Augsburg, KS 22 / 50, box 7.

26. SS-und Polizei Gericht Berlin III, Einstellungsverfügung.

27. SS-und Polizei Gericht Berlin III, Einstellungsverfügung.

28. Gerichts SS-Führer, den 7.6.1943, Betr. Strafsache gegen den SS-Standarten-führer Koch, an den Amtsgruppenchef D SS-Brigadeführer Glücks, NARA, Holdings of the Berlin Document Center, SS Officer Personnel Files, roll number A3343 SSO-190A.

29. Kogon, *Theory and Practice*, 290; see also *US v. Waldeck et al.*, 5223.

30. *US v. Waldeck et al.*, 5296.

31. See the following accounts of this incident: Kogon, *Theory and Practice*, 290; Konrad Morgen in *US v. Waldeck et al.*, 2752; Paulmann, Affidavit SS-64; Franz Eichhorn, "Barber to the Commandant," in *The Buchenwald Report*, ed. David A. Hackett (Boulder, CO: Westview Press, 1995), 123–124; Stefan Heymann, "The Trial of Koch," in *The Buchenwald Report*, 341.

32. Anklageschrift im Mordverfahren gegen Koch, Ilse, 50; Anke Schmeling, *Josias Erbprinz zu Waldeck und Pyrmont: Der politische Weg eines hohen SS-Führers* (Kassel: Gesamthochschul-Bibliothek, 1993), 96.

33. *US v. Waldeck et al.*, 5296.

34. *US v. Waldeck et al.*, 5296.

35. Nikolaus Wachsmann, *KL: A History of the Nazi Concentration Camps* (New York: Farrar, Straus and Giroux, 2015), 383–384.

36. Wachsmann, *KL*, 384; Smith, *Die Hexe von Buchenwald*, 76.

37. Heinrich Himmler, "Speech at Posen, October 4, 1943," in *Nazism: A Documentary Reader, 1919–1945*, vol. 3: *Foreign Policy, War and Racial Extermination*, ed. J. Noakes and G. Pridham (Exeter: University of Exeter Press, 2001), 617–618. See also Wachsmann, *KL*, 376.

38. Interrogation of Konrad Morgen, September 19, 1946, NARA, RG 238, War Crimes Records Collection, Records of the US Nuernberg War Crimes Trials Interrogations, 1946–1949, M 1019–47, 2–3.

39. See Konrad Morgen, Testimony before the International Military Tribunal at Nuremberg, August 6, 1946, *The Trial of the Major War Criminals before the International Military Tribunal at Nuremberg*, 20: 505; Interrogation of Konrad Morgen, September 4, 1946, NARA, RG 238, War Crimes Records Collection, Records of the US Nuernberg War Crimes Trials Interrogations, 1946–1949, M 1019–47, 8; Wachsmann, *KL*, 386.

40. For studies of Konrad Morgen, see James J. Weingartner, "Law and Justice in the Nazi SS: The Case of Conrad Morgen," *Central European History* 16, no. 3 (1983): 276–294; and Herlinde Pauer-Studer and J. David Velleman,

Konrad Morgen: The Conscience of a Nazi Judge (New York: Palgrave Macmillan, 2015).

41. Pauer-Studer and Velleman, *Conscience*, 43; Weingartner, "Law and Justice,"284.

42. Morgen himself makes the claim that he was demoted for a ruling in favor of the defendant in a "race defilement" case, but there is no evidence for this. See *US v. Waldeck et al.*, 2738.

43. Morgen Interrogation, September 4, 1946, 5.

44. Translation of Konrad Morgen's Statement, Oberursel, December 28, 1945 NARA, RG 549, War Crimes Case Files - Cases Tried, Box 440, 2.

45. Morgen, *Wesentliches Ermittlungsergebnis*, 4.

46. Morgen Interrogation, September 4, 1946, 10.

47. Morgen, *Wesentliches Ermittlungsergebnis*, 1.

48. SS-Reichsführer Himmler to Gruppenführer Burger, Chef des SS-Hauptamtes, March 12, 1943, StAA, Staatsanwaltschaft Augsburg, KS 22 / 50, box 7.

49. Morgen Interrogation, September 4, 1946, 11.

50. Interrogation of Konrad Morgen, January 18, 1947, NARA, RG 238, War Crimes Records Collection, Records of the US Nuernberg War Crimes Trials Interrogations, 1946–1949, M 1019–47, 2.

51. Translation of Morgen's Statement, December 28, 1945, 2.

52. Translation of Morgen's Statement, December 28, 1945, 3.

53. Translation of Morgen's Statement, December 28, 1945, 3.

54. See, for instance, the testimony of Prince Josias of Waldeck and Heinrich Nett in *US v. Waldeck et al.*, as well as Paulmann, Affidavit SS-64.

55. Translation of Morgen's Statement, December 28, 1945, 3.

56. Morgen, *Testimony before the International Military Tribunal*, 20: 509. In his biography of Hitler, John Toland appears to have fallen for Morgen's self-serving postwar claims, describing how Morgen spent the war engaged in a "lonesome attempt to end the Final Solution." John Toland, *Hitler* (Garden City, NY: Doubleday, 1976), 774.

57. Morgen Interrogation, September 4, 1946, 11.

58. Morgen Interrogation, September 4, 1946, 14.

59. Morgen Interrogation, September 4, 1946, 13–14.

60. Heymann, "The Trial of Koch," 341.

61. *US v. Waldeck et al.*, 2799.

62. *US v. Waldeck et al.*, 2882.

63. "Buchenwald: The Statistics of Buchenwald," Jewish Virtual Library, n.d., http://www.jewishvirtuallibrary.org/the-statistics-of-buchenwald.

64. As a witness before the International Tribunal at Nuremberg, for instance, Morgen testified with regard to killing centers such as Auschwitz that the SS "had nothing to do with this extermination." See Morgen, *Testimony before the International Military Tribunal*, 20: 505.

65. Morgen Interrogation, September 4, 1946, 12–13.

66. Morgen Interrogation, September 4, 1946, 13; Pauer-Studer and Velleman, *Conscience*, 48.

67. Abschrift, SS-Führungshauptamt, Bezug: Fernschreiben des SS-Richters Dr. Morgen von 24.8.43, NARA, Holdings of the Berlin Document Center, SS Officer Personnel Files, roll number A3343 SSO-190A.

68. SS-Reichsführer Himmler to Gruppenführer Burger, March 12, 1943.

69. *US v. Waldeck et al.*, 3714.

70. *US v. Waldeck et al.*, 3713.

71. *US v. Waldeck et al.*, 2928; Vernehmungsniederschrift von Erna Raible, May 3, 1949, StAA, Staatsanwaltschaft Augsburg, KS 22 / 50, 5.

72. *US v. Waldeck et al.*, 2747–2748, 2919.

73. The SS indictment of Karl Koch lists seven prisoner witnesses. See SS-und Polizeigericht z.b.V beim Hauptamt SS-Gericht, Anklageverfügung gegen SS-Standartenführer Karl Koch, Prien a / Ch., 17. August, 1944, StAM, Justizvollzugsanstalten 13948 / 2.

74. Morgen, *Testimony before the International Military Tribunal*, 20: 490–491.

75. *US v. Waldeck et al.*, 2752.

76. *US v. Waldeck et al.*, 2752.

77. Morgen, *Wesentliches Ermittlungsergebnis*, 54.

78. *US v. Waldeck et al.*, 2752; Eichhorn, "Barber to the Commandant," 123; Heymann, "The Trial of Koch," 341.

79. Holm Kirsten and Wolf Kirsten, eds., *Stimmen aus Buchenwald* (Göttingen: Wallstein, 2002), 68.

80. Hoven admitted to killing the prisoners Freudemann and May, but claimed it was not to silence them, as Morgen charged, but because they were dangerous criminals. See Pauer-Studer and Velleman, *Conscience*, 64.

81. Interrogation of Konrad Morgen, October 21, 1946, NARA, RG 238, War Crimes Records Collection, Records of the US Nuernberg War Crimes Trials Interrogations, 1946–1949, M 1019–47, 8; Pauer-Studer and Velleman, *Conscience*, 63.

82. "Extract from the Closing Brief Against Defendant Mrugowsky," *Trials of War Criminals before the Nuremberg Military Tribunals*, vol. 1: *The Medical Case*, 630–631.

83. "Extract from the Testimony of Prosecution Witness Dr. Eugen Kogon," *Trials of War Criminals before the Nuremberg Military Tribunals*, vol. 1: *The Medical Case*, 637–638.

84. Translation of Document NO-265 Prosecution Exhibit 287, Diary of the Division for Typhus and Virus Research at the Institute of Hygiene of the Waffen SS, 1941–1945, Entry of 30–31 December 1943, *Trials of War Criminals before the Nuremberg Military Tribunals*, vol. 1: *The Medical Case*, 569. See also Kogon, *Theory and Practice*, 291.

85. Pauer-Studer and Velleman, *Conscience*, 64.

86. For a compelling account of the Köhler case, see "Das Spiel is Aus—Arthur Nebe," *Der Spiegel*, August 1950, http://www.spiegel.de/spiegel/print/d-44447325.html.

87. Konrad Morgen, *Vorbemerkung zum Ermittlungsergebnis*, StAM, Justizvollzugsanstalten 13948 / 2, 2.

88. *US v. Waldeck et al.*, 2770.

89. Morgen, *Vorbemerkung zum Ermittlungsergebnis*, 1.

90. Morgen, *Wesentliches Ermittlungsergebnis*, 7–9; for currency conversion, see Historical Currency Converter, http://www.historicalstatistics.org/Currency converter.html, accessed April 15, 2022.

91. Morgen, *Wesentliches Ermittlungsergebnis*, 10.

92. Morgen, *Wesentliches Ermittlungsergebnis*, 13–14.

93. Morgen, *Wesentliches Ermittlungsergebnis*, 4.

94. Morgen, *Wesentliches Ermittlungsergebnis*, 17–18.

95. Morgen, *Wesentliches Ermittlungsergebnis*, 21–24.

96. Morgen, *Wesentliches Ermittlungsergebnis*, 24.

97. Morgen, *Wesentliches Ermittlungsergebnis*, 45.

98. Morgen, *Wesentliches Ermittlungsergebnis*, 44.

99. Morgen, *Wesentliches Ermittlungsergebnis*, 44.

100. Morgen, *Wesentliches Ermittlungsergebnis*, 45, 55–63.

101. Morgen, *Wesentliches Ermittlungsergebnis*, 48.

102. Morgen, *Wesentliches Ermittlungsergebnis*, 38.

103. Morgen, *Wesentliches Ermittlungsergebnis*, 38.

104. Anklageverfügung gegen SS-Standartenführer Karl Koch, 9.

105. Morgen, *Wesentliches Ermittlungsergebnis*, 38.

106. Morgen, *Wesentliches Ermittlungsergebnis*, 43.

107. Morgen, *Wesentliches Ermittlungsergebnis*, 38.

108. Morgen, *Wesentliches Ermittlungsergebnis*, 47.

109. Pauer-Studer and Velleman, *Conscience*, 51.

110. Morgen, *Wesentliches Ermittlungsergebnis*, 43.

111. Morgen, *Wesentliches Ermittlungsergebnis*, 47.

112. Morgen, *Wesentliches Ermittlungsergebnis*, 47.

113. Anklageverfügung gegen SS-Standartenführer Karl Koch, 2–4.

114. See Ernst Fraenkel, *The Dual State: A Contribution to the Theory of Dictatorship* (New York: Oxford University Press, 1940); Alan E. Steinweis and Robert D. Rachlin, "Introduction," in *The Law in Nazi Germany: Ideology, Opportunism, and the Perversion of Justice*, ed. Steinweis and Rachlin (New York: Berghahn, 2013), 1–2.

115. Steinweis and Rachlin, "Introduction," 2.

116. Pauer-Studer and Velleman, *Conscience*, 18.

117. Pauer-Studer and Velleman, *Conscience*, 18.

118. Pauer-Studer and Velleman, *Conscience*, 19.

119. Robert D. Rachlin, "Roland Freisler and the Volksgerichtshof," in *The Law in Nazi Germany: Ideology, Opportunism, and the Perversion of Justice*, ed. Alan E. Steinweis and Robert D. Rachlin (New York: Berghahn, 2013), 67.

120. Weingartner, "Law and Justice," 282.

121. Morgen Interrogation, September 4, 1946, 20–21.

122. Morgen Interrogation, September 4, 1946, 20; Günther Reinecke, *Testimony before the International Military Tribunal at Nuremberg*, 20: 442.

123. Morgen Interrogation, September 4, 1946, 21.

124. Aussage von Martin Sommer, 1967, IFZ, Akz. 4118 / 68, 26–28.

125. Aussage von Martin Sommer, 27–28.

126. Lutz Niethammer, ed., *Der "gesäuberte" Antifaschismus: Die SED und die roten Kapos von Buchenwald* (Berlin: Akademie, 1994), 61–62.

127. Aussage von Martin Sommer, 28.

128. Aussage von Martin Sommer, 32.

129. Aussage von Martin Sommer, 32; Morgen Interrogation, January 18, 1947, 2–5.

130. Aussage von Martin Sommer, 35–38; Morgen, *Wesentliches Ermittlungsergebnis*, 51–54.

131. Konrad Morgen to the Special Court of Inquiry (ZvB-Gericht), Weimar, September 11, 1944, http://nuremberg.law.harvard.edu/documents/2331-opinion -of-criminal-investigator?q=konrad+morgen#p.1.

132. Morgen Interrogation, January 18, 1947, 4.

133. Aussage von Martin Sommer, 38.

134. Aussage von Martin Sommer, 37–38.

135. Vernehmungsniederschrift von Erna Raible, 2.

136. Morgen Interrogation, January 18, 1947, 3.

137. Morgen Interrogation, January 18, 1947, 5.

138. *US v. Waldeck et al.*, 2811–2812.

139. Konrad Morgen to the Special Court of Inquiry.

140. At war's end, the cases against Hoven and Sommer were still pending. For the murder and abuse of Buchenwald inmates, Hoven would eventually be sentenced to death at the 1947 Doctors' Trial at Nuremberg, while Sommer would be sentenced to life in prison by a West German court in 1958.

141. Anklageschrift im Mordverfahren gegen Koch, Ilse, 51–52.

142. Anklageschrift im Mordverfahren gegen Koch, Ilse, 52.

143. *US v. Waldeck et al.*, 3714.

144. Aussage von Martin Sommer, 39.

145. Aussage von Martin Sommer, 40.

146. Vernehmungsniederschrift von Erna Raible, 2.

147. Vernehmungsniederschrift von Erna Raible, 5.

148. Anklageschrift im Mordverfahren gegen Koch, Ilse, 39.

149. Aussage von Martin Sommer, 42.

150. Aussage von Martin Sommer, 42.

151. Egon W. Fleck, Civ., and 1st Lt. Edward A. Tenenbaum, *Buchenwald: A Preliminary Report*, April 24, 1945, NARA RG 331, Records of Allied Operational and Occupation Headquarters, World War II—SHAEF—General Staff, G-5 Division, Secretariat Aug 1943–Jul 1945, box 50, 6.

152. Following the cessation of cremations at Buchenwald in March 1945, Himmler approved "emergency burials" in mass graves on the south slope of the Ettersberg hill. It is possible that Karl's body was disposed of here. See *Buchenwald Concentration Camp, 1937–1945*, ed. Gedenkstätte Buchenwald, compiled by Harry Stein, trans. Judith Rosenthal (Göttingen: Wallstein, 2004), 226.

153. Kogon, *Theory and Practice*, 292.

3. American Military Justice and the "Bitch of Buchenwald"

1. Stefan Heymann, "21,000 Prisoners Liberated," in *The Buchenwald Report*, ed. David Hackett (Boulder, CO: Westview Press, 1995), 3.

2. *Buchenwald Concentration Camp, 1937–1945*, ed. Gedenkstätte Buchenwald, compiled by Harry Stein, trans. Judith Rosenthal (Göttingen: Wallstein, 2004), 227.

3. David A. Hackett, "Introduction: Documenting the Nazi Camps: The Case of the Buchenwald Report," *The Buchenwald Report*, 4.

4. *The United States v. Josias Prince zu Waldeck, et al.*, Case no. 000-50-9, Denson Papers, Series II: Trials, 1945–2001, boxes 17–22 (5718 pages), 5307–5314; Eugen Kogon, *The Theory and Practice of Hell: The German Concentration Camps and the System behind Them* (New York: Farrar, Straus and Giroux, 2006), 280.

5. *Buchenwald Concentration Camp, 1937–1945*, 231.

6. Hermann Langbein, *Against All Hope: Resistance in the Nazi Concentration Camps 1938–1945* (New York: Paragon House, 1994), 352–353.

7. Egon W. Fleck, Civ., and 1st Lt. Edward A. Tenenbaum, *Buchenwald: A Preliminary Report*, April 24, 1945, NARA RG 331, Records of Allied Operational and Occupation Headquarters, World War II—SHAEF—General Staff, G-5 Division, Secretariat Aug 1943–Jul 1945, box 50, 11.

8. Kogon, *Theory and Practice of Hell*, 281.

9. *Buchenwald Concentration Camp, 1937–1945*, 235.

10. Fleck and Tenenbaum, *Preliminary Report*, 6.

11. Michael Hirsh, *The Liberators: America's Witnesses to the Holocaust* (New York: Bantam, 2010), 29–30.

12. Hirsh, *The Liberators*, 101; Charles R. Codman, *Drive* (Boston: Little, Brown, 1957), 283.

13. Fleck and Tenenbaum, *Preliminary Report*, 2.

14. Dan Stone, *The Liberation of the Camps* (New Haven: Yale University Press, 2016), 6.

15. Stone, *The Liberation of the Camps*, 71.

16. *Buchenwald Concentration Camp, 1937–1945*, 236.

17. Fleck and Tenenbaum, *Preliminary Report*, 2

18. *Atrocities and Other Conditions in Concentration Camps in Germany: Report of the Committee Requested by Gen. Dwight D. Eisenhower to the Congress of the United States, 1945*, NARA, RG 549, War Crimes Case Files, Cases Tried, box 444, 6.

19. Percy Knauth, *Germany in Defeat* (New York: Knopf, 1946), 39, 65.

20. John C. McManus, *Hell Before Their Very Eyes: American Soldiers Liberate Concentration Camps in Germany, April 1945* (Baltimore: Johns Hopkins University Press, 2015), 60.

21. *Death Mills,* directed by Billy Wilder and Hanus Burger (United States Department of War, 1945); Gene Currivan, "Nazi Death Factory Shocks Germans on Forced Tour," *New York Times,* April 18, 1945, 1, 8.

22. Currivan, "Nazi Death Factory," 8.

23. Currivan, "Nazi Death Factory," 8.

24. Subject: Information on the Infamous Concentration Camp at Buchenwald, Germany, February 14, 1945, NARA, RG 549, War Crimes Case Files, Cases Tried, box 437, 4–5.

25. Subject: Information on the Infamous Concentration Camp at Buchenwald, 1.

26. Fleck and Tenenbaum, *Preliminary Report,* 11.

27. Albert Rosenberg, interview with author, December 10, 2013, El Paso, TX; Hackett, "Introduction," *Buchenwald Report,* 14.

28. Hackett, "Introduction," *Buchenwald Report,* 1.

29. Eugen Kogon, "Main Report," *Buchenwald Report,* 64.

30. Gustav Wegerer, "Pathology," *Buchenwald Report,* 224.

31. Dr. Erich Wagner, *Ein Beitrag zur Tätowierungsfrage* (Jena: Universitätsanstalt für gerichtliche Medizin und naturwissenschaftliche Kriminalistik, 1940). At war's end, Wagner was arrested by American occupation authorities but managed to escape custody and live under a pseudonym in Bavaria until he was re-arrested by West German police in 1958. He died by suicide in prison in 1959 while awaiting trial.

32. Stefen Heymann, "Sidelights of the Koch Affair," *Buchenwald Report,* 338.

33. Lt. Col. Raymond C. Givens, *Report of Investigation of Alleged War Crime,* to Commanding General, Third US Army, June 3, 1945. NARA, RG 549, War Crimes Case Files, Cases Tried, box 446, 3.

34. Major M. C. Reuben Cares, Chief of Pathology, Seventh Medical Laboratory, Subject: Identification of Tattooed Human Hides, May 25, 1945, NARA, RG 549, War Crimes Case Files, Cases Tried, box 437.

35. Givens, *Report of Investigation of Alleged War Crime,* 3.

36. Hugo Beher's Personal Testimony, May 27, 1945, NARA, RG 549, War Crimes Case Files, Cases Tried, box 439.

37. For the War Crimes Office, Perpetuation of Testimony of 2nd Lt. William Powell, August 3, 1945, NARA, RG 549, War Crimes Case Files, Cases Tried, box 446.

38. Givens, *Report of Investigation of Alleged War Crime,* 5.

39. Report of the Committee Requested by Gen. Dwight D. Eisenhower through the Chief of Staff, Gen. George C. Marshall to the United States Congress Relative to Atrocities and Other Conditions in Concentration Camps in Germany, May 15, 1945, NARA, RG 549, War Crimes Case Files, Cases Tried, box 444, 7.

40. See NARA, RG 549, War Crimes Case Files—Cases Tried.

41. Katrin Grieser, "Die Dachauer Buchenwald-Prozesse: Anspruch und Wirklichkeit—Anspruch und Wirkung," in *Dachauer Prozesse: NS-Verbrechen vor amerikanischen Militärgerichten in Dachau 1945–1948*, ed. Ludwig Eiber and Robert Siegel (Göttingen: Wallstein, 2007), 161.

42. *US v. Waldeck et al.*, 3722.

43. *US v. Waldeck et al.*, 3716.

44. Interrogation of Ilse Koch, Ludwigsburg, June 16, 1945, NARA, RG 549, War Crimes Case Files, Cases Tried, box 440, 1, 4.

45. Interrogation of Ilse Koch, June 16, 1945, 1–2.

46. Interrogation of Ilse Koch, June 16, 1945, 2–3.

47. Interrogation of Ilse Koch, June 16, 1945, 3.

48. *US v. Waldeck et al.*, 3717.

49. *US v. Waldeck et al.*, 3717.

50. Arthur L. Smith, Jr., *Die Hexe von Buchenwald* (Weimar: Böhlau, 1995), 109.

51. Alison Owings, *Frauen: German Women Recall the Third Reich* (New Brunswick, NJ: Rutgers University Press, 1993), 336–337.

52. Winston Churchill, Franklin Roosevelt, and Joseph Stalin, "Moscow Declaration, November 1, 1943," in *The Nuremberg War Crimes Trial, 1945–1946: A Documentary History*, ed. Michael Marrus (Boston: Bedford Books, 1997), 20–21.

53. Report—War Crimes Activities, August 17, 1949, attached to Document: Headquarters-United States Forces European Theatre to Commanding General, Third Army Area, re. War Crimes Trial Cases, October 14, 1946, NARA, RG 549, General Admin., box 9.

54. Lisa Yavnai, "Military Justice: The U.S. Army War Crimes Trials in Germany 1944–1947" (PhD diss., London School of Economics and Political Science, 2007), 126.

55. Report—War Crimes Activities, August 17, 1949.

56. JCS 1023 / 10—Directive on the Identification and Apprehension of Persons Suspected of War Crimes or Other Offenses and Trial of Certain Offenders, July 8, 1945, NARA, RG 549, General Admin., box 1.

57. Rules of Procedure in Military Government Courts, June 1945, reproduced in Holder Lessing, *Der Erste Dachauer Prozess, 1945–1946* (Baden-Baden: Nomos, 1993), Appendix 5. For a thorough exploration and explanation of the American military trial system at Dachau see Tomaz Jardim, *The Mauthausen Trial: American Military Justice in Germany* (Cambridge, MA: Harvard University Press, 2012).

58. William Denson, interview by Joan Ringelheim, August 25, 1994, video, USHMM Film and Video Archive, RG-50.030*0268.

59. William Denson, List of Memorized Passages from Scripture, Age 16, Denson Papers, Series I: Personal, box 1.

60. See Yavnai, "Military Justice," Appendix.

61. "He Sent 97 Nazis to the Gallows," *Newsday*, April 23, 1990, Denson Papers, Series I: Personal, box 1, folder 5.

62. William Denson, interview by Joshua Greene, in *Dachau: Justice on Trial*, First Draft Script, Denson Papers, Series I: Personal, box 1, folder 4.

63. William Denson, interview by Joan Ringelheim.

64. Dr. Eugen Kogon, Case Analysis Pertaining to the Buchenwald Case, February 11, 1947, Denson Papers, Series II: Trials, folder 96.

65. William Denson, Untitled and Undated Speech to Women's Group, Denson Papers, Series I: Personal, box 3, folder 33.

66. "Nuremberg Prosecutor Reflects on History's Judgment of Evil," *New York Times*, May 6, 1990.

67. William Denson, interview by Joan Ringelheim.

68. Stuart Vincent, "Crimes Almost Beyond Belief," *Newsday*, April 23, 1990, II:4.

69. Lt. Col. C. E. Straight, Report of the Deputy Judge Advocate for War Crimes, European Command, June 1944 to July 1948, NARA, RG 549, General Admin., box 13, 160.

70. Jardim, *The Mauthausen Trial*, 93.

71. "Charge and Particulars," Review and Recommendations of the Deputy Judge Advocate for War Crimes, *United States v. Josias Prince zu Waldeck et al.*, 15. November 1947, NARA, RG 549, War Crimes Case Files, Cases Tried, box 425, 1.

72. William D. Denson, Robert L. Kunzig, and Solomon Surowitz, *An Information Booklet on the Buchenwald Concentration Camp Case*, Denson Papers, Series II: Trials, folder 90.

73. "31 Buchenwald Officials to Stand Trial in April," *Stars and Stripes*, March 9, 1947.

74. Smith, *Die Hexe von Buchenwald*, 119.

75. "Frau Koch Gives Birth to 7-lb. Boy," *Washington Post*, October 31, 1947; "Ilse Koch Has Baby," *New York Times*, October 30, 1947; "Former Nazi Camp Leader Has Her Baby," *Lima (Ohio) News*, October 30, 1947.

76. For details of the pregnancy and official conclusions, see Hearings before the Investigations Subcommittee of the Committee on Expenditures in the Executive Departments, United States Senate, Eightieth Congress; Part 5: December 8 and 9, 1948 (Washington: United States Government Printing Office, 1949), 1026–1027.

77. *US v. Waldeck et al.*, 16–17.

78. *US v. Waldeck et al.*, 17.

79. *US v. Waldeck et al.*, 43.

80. *US v. Waldeck et al.*, 53.

81. "31 Buchenwald Officials to Stand Trial in April," *Stars and Stripes*, March 9, 1947; "Made Lampshade of Victims' Skin, Nazi Widow Tried," *Toronto Daily Star*, April 11, 1947; "Frau Koch Disavows Buchenwald Crimes," *New York Times*, July 11, 1947; "22 Nazis to Hang for Atrocities at Buchenwald," *Globe and Mail*, August 15, 1947; see also *Stars and Stripes*, April 12, 1947, as quoted in Smith, *Die Hexe von Buchenwald*, 117.

82. James O'Donnell, "The Witch of Buchenwald: The Record of a Sadist," *Newsweek*, July 28, 1947.

83. *US v. Waldeck et al.*, 300–301.

84. *US v. Waldeck et al.*, 301, 937.

85. *US v. Waldeck et al.*, 444, 462.

86. *US v. Waldeck et al.*, 1660–1661, 1681–1682.

87. *US v. Waldeck et al.*, 1113–1114, 1120–1122.

88. *US v. Waldeck et al.*, 1750–1753.

89. *US v. Waldeck et al.*, 112.

90. *US v. Waldeck et al.*, 76.

91. *US v. Waldeck et al.*, 550.

92. *US v. Waldeck et al.*, 355, 373.

93. *US v. Waldeck et al.*, 374.

94. *US v. Waldeck et al.*, 400.

95. *US v. Waldeck et al.*, 375.

96. *US v. Waldeck et al.*, 1235–1236.

97. *US v. Waldeck et al.*, 1252.

98. *US v. Waldeck et al.*, 1234.

99. *US v. Waldeck et al.*, 1257–1260.

100. *US v. Waldeck et al.*, 1253–1254.

101. *US v. Waldeck et al.*, 1261–1262.

102. *US v. Waldeck et al.*, 1274.

103. *US v. Waldeck et al.*, 1401; Sworn Statement of Herbert Froboess, Munich, November 3, 1948, NARA, RG 549, War Crimes Case Files, Cases Tried, box 436.

104. *US v. Waldeck et al.*, 1361.

105. *US v. Waldeck et al.*, 1366.

106. *US v. Waldeck et al.*, 1367.

107. *US v. Waldeck et al.*, 1363–1364.

108. *US v. Waldeck et al.*, 1365, 1363.

109. *US v. Waldeck et al.*, 1384.

110. *US v. Waldeck et al.*, 1395.

111. *US v. Waldeck et al.*, 1392–1394.

112. *US v. Waldeck et al.*, 4810–4818.

113. *US v. Waldeck et al.*, 1400.

114. *US v. Waldeck et al.*, 1778.

115. *US v. Waldeck et al.*, 1945–1947.

116. *US v. Waldeck et al.*, 4140.

117. *US v. Waldeck et al.*, 1965, 2001, 2329.

118. *US v. Waldeck et al.*, 2326.

119. *US v. Waldeck et al.*, 2330.

120. *US v. Waldeck et al.*, 2330–2331.

121. *US v. Waldeck et al.*, 2805–2806.

122. *US v. Waldeck et al.*, 2807.

123. *US v. Waldeck et al.*, 2829, 2831.

124. *US v. Waldeck et al.*, 2830.

125. *US v. Waldeck et al.*, 2901.

126. *US v. Waldeck et al.*, 2902.

127. *US v. Waldeck et al.*, 2903.

128. *US v. Waldeck et al.*, 2907.

129. *US v. Waldeck et al.*, 2929.

130. *US v. Waldeck et al.*, 2964–2970, 2971–2975.

131. *US v. Waldeck et al.*, 3696.

132. *US v. Waldeck et al.*, 3706.

133. *US v. Waldeck et al.*, 3711.

134. *US v. Waldeck et al.*, 3706–3707.
135. *US v. Waldeck et al.*, 3708.
136. *US v. Waldeck et al.*, 3713.
137. *US v. Waldeck et al.*, 3717.
138. *US v. Waldeck et al.*, 3714–3715.
139. *US v. Waldeck et al.*, 3717.
140. *US v. Waldeck et al.*, 3718.
141. *US v. Waldeck et al.*, 3721–3722.
142. *US v. Waldeck et al.*, 3723.
143. *US v. Waldeck et al.*, 3726.
144. *US v. Waldeck et al.*, 3733.
145. *US v. Waldeck et al.*, 3726.
146. *US v. Waldeck et al.*, 3727.
147. *US v. Waldeck et al.*, 3727.
148. *US v. Waldeck et al.*, 3740.
149. "Frau Koch Disavows Buchenwald Crimes," *New York Times*, July 11, 1947.
150. *US v. Waldeck et al.*, 43.
151. Denson et al., *Information Booklet.*
152. Denson et al., *Information Booklet.*

4. Clemency, Controversy, and the Koch Case in the US Senate

1. *The United States v. Josias Prince zu Waldeck et al.*, Case no. 000-50-9, Denson Papers, Series II: Trials, 1945–2001, boxes 17–22 (5718 pages), 5692.
2. *U.S. v. Waldeck et al.*, 5693.
3. Hearings Before the Investigations Subcommittee of the Committee on Expenditures in the Executive Departments, United States Senate, Eightieth Congress; Part 5: December 8 and 9, 1948 (Washington, DC: United States Government Printing Office, 1949), 1088.
4. James O'Donnell, "The Witch of Buchenwald: The Record of a Sadist," *Newsweek*, July 28, 1947.
5. *U.S. v. Waldeck et al.*, 5709.
6. *U.S. v. Waldeck et al.*, 5709–5710.
7. *U.S. v. Waldeck et al.*, 5711.
8. *U.S. v. Waldeck et al.*, 5711.
9. *U.S. v. Waldeck et al.*, 5711–5717.
10. "War Crimes: The Widow and Her Friend," *Time*, August 25, 1947.

11. "Ilse Koch 'Concentration Camp Murderess' War Crimes Trial," Universal Newsreels, October 28, 1948, https://www.youtube.com/watch?v=I_zCP6J9OhY.

12. *U.S. v. Waldeck et al.*, 5713.

13. "Frau Koch, 30 Others Found Guilty of Buchenwald Crimes," *Washington Post*, August 13, 1947.

14. *U.S. v. Waldeck et al.*, 5711–5717.

15. Sworn Affidavit of Captain Emanuel Lewis, United States Air Forces in Europe, October 11, 1948, NARA, RG 549, War Crimes Case Files, Cases Tried, box 457.

16. Petition for Clemency for Ilse Koch, to General Lucius D. Clay, September 18, 1947, NARA, RG 549, War Crimes Case Files, Cases Tried, box 457.

17. Petition for Clemency for Ilse Koch.

18. Maj. Carl E. Whitney, Cpt. Emanuel Lewis, et al., Petition for Review, *The United States v. Josias Prince zu Waldeck, et al.*, October 3, 1947, NARA, RG 549, War Crimes Case Files, Cases Tried, Box 437, 1.

19. Whitney et al., Petition for Review, 27–28.

20. Whitney et al., Petition for Review, 63.

21. Whitney et al., Petition for Review, 63.

22. Whitney et al., Petition for Review, 64.

23. "Frau Koch Gives Birth to 7-lb. Boy," *Washington Post*, October 31, 1947, B11; "Ilse Koch Has Baby," *New York Times*, October 30, 1947, 16.

24. Letter of August Bender, reproduced in the documentary film *Ilse Koch—Die Hexe von Buchenwald*, dir. André Meier and Pepe Pippig, 2012.

25. Richard A. Schneider, Memorandum for Col. Harbaugh, Subject: Reduction of Sentence of Ilse Koch, October 6, 1948, NARA, RG 549, War Crimes Case Files, Cases Tried, box 436, 1.

26. Schneider, Memorandum for Col. Harbaugh, 2.

27. Schneider, Memorandum for Col. Harbaugh, 1.

28. Harold E. Kuhn, Memorandum to Col. Harbaugh, Subject: Sentence of Ilse Koch, October 1, 1948, NARA, RG 549, War Crimes Case Files, Cases Tried, box 436, 1.

29. Kuhn, Memorandum to Col. Harbaugh.

30. Maj. Thomas C. Marmon, Memorandum for Col. Harbaugh, Subject: Reduction of the War Crimes Sentence of Ilse Koch, October 4, 1948, NARA, RG 549, War Crimes Case Files, Cases Tried, box 436, 1.

31. Marmon, Memorandum for Col. Harbaugh.

32. Review and Recommendations of the Deputy Judge Advocate for War Crimes, *United States v. Josias Prince zu Waldeck, et al.*, November 15, 1947, NARA, RG 549, War Crimes Case Files, Cases Tried, box 426, 87.

33. Supplemental and Special Report of War Crimes Board of Review no. 5, *United States v. Josias Prince zu Waldeck, et al.*, October 6, 1948, NARA, RG 549, War Crimes Case Files, Cases Tried, box 436, 2.

34. Supplemental and Special Report of War Crimes Board of Review no. 5, 2.

35. Col. J. L. Harbaugh, Jr., Worksheet, Defendant # 15—Ilse Koch, NARA, RG 549, War Crimes Case Files, Cases Tried, box 436, 3.

36. Harbaugh, Worksheet, 3.

37. Harbaugh, Worksheet, 3.

38. Recommendation of the Judge Advocate, *United States v. Josias Prince zu Waldeck, et al.*, May 7, 1948, NARA, RG 549, War Crimes Case Files, Cases Tried, box 437, 2.

39. Lucius D. Clay, *Decision in Germany* (Garden City, NY: Doubleday, 1950), 254.

40. Clay, *Decision in Germany*, 254.

41. Ilse Koch to Captain Emanuel Lewis, June 19, 1948, NARA, RG 549, War Crimes Case Files, Cases Tried, box 436.

42. Ilse Koch to the War Crimes Branch, Judge Advocate Division (EUCOM), August 16, 1948, NARA, RG 549, War Crimes Case Files, Cases Tried, box 457.

43. War Crimes Branch, Judge Advocate Division, Case no. 000-50-9, Accused: Ilse Koch, Recommendation, September 14, 1948, NARA, RG 549, War Crimes Case Files, Cases Tried, Box 436.

44. Hearings before the Investigations Subcommittee, December 8 and 9, 1948, 1095.

45. "Ilse Koch's Term in Prison Reduced to Four Years," *Stars and Stripes*, September 17, 1948; Headquarters, European Command, Public Information Division, "EUCOM Issues Report on Sentence Reductions for Buchenwald Camp Criminals," September 17, 1948, NARA, RG 549, War Crimes Case Files, Cases Tried, box 443.

46. "Strange Clemency," Washington Post, September 20, 1948, 10.

47. "Clemency for the Queen of Buchenwald," Asheville Citizen-Times, September 23, 1948, 4.

48. Department of Army, Public Information Division, The Ilse Koch Case—Digest of Editorial Comment, Radio Comment and Press Opinion,

17 September–18 October, 1948, Denson Papers, Series II: Trials, box 15, folder 91.

49. The Ilse Koch Case—Digest of Editorial Comment.

50. The Ilse Koch Case—Digest of Editorial Comment.

51. The Ilse Koch Case—Digest of Editorial Comment.

52. The Ilse Koch Case—Digest of Editorial Comment.

53. "Second Look at the Koch Case," Asheville Citizen-Times, September 30, 1948, 4.

54. The Ilse Koch Case—Digest of Editorial Comment.

55. William D. Denson, "Ilse Koch," letter to the editor, *Washington Post*, September 23, 1948, 10.

56. William D. Denson, "Frau Ilse Koch a Sadist from Some Tortured Other World, Prosecutor Says; Assails Cut in Her Sentence," *St. Louis Post-Dispatch*, September 26, 1948.

57. Denson, "Frau Ilse Koch a Sadist."

58. See Leon B. Poullada Personal Papers, administrative information, abstract, John F. Kennedy Presidential Library, https://www.jfklibrary.org/asset-viewer/archives/LBPPP.

59. Leon Poullada, "The Trial of Ilse Koch: 'Former Counsel in War Crimes Cases Says Assembly-Line Technique Flouted Principles of Justice,'" *Washington Evening Star*, October 2, 1948.

60. Poullada, "The Trial of Ilse Koch."

61. John O'Donnell, "Capitol Stuff," *New York Daily News*, October 4, 1948.

62. Edwin C. Hartrich, "The Evidence against Ilse Koch," *New York Herald Tribune*, October 13, 1948.

63. Hartrich, "The Evidence against Ilse Koch."

64. See The Ilse Koch Case—Digest of Editorial Comment.

65. Lucius D. Clay, *The Papers of General Lucius D. Clay, Germany, 1945–1949*, ed. Jean Edward Smith, 2 vols. (Bloomington: Indiana University Press, 1974), 2: 881.

66. "Clay Says Record Did Not Warrant Ilse's Life Term," *Stars and Stripes*, October 22, 1948.

67. The Ilse Koch Case—Digest of Editorial Comment.

68. "Isacson Pickets Clay: Heads Group Demanding General's Recall from Germany," *New York Times*, October 22, 1948.

69. "Clay Heckled Here; 800 Pickets Routed," *New York Times*, May 25, 1950.

70. "Clay Heckled Here; 800 Pickets Routed."

71. Poster: "Shall Ilse Koch Go Free?" Protest Meeting, Brooklyn Jewish Center, October 21, 1948, Denson Papers, Series II: Trials, box 15, folder 92.

72. William Denson to Bryan F. LaPlante, Chief, Washington Area Security Branch, Office of Security and Intelligence, re. Speech to Be Made before the American Jewish Congress, October 21, 1948, Denson Papers, Series II: Trials, box 15, folder 92.

73. "Gieseking Agrees to Quit U.S. without Giving Concert Here," *New York Times*, January 25, 1949.

74. "German Exhibits Draw Picket Line," *New York Times*, April 10, 1949.

75. Woody Guthrie, "Ilse Koch," in Will Kaufman, *Woody Guthrie: American Radical* (Champaign: University of Illinois Press, 2015), 156.

76. "Hope to Reverse Leniency to Koch," *New York Post*, September 26, 1948.

77. Hearings before the Investigations Subcommittee, December 8 and 9, 1948, 1022; Arthur L. Smith, Jr., *Die Hexe von Buchenwald* (Weimar: Böhlau, 1995), 155.

78. Committee on International Relations, Selected Executive Session Hearings of the Committee, 1943–1950: Problems of World War Two and Its Aftermath, Pt. 2 (Washington, DC: US Government Printing Office, 1976), 16.

79. Homer Ferguson, Conduct of the Ilse Koch War Crimes Trial, Interim Report of the Investigations Subcommittee of the Committee on Expenditures in the Executive Departments, December 27, 1948, Denson Papers, Series II: Trials, box 15, folder 91, 1.

80. Ferguson, Conduct of the Ilse Koch War Crimes Trial, 2.

81. Hearings before the Investigations Subcommittee, December 8 and 9, 1948, 999–1001.

82. Hearings before the Investigations Subcommittee, December 8 and 9, 1948, 1002.

83. Hearings before the Investigations Subcommittee, December 8 and 9, 1948, 1002.

84. Hearings before the Investigations Subcommittee, December 8 and 9, 1948, 1005.

85. Hearings before the Investigations Subcommittee, December 8 and 9, 1948, 1012.

86. Hearings before the Investigations Subcommittee, December 8 and 9, 1948, 1011.

87. Hearings before the Investigations Subcommittee, December 8 and 9, 1948, 1014.

88. Hearings before the Investigations Subcommittee, December 8 and 9, 1948, 1014.

89. Hearings before the Investigations Subcommittee, December 8 and 9, 1948, 1024.

90. Hearings before the Investigations Subcommittee, December 8 and 9, 1948, 1025.

91. Hearings before the Investigations Subcommittee, December 8 and 9, 1948, 1026.

92. Hearings before the Investigations Subcommittee, December 8 and 9, 1948, 1027.

93. Hearings before the Investigations Subcommittee, December 8 and 9, 1948, 1026.

94. "Royall Asks Clay to Study Second Trial of Ilse Koch," *Stars and Stripes*, September 30, 1948.

95. General Lucius Clay to Secretary of the Army Kenneth Royall, October 2, 1948, NARA, RG 549, War Crimes Case Files, Cases Tried, box 441.

96. Clay to Royall, October 2, 1948.

97. "The Bitch Again," *Time*, October 4, 1948.

98. "Ferguson Will Give Ilse Koch Case Data," *New York Times*, October 20, 1948; Smith, *Die Hexe von Buchenwald*, 155.

99. "Army Gets Koch Records—Will Relay Papers on War Crime Case to President," *New York Times*, October 21, 1948.

100. General Lucius D. Clay to Secretary Royall, Subject: Second Trial of Ilse Koch, November 28, 1948, NARA, RG 549, War Crimes Case Files, Cases Tried, box 441, 9.

101. Clay to Royall, November 28, 1948, 10, 12.

102. Clay to Royall, November 28, 1948, 12.

103. "Trial of Ilse Koch by Germans Urged—Frankfurt Editor Says Unheard Witnesses Could Add Data to Charges against Her," *New York Times*, October 9, 1948.

104. "New Trial of Ilse Koch Promised by Bavarian," *New York Times*, October 10, 1948; "Denazi Trial Scheduled for Ilse on Release," *Stars and Stripes*, October 10, 1948.

105. "New Ilse Koch Trial Up—Bavarian Official Says German Will 'No Doubt' Press Action," *New York Times*, October 17, 1948.

106. Ferguson, Conduct of the Ilse Koch War Crimes Trial, 2.

107. "Senators Will Open Public Hearings on Koch Case Oct. 15," *Stars and Stripes*, October 4, 1948.

108. "Senators Bar Open Hearings on Koch Case; Berlin Crisis Seen as Factor in the Decision," *New York Times*, December 10, 1948.

109. Hearings before the Investigations Subcommittee, December 8 and 9, 1948, 1035.

110. Hearings before the Investigations Subcommittee, December 8 and 9, 1948, 1042.

111. Hearings before the Investigations Subcommittee, December 8 and 9, 1948, 1057.

112. Hearings before the Investigations Subcommittee, December 8 and 9, 1948, 1060.

113. Hearings before the Investigations Subcommittee, December 8 and 9, 1948, 1075.

114. Hearings before the Investigations Subcommittee, December 8 and 9, 1948, 1085.

115. Hearings before the Investigations Subcommittee, December 8 and 9, 1948, 1091.

116. Hearings before the Investigations Subcommittee, December 8 and 9, 1948, 1080.

117. Hearings before the Investigations Subcommittee, December 8 and 9, 1948, 1081.

118. Hearings before the Investigations Subcommittee, December 8 and 9, 1948, 1086.

119. Hearings before the Investigations Subcommittee, December 8 and 9, 1948, 1113–1118.

120. Hearings before the Investigations Subcommittee, December 8 and 9, 1948, 1098.

121. Hearings before the Investigations Subcommittee, December 8 and 9, 1948, 1108.

122. Hearings before the Investigations Subcommittee, December 8 and 9, 1948, 1108.

123. Hearings before the Investigations Subcommittee, December 8 and 9, 1948, 1119.

124. Hearings before the Investigations Subcommittee, December 8 and 9, 1948, 1119.

125. Hearings before the Investigations Subcommittee, December 8 and 9, 1948, 1134.

126. Hearings before the Investigations Subcommittee, December 8 and 9, 1948, 1133.

127. Hearings before the Investigations Subcommittee, December 8 and 9, 1948, 1136.

128. Hearings before the Investigations Subcommittee, December 8 and 9, 1948, 1142.

129. Hearings before the Investigations Subcommittee, December 8 and 9, 1948, 1146.

130. Hearings before the Investigations Subcommittee, December 8 and 9, 1948, 1142, 1147.

131. Hearings before the Investigations Subcommittee, December 8 and 9, 1948, 1168.

132. Ferguson, Conduct of the Ilse Koch War Crimes Trial, 17–19.

133. Ferguson, Conduct of the Ilse Koch War Crimes Trial, 22.

134. Ferguson, Conduct of the Ilse Koch War Crimes Trial, 22–23.

135. Ferguson, Conduct of the Ilse Koch War Crimes Trial, 22.

136. Ferguson, Conduct of the Ilse Koch War Crimes Trial, 24.

137. "Ilse Koch Claims U.S. Court Suppressed Her Evidence," *Washington Post,* October 4, 1948.

138. "Ilse Koch 'Furious,' Claims Innocence," *Stars and Stripes,* September 25, 1948.

139. "Frau Koch Silent," *New York Times,* September 30, 1948.

140. "Ilse Koch 'Furious,' Claims Innocence."

5. New Charges, New Challenges in a Divided Germany

1. William D. Denson and Robert L. Kunzig, "Why Should Ilse Koch Go Free?" *Look,* January 4, 1949, 37.

2. Denson and Kunzig, "Why Should Ilse Koch Go Free?"

3. "New Trial for Ilse Koch Is Essential," *Philadelphia Inquirer,* December 28, 1948.

4. "The Case of Ilse Koch," *New York Times,* December 28, 1948; "Beast of Buchenwald," *Washington Post,* December 28, 1948.

5. "Justice in the Koch Case," *Washington Star,* December 28, 1948.

6. Homer Ferguson, Conduct of the Ilse Koch War Crimes Trial, Interim Report of the Investigations Subcommittee of the Committee on Expenditures

in the Executive Departments, December 27, 1948, Denson Papers, Series II: Trials, box 15, folder 91, 24.

7. Wade M. Fleischer, Analysis of the Unintroduced Evidence Concerning Ilse Koch, Memorandum for Colonel Harbaugh, January 12, 1949, NARA, RG 549, War Crimes Case Files, Cases Tried, box 441.

8. Colonel J. L. Harbaugh, JAGD, Memorandum for Colonel Fleischer, January 25, 1949, NARA, RG 549, War Crimes Case Files, Cases Tried, box 441.

9. Colonel J. L. Harbaugh JAG, Memorandum for the Commander-in-Chief, European Command [Clay], Subject: Second Trial of Ilse Koch, February 2, 1949, NARA, RG 549, War Crimes Case Files, Cases Tried, box 441.

10. Col. Wade M. Fleischer, Memorandum for Col Harbaugh, Subject: Retrial of Ilse Koch Before a US Military Commission for Offenses in Violation of German Law, February 9, 1949, NARA, RG 549, War Crimes Case Files, Cases Tried, box 441.

11. CINCEUR Clay to Secretary Royall, February 7, 1949, NARA, RG 549, War Crimes Case Files, Cases Tried, box 441.

12. "Warum Ilse Koch begnadigt wurde," *Tägliche Runschau*, September 19, 1948; the December 29, 1948, issue of the *Tägliche Rundschau* included a cartoon with a caption that read "Don't worry, Ilse, people of your ilk are protected by democracy." See Alexandra Przyrembel, "Transfixed by an Image: Ilse Koch, the 'Kommandeuse' of Buchenwald," *German History* 19, no. 3 (2001): 369–399, 394.

13. "Ein weiterer Beweis," *Berliner Zeitung*, September 18, 1948.

14. Protest gegen die Revision des Buchenwaldurteils, Berliner VVN Pressestelle, September 13, 1948, BwA, Prozesse gegen Ilse Koch, folder 81-2-1.

15. President of the Legislature of Thuringia, Resolution of the Legislature of Thuringia, Weimar, October 7, 1948, NARA, RG 549, War Crimes Case Files, Cases Tried, box 441.

16. Dr. Johann Ilkow to Headquarters European Command, Office of the Judge Advocate, Brig General J. L. Harbaugh, Jr., Second Report on State of Affairs, April 15, 1949, NARA, RG 549, War Crimes Case Files, Cases Tried, box 441; "Germans Debate Right to Try Ilse upon Release by US," *Stars and Stripes*, April 25, 1949.

17. Dr. Rossmann, Judge of the Amstgericht, Warrant of Arrest, Weimar, November 16, 1948, NARA, RG 549, War Crimes Case Files, Cases Tried, box 441.

18. Thuringia Ministry of Justice to the German Department of Justice of the Soviet Zone of Occupation in Germany at Berlin, Subject: Proceedings

against Frau Ilse Koch for Crimes Committed against Humanity, December 2, 1948, NARA, RG 549, War Crimes Case Files, Cases Tried, box 441.

19. Press Release, Headquarters, European Command, Evidence in Ilse Koch Case Made Available to Germans, March 22, 1949, NARA, RG 549, War Crimes Case Files, Cases Tried, box 441.

20. "Koch May Get Trial in East," *Stars and Stripes*, March 24, 1949.

21. "Group Asks Ilse Koch Trial in German Zone," *Stars and Stripes*, April 14, 1949; "Germans Debate Right to Try Ilse upon Release by US," *Stars and Stripes*, April 25, 1949.

22. W. M. Fleischer, draft memorandum, April 27, 1949, NARA, RG 549, War Crimes Case Files, Cases Tried, box 441.

23. Ilkow, Second Report on State of Affairs.

24. Ilkow, Second Report on State of Affairs.

25. For information on Ilkow, see BayHStA, MJu 25339, Personalbogen und Lebenslauf in Personalakt Dr. Johann Ilkow; Andreas Eichmüller, "Der Ilse Koch-Prozess in Augsburg 1950 / 51," in *Vor 70 Jahren—Stunde Null für die Justiz?* ed. Arnd Koch and Herbert Veh (Augsburg: Nomos, 2017), 99–100; Edith Raim, *Nazi Crimes against Jews and German Post-War Justice* (Berlin: De Gruyter, 2014), 253 f.

26. JAG Col. J. L Harbaugh, Jr., Memorandum for J. A. Miles, Re: Conference with Dr. Ilkow in the Koch Case, March 8, 1949, NARA, RG 549, War Crimes Case Files, Cases Tried, box 441.

27. Ilkow, Second Report on State of Affairs.

28. Ilkow, Second Report on State of Affairs.

29. Quoted in Przyrembel, "Transfixed by an Image," 393.

30. Harbaugh, Memorandum for J. A. Miles.

31. Ilkow, Second Report on State of Affairs.

32. Dr. Johann Ilkow to William D. Denson, Subject: Proceedings against Ilse Koch, April 4, 1949, Denson Papers, Series II: Trials, box 16, folder 94.

33. Vernehmungsniederschrift von Ilse Koch, Landsberg, April 29, 1949, StAA, Staatsanwaltschaft Augsburg, KS 22 / 50, 6.

34. Col. Wade M. Fleischer, Memorandum for Col. Gunn, Subject: Present Status of the Ilse Koch Case, May 17, 1949, NARA, RG 549, War Crimes Case Files, Cases Tried, box 437.

35. Harbaugh, Memorandum for J. A. Miles.

36. Dr. Johann Ilkow, Antrag auf Eröffnung der gerichtlichen Voruntersuchung, May 15, 1949, StAA, Staatsanwaltschaft Augsburg, KS 22 / 50, box 1, folder 1.

37. For a discussion of German legal procedure, see Devin O. Pendas, *The Frankfurt Auschwitz Trial, 1963–1965* (Cambridge: Cambridge University Press, 2006), 50, 119–121.

38. Eichmüller, "Der Ilse Koch-Prozess in Augsburg," 102.

39. Eichmüller, "Der Ilse Koch-Prozess in Augsburg," 102.

40. Ilkow, Antrag auf Eröffnung der gerichtlichen Voruntersuchung.

41. Der Obserstaatsanwalt bei dem Landgericht augsburg, an das Bayerische Staatsministerium der Justiz, Bamberg, May 15, 1950, StAA, Staatsanwaltschaft Augsburg, KS 22 / 50.

42. Friedrich Thumm, Zeugenaussagen, June 17, 1949, and July 29, 1949, StAA, Staatsanwaltschaft Augsburg, KS 22 / 50, box 1, folder 1.

43. See, for example, the depositions of witnesses Josef Tennenbaum, Karl Lucas, Robert Sperl, Alfons Baer, Karl Wahl, Fritz Luithardt, and Eugen Ochs, StAA, Staatsanwaltschaft Augsburg, KS 22 / 50, box 1, folder 1.

44. Josef Warscher, Zeugenaussage, June 23, 1949, StAA, Staatsanwaltschaft Augsburg, KS 22 / 50, box 1, folder 1.

45. Emil Carlebach, Zeugenaussage, May 10, 1949, StAA, Staatsanwaltschaft Augsburg, KS 22 / 50, box 1, folder 1.

46. Erich Bormann, Zeugenaussage, June 24, 1949, StAA, Staatsanwaltschaft Augsburg, KS 22 / 50, box 1, folder 1.

47. Leopold Lukasik, Zeugenaussage, July 23, 1949, StAA, Staatsanwaltschaft Augsburg, KS 22 / 50, box 1, folder 1.

48. Willi Bleicher, Zeugenaussage, June 24, 1949, StAA, Staatsanwaltschaft Augsburg, KS 22 / 50, box 1, folder 1.

49. Clemens Bukowski, Zeugenaussage, June 29, 1949, StAA, Staatsanwaltschaft Augsburg, KS 22 / 50, box 1, folder 1.

50. Col. Wade M. Fleischer, Memorandum for the Judge Advocate, Subject: Trial of Ilse Koch by German Court, June 28, 1949, NARA, RG 549, War Crimes Case Files, Cases Tried, box 441.

51. Dr. Johann Ilkow to Headquarters European Command, Office of the Judge Advocate, Col. Wade M. Fleischer, et al., Subject: Proceedings against Ilse Koch, June 27, 1949, NARA, RG 549, War Crimes Case Files, Cases Tried, box 441.

52. Ilkow to Headquarters European Command, June 27, 1949.

53. Ilkow to Headquarters European Command, June 27, 1949.

54. Ilkow to Headquarters European Command, June 27, 1949.

55. Gert Heidenreich, "Freiheit im Freistaat: Polizeiaktion gegen Münchner Verlage—Hintergrund: die Vergangenheit des bayerischen Innenministers Alfred Seidl," *Die Zeit*, October 20, 1978.

56. See, for instance, Senate Resolution No. 48, State of Ohio, May 5, 1949; Senate Concurrent Resolution No. 26, Michigan State Legislature, April 14, 1949; Resolution Adopted at the Meeting of the Department of Michigan Catholic War Veterans, April 10, 1949; all in NARA, RG 549, War Crimes Case Files, Cases Tried, box 441; "2000 Expected at Rally to Protest Plan," *Detroit Times*, May 5, 1949.

57. See, for instance, Oberlandesgerichtsrat Dr. Jagomast to Werner Katz, New York, August 17, 1949, StAA, Staatsanwaltschaft Augsburg, KS 22 / 50, box 1, folder 5.

58. Depositions of Simon Barsam, September 9, 1949, and Moritz Schwarzwald (no date visible), NARA, RG 549, War Crimes Case Files, Cases Tried, box 441.

59. Deposition of Paul Wallentin, September 12, 1949, NARA, RG 549, War Crimes Case Files, Cases Tried, box 441.

60. Depositions of Abner Rand (no date visible), and Michael Sprechmann, September 2, 1949, NARA, RG 549, War Crimes Case Files, Cases Tried, box 441.

61. Depositions of Karl Press (no date visible), Siegmund Flamm (no date visible), Arthur Albers, August 17, 1949, and Ernst Federn, September 12, 1949, NARA, RG 549, War Crimes Case Files, Cases Tried, box 441.

62. Deposition of Bruno Kriss (no date visible), NARA, RG 549, War Crimes Case Files, Cases Tried, box 441.

63. Office of Military Government for Bavaria to Legal Division, Office of Military Government for Germany, Subject: Ilse Koch, July 6, 1949, NARA, RG 549, War Crimes Case Files, Cases Tried, box 441.

64. See, for example, responses to questions re. Thumm in the depositions of Kurt Sitte, Paul Heller, Kurt Glass, Ludwig Scheinbrunn, and Peter Zenkl, NARA, RG 549, War Crimes Case Files, Cases Tried, box 441.

65. Deposition of Jacob Werber (no date visible), NARA, RG 549, War Crimes Case Files, Cases Tried, box 441.

66. Deposition of Paul Heller, August 30, 1949, NARA, RG 549, War Crimes Case Files, Cases Tried, box 441.

67. Deposition of Jacob Werber.

68. Deposition of Ludwig Scheinbrunn, September 10, 1949, NARA, RG 549, War Crimes Case Files, Cases Tried, box 441.

69. Depositions of Kurt Sitte, September 8, 1949, and Peter Zenkl, August 30, 1949, NARA, RG 549, War Crimes Case Files, Cases Tried, box 441.

70. Arthur L. Smith, Jr., *Die Hexe von Buchenwald* (Weimar: Böhlau, 1995), 182.

71. Dr. Johann Ilkow to Col. Wade M. Fleischer, Office of the Judge Advocate, Subject: Ilse Koch, September 21, 1949, NARA RG 549, War Crimes Case Files, Cases Tried, box 441.

72. Der Oberstaatsanwalt bei dem Landgericht Augsburg, Antrag auf Erlass eines Haftbefehls, September 22, 1949; Der Untersuchungsrichter des Landgerichts Augsburg, Haftbefehl, September 30, 1949, StAA, Staatsanwaltschaft Augsburg, KS 22 / 50, box 8, folder 2.

73. Dr. Alfred Seidl an den Bayerischen Verfassungsgerichtshof, Verfassungsbeschwerde der Beschuldigten Ilse Koch, October 10, 1949, StAA, Staatsanwaltschaft Augsburg, KS 22 / 50, box 1, folder 2; Dr. Johann Ilkow to Colonel Robert A. Chandler re. Proceedings against Ilse Koch, October 20, 1949, NARA, RG 549, War Crimes Case Files, Cases Tried, box 441.

74. "Ilse's Lawyer Asks Ouster of Non-Nazi Trial Officials," *Stars and Stripes,* October 21, 1949.

75. Devin Pendas, *Democracy, Nazi Trials, and Transitional Justice in Germany, 1945– 1950* (New York: Cambridge University Press, 2020), 68.

76. Eichmüller, "Der Ilse Koch-Prozess in Augsburg," 109.

77. Ilkow to Chandler, October 20, 1949.

78. Dr. Johann Ilkow, an das Bayerische Staastsministerium der Justiz, October 20, 1949, StAA, Staatsanwaltschaft Augsburg, KS 22 / 50, box 1, folder 2.

79. "Ilse Freed; Jailed by Germans," *Stars and Stripes,* October 18, 1949.

80. "Ilse Freed; Jailed by Germans."

81. "Freedom Shortlived for Infamous Ilse," *Pacific Stars and Stripes,* October 18, 1949.

82. "Ilse Freed; Jailed by Germans."

83. "Ilse Freed; Jailed by Germans."

84. Ilkow to Chandler, October 20, 1949.

85. Ilkow to Chandler, October 20, 1949.

86. Dr. Alfred Seidl an die Strafkammer des Landgerichts Augsburg, Betrifft: Verfahren gegen Ilse Koch, October 19, 1949, StAA, Staatsanwaltschaft Augsburg, KS 22 / 50, box 1, folder 2.

87. Ilkow to Chandler, October 20, 1949.

88. "Extradition Asked for Ilse," *Stars and Stripes,* October 25, 1949.

89. Dr. Johann Ilkow to Col. Robert L. Chandler, Judge Advocate Division, EUCOM, Subject: Criminal Proceedings against Ilse Koch, November 16, 1949, NARA, RG 549, War Crimes Case Files, Cases Tried, box 441.

90. Ilkow to Chandler, November 16, 1949.

91. Eichmüller, "Der Ilse Koch-Prozess in Augsburg," 105.

92. Hauptwachtmeisterin Therese Raith, U. Gef. 48—Koch, Ilse, October 17, 1949–November 9, 1949, StAA, Staatsanwaltschaft Augsburg, KS 22 / 50, box 2, folder 6.

93. Dr. Alfred Seidl, an die 1. Strafkammer des Landgerichts Augsburg, January 16, 1950, StAA, Staatsanwaltschaft Augsburg, KS 22 / 50, box 1, folder 4.

94. Beschluss der 1. Strafkammer des Landgerichts Augsburg vom January 25, 1950, in dem Strafverfahren gegen Ilse Koch wegen Mordes, StAA, Staatsanwaltschaft Augsburg, KS 22 / 50, box 2, folder 6.

95. Direktion der Heil-und Pflegeanstalt Erlangen, Kurz-Gutachten über den Geisteszustand von Ilse Koch, April 3, 1950, StAA, Staatsanwaltschaft Augsburg, KS 22 / 50, box 2, folder 6.

96. Dr. Sighart, Direktor, Ärztliches Gutachten, Günzburg, April 5, 1950, StAA, Staatsanwaltschaft Augsburg, KS 22 / 50, box 5, 6.

97. Sighart, Ärztliches Gutachten, 5.

98. Der Untersuchungsrichter des Landgerichts Augsburg Dr. Jagomast, z.Zt, Aichach, den April 4, 1950, StAA, Staatsanwaltschaft Augsburg, KS 22 / 50, box 2, folder 6.

99. Eichmüller, "Der Ilse Koch-Prozess in Augsburg," 106.

100. Eichmüller, "Der Ilse Koch-Prozess in Augsburg," 107.

6. The Augsburg Trial of Ilse Koch

1. Devin O. Pendas, *The Frankfurt Auschwitz Trial, 1963–1965* (Cambridge: Cambridge University Press, 2006), 90. My discussion of the function of the German judicial system here draws heavily on Devin Pendas's excellent study of the Frankfurt Auschwitz trial, and in particular his chapter "The Trial Actors," 80–103.

2. Pendas, *The Frankfurt Auschwitz Trial,* 59.

3. Pendas, *The Frankfurt Auschwitz Trial,* 90.

4. Pendas, *The Frankfurt Auschwitz Trial,* 90.

5. Pendas, *The Frankfurt Auschwitz Trial,* 89.

6. The Chief Prosecutor of the Landgericht Augsburg, Indictment of Ilse Koch, May 10, 1950, NARA, RG 549, War Crimes Case Files, Cases Tried, box 436. In the English translation prepared for US authorities and used here, the indictment uses the terms "abetting" rather than "incitement," and "dangerous" rather than "grievous" bodily harm, yet I have used the latter terms as they represent more accurate translations of the German.

7. Indictment of Ilse Koch, 36.

8. Pendas, *The Frankfurt Auschwitz Trial*, 56–57.

9. Indictment of Ilse Koch, 37–38.

10. Indictment of Ilse Koch, 63.

11. Indictment of Ilse Koch, 74.

12. Indictment of Ilse Koch, 65.

13. Indictment of Ilse Koch, 68.

14. Indictment of Ilse Koch, 84–85.

15. Indictment of Ilse Koch, 91.

16. Indictment of Ilse Koch, 111.

17. Indictment of Ilse Koch, 93.

18. Indictment of Ilse Koch, 119.

19. Indictment of Ilse Koch, 132.

20. Indictment of Ilse Koch, 133.

21. Indictment of Ilse Koch, 133.

22. Der Oberstaatsanwalt bei dem Landgericht Augsburg an den Herrn Vorsitzender der Strafkammer des Landgerichts Augsburg, Betrifft: Strafverfahren gegen Ilse Koch, May 10, 1950, StAA, Staatsanwaltschaft Augsburg, KS 22 / 50, box 2, folder 9.

23. Der Obserstaatsanwalt bei dem Landgericht Augsburg an das Bayerische Staatsministerium der Justiz, Bamberg, May 15, 1950, StAA, Staatsanwaltschaft Augsburg, KS 22 / 50.

24. Andreas Eichmüller, "Der Ilse Koch-Prozess in Augsburg 1950 / 51," in *Vor 70 Jahren—Stunde Null für die Justiz?* ed. Arnd Koch and Herbert Veh (Augsburg: Nomos, 2017), 110.

25. Ilkow an das Bayerische Staatsministerium der Justiz, May 15, 1950.

26. Court proceedings against Sommer eventually began in 1955, but were broken off when a doctor's examination declared him "physically unfit to stand trial." Yet after Sommer remarried in 1956, fathered a child, and applied for an increase in his veterans pension, West German authorities again took up his case. Following court proceedings in Bayreuth, Sommer was sentenced to life

imprisonment in 1958 and remained incarcerated until his death in 1988. See "West Germany: The Monster," *Time*, July 14, 1958; "Beast of Buchenwald Found Fit to Marry, Avoided Trial as Sick Man," *Jewish Telegraph Agency*, August 2, 1956.

27. Dr. Johann Ilkow, Personalbogen und Lebenslauf, BayHStA, MJu 25339. Ilkow would continue to suffer from ill health; he died in 1958 at the age of fifty-eight from a bleeding ulcer.

28. "Die Anklageschrift gegen Ilse Koch," *Schwäbische Landeszeitung*, November 25, 1950.

29. Eichmüller, "Der Ilse Koch-Prozess in Augsburg," 111.

30. Eichmüller, "Der Ilse Koch-Prozess in Augsburg," 112.

31. Eichmüller, "Der Ilse Koch-Prozess in Augsburg," 112.

32. "Die 'Kommandeuse' weiss von nichts," *Schwäbische Landeszeitung*, November 29, 1950.

33. Arthur L. Smith, Jr., *Die Hexe von Buchenwald* (Weimar: Böhlau, 1995), 188.

34. "Ilse Koch—eine redliche Waschfrau," *Süddeutsche Zeitung*, November 29, 1950.

35. "Inmates Skinned, Koch Trial Hears," *New York Times*, November 29, 1950.

36. "Ein Lampenschirm aus Menschenhaut," *Frankfurter Allgemeine Zeitung*, November 30, 1950.

37. "Ilse Kochs ständiges 'Stimmt nicht!'" *Schwäbische Landeszeitung*, December 1, 1950.

38. "Ilse Koch—eine redliche Waschfrau," *Süddeutsche Zeitung*, November 29, 1950.

39. "Inmates Skinned, Koch Trial Hears," *New York Times*, November 29, 1950.

40. Pendas, *The Frankfurt Auschwitz Trial*, 84.

41. See Alexandra Przyrembel, "Transfixed by an Image: Ilse Koch, the 'Kommandeuse' of Buchenwald," *German History* 19, no. 3 (2001): 369–399, 384.

42. "Ilse Kochs ständiges 'Stimmt nicht!'" *Schwäbische Landeszeitung*, December 1, 1950.

43. "Die bestgehasste Person von Buchenwald," *Süddeutsche Zeitung*, December 1, 1950; "Ilse Koch ohne Offentlichkeit," *Schwäbische Landeszeitung*, December 2, 1950.

44. "Germans Give Ilse Koch Life Term for Crimes against Countrymen," *New York Times*, January 16, 1950.

45. "Ilse Koch hat doch Nerven," *Frankfurter Allgemeine Zeitung*, December 7, 1950.

46. "Uebergewicht auf Seite der Anklage," *Schwäbische Landeszeitung*, December 8, 1950.

47. "Ilse Kochs ständiges 'Stimmt nicht!'" *Schwäbische Landeszeitung*, December 1, 1950.

48. "Koch Court Rejects Testimony of Two for Prosecution," *Stars and Stripes*, December 21, 1950.

49. "Ilse Kochs 'reines Gewissen'" *Süddeutsche Zeitung*, December 7, 1950.

50. "Zwischenfall," *Frankfurter Allgemeine Zeitung*, December 8, 1950.

51. "Zwischenfall," *Frankfurter Allgemeine Zeitung*, December 8, 1950.

52. "Ilse Koch spielt die Rasende," *Frankfurter Allgemeine Zeitung*, December 12, 1950; "IK in Frenzy; Doctors Watch Her," *New York Times*, December 12, 1950.

53. "Ilse Kochs Flucht in die Krankheit," *Süddeutsche Zeitung*, December 12, 1950.

54. "Ilse Koch spielt die Rasende," *Frankfurter Allgemeine Zeitung*, December 12, 1950.

55. "Ilse Koch macht in Intermezzis," *Schwäbische Landeszeitung*, December 15, 1950.

56. "Wieder ohne Ilse Koch," *Schwäbische Landeszeitung*, December 15, 1950.

57. "Lebenslänglich für Ilse Koch beantragt," *Süddeutsche Zeitung*, January 12, 1951; Eichmüller, "Der Ilse Koch-Prozess in Augsburg," 120.

58. "Prügel wegen einer Tasse," *Frankfurter Allgemeine Zeitung*, December 20, 1950; Eichmüller, "Der Ilse Koch-Prozess in Augsburg," 118.

59. "Ilse Koch will nichts mehr essen," *Schwäbische Landeszeitung*, January 5, 1951.

60. "Zwischenfälle im Prozess gegen Ilse Koch," *Frankfurter Allgemeine Zeitung*, December 30, 1950.

61. "Ilse Koch ohne Offentlichkeit," *Schwäbische Landeszeitung*, December 2, 1950.

62. "Zwischenfälle im Prozess gegen Ilse Koch," *Frankfurter Allgemeine Zeitung*, December 30, 1950.

63. "Koch-Prozess beleuchtet SS-Gerichtbarkeit," *Süddeutsche Zeitung*, December 2 / 3, 1950.

64. "Zwischenfälle im Prozess gegen Ilse Koch," *Frankfurter Allgemeine Zeitung*, December 30, 1950.

65. "Hängen—das war alles," *Frankfurter Allgemeine Zeitung*, January 10, 1951.

66. "Amerikanisches Recht—harte Nuss für deutsche Juristen," *Süddeutsche Zeitung*, December 9 / 10, 1950.

67. "Hängen—das war alles," *Frankfurter Allgemeine Zeitung*, January 10, 1951.

68. "Kogon ohne unmittelbare Wahrnehmung," *Schwäbische Landeszeitung*, January 10, 1951.

69. "Ilse Kochs Flucht in die Krankheit," *Süddeutsche Zeitung*, December 12, 1950.

70. "Dr. Kogon kann nicht kommen," *Schwäbische Landeszeitung*, January 8, 1951.

71. Dr. Eugen Kogon an das Schwurgericht Augsburg, January 4, 1951, StAA, Staatsanwaltschaft Augsburg, KS 22 / 50, box 2, folder 8.

72. "Dr. Kogon kann nicht kommen," *Schwäbische Landeszeitung*, January 8, 1951.

73. "Kogon ohne unmittelbare Wahrnehmung," *Schwäbische Landeszeitung*, January 10, 1951.

74. "Kogon als Zeuge," *Frankfurter Allgemeine Zeitung*, January 9, 1951.

75. "Zuchthaus für Ilse Koch beantragt," *Frankfurter Allgemeine Zeitung*, January 12, 1951; "Lebenslänglich für Ilse Koch beantragt," *Süddeutsche Zeitung*, January 12, 1951.

76. "Plakatdemonstrationen gegen Ilse Koch," *Schwäbische Landeszeitung*, January 13, 1951; "Zuchthaus für Ilse Koch beantragt," *Frankfurter Allgemeine Zeitung*, January 12, 1951.

77. "Zuchthaus für Ilse Koch beantragt," *Frankfurter Allgemeine Zeitung*, January 12, 1951.

78. "Lebenslänglich für Ilse Koch beantragt," *Süddeutsche Zeitung*, January 12, 1951.

79. "Plakatdemonstrationen gegen Ilse Koch," *Schwäbische Landeszeitung*, January 13, 1951.

80. "Zuchthaus für Ilse Koch beantragt," *Frankfurter Allgemeine Zeitung*, January 12, 1951.

81. "Ilse Koch-Verhandlung beendet," *Süddeutsche Zeitung*, January 13, 1951.

82. "Ilse Koch-Verhandlung beendet," *Süddeutsche Zeitung*, January 13, 1951.

83. "Ilse Koch Tobt," *Frankfurter Allgemeine Zeitung*, January 15, 1951; Smith, *Die Hexe von Buchenwald*, 199.

84. LG Augsburg, Urteil vom 15.01.1951, KS 22 / 50, in *Justiz und NS-Verbrechen: Sammlung deutcher Strafurteile wegen nationalsozialistischer Tötungsverbrechen*, vol. 8 (Amsterdam: Amsterdam University Press, 2011), 31.

85. "Lebenslänglich für Ilse Koch," *Frankfurter Allgemeine Zeitung*, January 16, 1951.

86. "Germans Give Ilse Koch Life Term for Crimes against Countrymen," *New York Times*, January 16, 1951.

87. "Lebenslänglich für Ilse Koch," *Frankfurter Allgemeine Zeitung*, January 16, 1951.

88. LG Augsburg, Urteil, 57–67.

89. LG Augsburg, Urteil, 94.

90. LG Augsburg, Urteil, 100–102.

91. LG Augsburg, Urteil, 102–103.

92. LG Augsburg, Urteil, 103.

93. LG Augsburg, Urteil, 121.

94. LG Augsburg, Urteil, 122.

95. LG Augsburg, Urteil, 124.

96. LG Augsburg, Urteil, 126–127.

97. LG Augsburg, Urteil, 128.

98. For a thorough study of this issue, see Norbert Frei, *Adenauer's Germany and the Nazi Past: The Politics of Amnesty and Integration* (New York: Columbia University Press, 2002).

99. For an interesting study of how the focus on sadists and "excess perpetrators" at the Frankfurt Auschwitz trial contributed to similar outcomes, see Rebecca Wittmann, *Beyond Justice: The Auschwitz Trial* (Cambridge, MA: Harvard University Press, 2005).

100. "Zum drittenmal die 'Kommandeuse von Buchenwald,'" *Die Zeit*, December 7, 1950.

7. The Long Years After

1. "Doppelte Revision im Falle Ilse Koch," *Schwäbische Landeszeitung*, January 19, 1951; Arthur L. Smith, Jr., *Die Hexe von Buchenwald* (Weimar: Böhlau, 1995), 200.

2. Revisionsbegründung des Rechtsanwalts Dr. Alfred Seidl in München in Sachen Koch, Ilse, June 23, 1951, StAA, Staatsanwaltschaft Augsburg, KS 22 / 50, box 2, folder 10.

3. Strafsenat des Bundesgerichtshofs in der Sitzung vom 22. April, 1952, Strafsache gegen die Witwe Ilse Koch . . . , wegen Anstiftung zum Morde und zum versuchten Morde, StAA, Staatsanwaltschaft Augsburg, KS 22 / 50, box 2, folder 10, 5.

4. Strafsenat des Bundesgerichtshofs in der Sitzung vom 22. April, 1952, 8.

5. Strafsenat des Bundesgerichtshofs in der Sitzung vom 22. April, 1952, 10.

6. The prison doctor noted, for instance, that on May 31, 1951, she had "disturbed the peace of the prison, screaming and carrying-on," and had to be given an injection to calm down. Anstaltsarzt, Strafanstalt Aichach, May 31, 1951, StAM, Justizvollzugsanstalten 13948 / 0.

7. Strafanstalt Aichach, Besucherbuch, StAM, Justizvollzugsanstalten 13948 / 2.

8. Gisela Koch, phone interview with author, September 17, 2013. Aichach records indicate that following Gisela's 1953 visit, she did not visit again until 1958. See Beamtenkonferenz (Nachprüfung), Z 596—Koch, Ilse, August 6, 1964, StAM, Justizvollzugsanstalten 13948 / 2.

9. Beamtenkonferenz (Nachprüfung), Z 596—Koch, Ilse, August 6, 1964.

10. Ilse Koch to mother Anna Köhler, August 10, 1952, StAM, Justizvollzugsanstalten 13948 / 4.

11. "Jail Tames Nazis' 'Witch of Buchenwald,'" *Stars and Stripes,* April 19, 1955.

12. Ilse Koch to daughter Gisela, November 4, 1956, StAM, Justizvollzugsanstalten 13948 / 6.

13. Ilse Koch to son Artwin, July 8, 1957, StAM, Justizvollzugsanstalten 13948 / 6.

14. Ilse Koch to daughter Gisela, June 29, 1962, courtesy of Gisela Koch.

15. Ilse Koch to mother Anna Köhler, August 10, 1952, StAM, Justizvollzugsanstalten 13948 / 4.

16. Ilse Koch to Gisela, June 29, 1962.

17. "Camp 'Witch' Pens Poetry for Solace," *Stars and Stripes,* September 7, 1952.

18. Ilse Koch to Artwin, July 8, 1957.

19. Ilse Koch to son Artwin, June 5, 1955, StAM, Justizvollzugsanstalten 13948 / 6.

20. Ilse Koch, Address Book, StAM, Justizvollzugsanstalten 13948 / 3.

21. Ilse Koch to daughter Gisela, February 12, 1965, StAM, Justizvollzugsanstalten 13948 / 5.

22. For a history of Stille Hilfe, see Oliver Schröm and Andrea Röpke, *Stille Hilfe für braune Kameraden: Das geheime Netzwerk der Alt- und Neonazis* (Berlin: Ch. Links, 2001).

23. Gisela Koch, interview with author, September 17, 2013.

24. H. E. Prinzessin von Isenburg to Konrad Adenauer, March 1, 1955, StAA, Staatsanwaltschaft, KS 22 / 50, box 4.

25. Anna Köhler to Konrad Adenauer, March 1, 1955, StAA, Staatsanwaltschaft, KS 22 / 50, box 4.

26. Frauenstrafanstalt Aichach, an die Staatsanwaltschaft beim Landgericht Augsburg, May 12, 1955, StAA, Staatsanwaltschaft KS 22 / 50, box 4.

27. Ilse Koch to Alfred Seidl, November 18, 1955, StAM, Justizvollzugsanstalten 13948 / 6.

28. Rechtsanwalt Dr. Alfred Seidl, Gnadengesuch, an das Bayerische Staatsministerium der Justiz, June 4, 1957, StAA, Staatsanwaltschaft, KS 22 / 50, box 4, 4.

29. Alfred Seidl, Gnadengesuch, 12.

30. Alfred Seidl, Gnadengesuch, 17–19.

31. Strafanstalt Aichach, Gutachten aus Anlass des Gnadengesuches, an den Oberstaatsanwalt, July 13, 1957, StAA, Staatsanwaltschaft, KS 22 / 50, box 4.

32. Ilse Koch to the Bavarian Ministry of Justice, August 29, 1957, StAA, Staatsanwaltschaft, KS 22 / 50, box 4.

33. Son Artwin, an das Oberste Bundesgericht, November 1, 1957, StAA, Staatsanwaltschaft KS 22 / 50, box 4.

34. Ilse Koch to the Bavarian Ministry of Justice, June 1, 1960, StAA, Staatsanwaltschaft, KS 22 / 50, box 4.

35. Ilse Koch to the Bavarian Ministry of Justice, October 19, 1961, StAA, Staatsanwaltschaft, KS 22 / 50, box 4.

36. Europarat, Generalsekretariat, European Commission for Human Rights, March 13, 1962, StAM, Justizvollzugsanstalten 13948 / 7.

37. Frauenstrafanstalt Aichach an den Herrn Oberstaatsanwalt beim Landgericht Augsburg, December 11, 1961, StAA, Staatsanwaltschaft, KS 22 / 50, box 4.

38. Zusammenstellung der gemeldeten und beobachten Auffälligkeiten der Strafgefangenen Ilse Koch, February 1, 1963, to January 31, 1964, StAM, Justizvollzugsanstalten 13948 / 9 (hereafter Zusammenstellung).

39. Ilse Koch to the European Commission on Human Rights, July 19, 1963, StAM, Justizvollzugsanstalten 13948 / 8.

40. Ilse Koch to daughter Gisela, October 11, 1963, in Zusammenstellung.

41. Ilse Koch to son Artwin, November 8, 1963, in Zusammenstellung.

42. For a few examples among many, see cover illustrations of the June 1933, June 1934, June 1935, August 1935, and December 1938 issues of *Der Stürmer.*

43. Gisela Koch to Frauenanstalt Aichach, January 23, 1964, StAM, Justizvollzugsanstalten 13948 / 5.

44. Gisela Koch to Tomaz Jardim, September 19, 2013; Frauenstrafanstalt Aichach, an die Staatsanwaltschaft bei dem Landgericht Augsburg, March 13, 1967, StAA, Staatsanwaltschaft, KS 22 / 50, box 4.

45. Anstaltarzt Dr. J. S. Weilscher an Direktor Schober, February 16, 1964, StAM, Justizvollzugsanstalten 13878.

46. Nervenkrankenhaus des Bezirks Oberbayern, Haar bei München, an die Direktion Frauenstrafanstalt Aichach, Betr.: Nervenärztlicher Bericht über die Strafgefangene Ilse Koch, July 21, 1964, StAA, Staatsanwaltschaft, KS 22 / 50, box 4.

47. Ilse Koch to the Bavarian Ministry of Justice, August 13, 1964, StAA, Staatsanwaltschaft, KS 22 / 50, box 4.

48. Abschiedsbrief der Gefg. Z. 596, Koch, Ilse, an ihre Tochter Gisela, August 14, 1964, StAM, Justizvollzugsanstalten 13948 / 9.

49. Frauenstrafanstalt Aichach, an die Staatsanwaltschaft bei dem Landgericht Augsburg, September 14, 1964, StAA, Staatsanwaltschaft KS 22 / 50, box 4.

50. Generalbundesanwalt Dr. Max Güde, an den Ministerpräsidenten des Freistaats Bayern, Herrn Dr. Goppel, January 27, 1965, StAA, Staatsanwaltschaft KS 22 / 50, box 4.

51. Dr. Ehard, Bayer, Staatsminister der Justiz, an Herrn Bundestagsabgeordneten Dr. Max Güde, July 22, 1965, StAM, Justizvollzugsanstalten 13948 / 5.

52. "Ilse Koch's Posthumous Rehabilitation Sought by Son," *New York Times*, May 7, 1971.

53. Uwe Köhler to Ilse Koch, December 15, 1966, StAM, Justizvollzugsanstalten 13948 / 2.

54. Ilse Koch to Uwe Köhler, December 19, 1966, StAM, Justizvollzugsanstalten 13948 / 2.

55. Beamtenkonferenz (Nachprüfung), Z 596—Koch, Ilse, August 3, 1967, StAM, Justizvollzugsanstalten 13948 / 2.

56. "Ilse Koch's Posthumous Rehabilitation Sought by Son."

57. "Ilse Koch's Posthumous Rehabilitation Sought by Son."

58. Beamtenkonferenz (Nachprüfung), Z 596—Koch, Ilse, August 3, 1967.

59. Ilse Koch to Hans-Günther Pfitzner, May 11, 1966, StAM, Justizvollzugsanstalten 13948 / 5.

60. Dr. Hans-Günther Pfitzner, Antrag auf Bewährung aus Gnade, April 17, 1967, StAA, Staatsanwaltschaft, KS 22 / 50, box 4.

61. Frauenstrafanstalt Aichach, an die Staatsanwaltschaft bei dem Landgericht Augsburg, June 6, 1967, StAA, Staatsanwaltschaft 22 / 50, box 4.

62. Ilse Koch to the Bavarian Ministry of Justice, May 19, 1967, StAA, Staatsanwaltschaft KS 22 / 50, box 4.

63. Der Oberstaatsanwalt bei dem Landgericht Augsburg, an den Herrn Generalstaatsanwalt bei dem Oberlandesgerticht, June 21, 1967, StAA, Staatsanwaltschaft KS 22 / 50, box 4.

64. Andreas Eichmüller, "Der Ilse Koch-Prozess in Augsburg 1950 / 51," in *Vor 70 Jahren—Stunde Null für die Justiz?* ed. Arnd Koch and Herbert Veh (Augsburg: Nomos, 2017), 125–126.

65. Alexandra Przyrembel, "Transfixed by an Image: Ilse Koch, the 'Kommandeuse' of Buchenwald," *German History* 19, no. 3 (2001): 369–399, 399.

66. Hans-Günther Pfitzner to Ilse Koch, August 10, 1967, StAM, Justizvollzugsanstalten 13948 / 2.

67. Ilse Koch to Hans-Günther Pfitzner, August 26, 1967, StAM, Justizvollzugsanstalten 13948 / 2.

68. Ilse Koch to son Uwe, September 1, 1967, StAM, Justizvollzugsanstalten 13948 / 2.

69. Ilse Koch, note to son Uwe, September 1, 1967, StAM, Justizvollzugsanstalten 13948 / 2.

70. Frauenstrafanstalt Aichach, Betrifft: Selbstmord der Strafgefangenen Ilse Koch, September 6, 1967, StAM, Justizvollzugsanstalten 13948 / 2.

71. Frauenstrafanstalt Aichach, Betrifft: Selbstmord der Strafgefangenen Ilse Koch, September 6, 1967, StAM, Justizvollzugsanstalten 13948 / 2.

72. "Ilse Koch nahm sich das Leben," *Augsburger Allgemeine Zeitung*, September 4, 1967.

73. "Ilse Kochs Freitod kam völlig überraschend," *Aichacher Zeitung*, September 4, 1967; Frauenstrafanstalt Aichach an das Bayerische Staatsministerium der Justiz, September 7, 1967, StAM, Justizvollzugsanstalten 13948 / 2.

74. "Best Years of Her Life," *Newsweek*, September 18, 1967.

75. Anstaltsleitung, telegram to Uwe Köhler and Gisela Koch, September 2, 1967, StAM, Justizvollzugsanstalten 13878 / 2.

76. Gisela Koch, interview with author, September 17, 2013.

77. "Best Years of Her Life," *Newsweek*, September 18, 1967.

Epilogue

1. "Der Tod der Ilse Koch," *Die Zeit*, September 8, 1967; "'Kommandeuse' von Buchenwald erhängt in der Zelle aufgefunden," *Frankfurter Allgemeine Zeitung*, September 4, 1967; "Ilse Koch hat sich erhängt," *Süddeutsche Zeitung*, September 4, 1967.

2. Gerhard Mauz, "Die Kommandeuse und die Kollektivschuld," *Der Spiegel*, September 10, 1967.

3. William D. Denson, "Frau Ilse Koch a Sadist from Some Tortured Other World, Prosecutor Says; Assails Cut in Her Sentence," *St. Louis Post-Dispatch*, September 26, 1948.

4. See *The United States v. Josias Prince zu Waldeck, et al.*, Case no. 000-50-9, Denson Papers, Series II: Trials, 1945–2001, boxes 17–22 (5718 pages); Susannah Heschel, "Does Atrocity Have a Gender?" in *Lessons and Legacies*, vol. 6: *New Currents in Holocaust Research*, ed. Jeffry M. Diefendorf (Evanston, IL: Northwestern University Press, 2004), 305; Christina Herkommer, "Women under National So-

cialism: Women's Scope for Action and the Issue of Gender," in *Ordinary People as Mass Murderers: Perpetrators in Comparative Perspectives,* ed. O. Jensen and C. Szejnmann (New York: Palgrave Macmillan, 2008), 114.

5. Dr. Sighart, Direktor, Ärztliches Gutachten, Günzburg, April 5, 1950, StAA, Staatsanwaltschaft Augsburg KS 22 / 50, box 5, 5.

6. Homer Ferguson, Conduct of the Ilse Koch War Crimes Trial, Interim Report of the Investigations Subcommittee of the Committee on Expenditures in the Executive Departments, December 27, 1948, Denson Papers, Series II: Trials, box 15, folder 91, 22.

7. LG Augsburg, Urteil vom 15.01.1951, KS 22 / 50, in *Justiz und NS-Verbrechen: Sammlung deutcher Strafurteile wegen nationalsozialistischer Tötungsverbrechen,* vol. 8 (Amsterdam: Amsterdam University Press, 2011), 126–127; "Lebenslänglich für Ilse Koch," *Frankfurter Allgemeine Zeitung,* January 16, 1951.

8. Mark Drumbl and Solange Mouthaan, "'A Hussy Who Rode on Horseback in Sexy Underwear in Front of the Prisoners': The Trials of Buchenwald's Ilse Koch," *International Criminal Law Review* 21, no. 2 (2021): 280–312, 305.

9. Woody Guthrie, "Ilse Koch," in Will Kaufman, *Woody Guthrie: American Radical* (Champaign: University of Illinois Press, 2015); Leon Uris, *Exodus* (New York: Doubleday, 1958) 96; Sylvia Plath, "Lady Lazarus," *Ariel—Poems by Sylvia Plath* (New York: Farber and Farber, 1965).

10. "Der Tod der Ilse Koch," *Die Zeit,* September 8, 1967; "Ilse Koch hat sich erhängt," *Süddeutsche Zeitung,* September 4, 1967; "'Kommandeuse' von Buchenwald erhängt in der Zelle aufgefunden," *Frankfurter Allgemeine Zeitung,* September 4, 1967; "Ilse Koch Hangs Herself in Cell," *New York Times,* September 2, 1967; "Hangs Self: German 'Bitch of Buchenwald' Dies a Suicide," *Washington Post,* September 3, 1967.

11. James O'Donnell, "The Witch of Buchenwald: The Record of a Sadist," *Newsweek,* July 28, 1947; "31 Buchenwald Officials to Stand Trial in April," *Stars and Stripes,* March 9, 1947; *Stars and Stripes,* April 12, 1947, as quoted in Arthur L. Smith, Jr., *Die Hexe von Buchenwald* (Weimar: Böhlau, 1995), 117; "Ilse Koch Claims U.S. Court Suppressed Her Evidence," *Washington Post,* October 4, 1948.

12. "Ilse Koch Hangs Herself in Cell," *New York Times,* September 2, 1967.

13. "Hangs Self: German 'Bitch of Buchenwald' Dies a Suicide," *Washington Post,* September 3, 1967.

14. "Best Years of Her Life," *Newsweek,* September 18, 1967.

15. Joseph Como, *Bitch of Buchenwald: The Sex Life of Ilse Koch* (New York: Ophelia Press, 1971), i–ii.

16. *Ilsa, She Wolf of the SS*, directed by Don Edmonds (USA, 1975); Lynn Rapaport, "Holocaust Pornography: Profaning the Sacred in *Ilsa, She Wolf of the SS*," *Shofar: An Interdisciplinary Journal of Jewish Studies* 22, no. 1 (2003).

17. Rapaport, "Holocaust Pornography," 58, 71.

18. Rapaport, "Holocaust Pornography," 71.

19. *The Most Evil Men and Women in History*, 15 episodes, Uden Associates Productions (USA, 2001).

20. Nora McGreevy, "95-Year-Old Nazi Camp Secretary Charged as Accessory in 10,000 Murders," *Smithsonian*, February 9, 2021.

21. Alison Maloney, "'War Witches': Female Nazi Guards Tortured and Killed Thousands, Beat Naked Women to Death & 'Made Lampshades from Human Skin,'" *The Sun*, February 10, 2021.

22. Sam Elliot, "Inside Life of Female Nazi Prison Camp Guard Who Made Lampshades out of Human Skin," *Daily Star*, February 11, 2021.

23. Andreas Eichmüller, "Der Ilse Koch-Prozess in Augsburg 1950 / 51," in *Vor 70 Jahren—Stunde Null für die Justiz?* ed. Arnd Koch and Herbert Veh (Augsburg: Nomos, 2017), 125–126.

Acknowledgments

I could never have completed this book without the help of the people and institutions I have had the honor of working with over the course of the last decade. Though writing a book is at times an all too solitary enterprise, the wise counsel, patience, and emotional support offered up by my friends, family, and colleagues were foundational. First and foremost, I owe my deepest gratitude to Oliver Glatz, whose research assistance could not have been more helpful or insightful as we sorted through mountains of German legal documents and puzzled through various linguistic, archival, and historical quandaries together. Likewise, I am indebted to the eminently helpful archivists and staff at the National Archives in College Park, MD, the United States Holocaust Memorial Museum, Yale University Library Manuscripts and Archives, the Augsburg and Munich State Archives, the Berlin State Library, the Institute for Contemporary History in Munich, the Fritz Bauer Institute, and the archives of the Buchenwald, Sachsenhausen, Dachau, and Majdanek memorial sites.

This book benefited immeasurably from the efforts of a number of people who read draft chapters and provided their exceptionally valuable feedback. First, my wife, Ella Street, a most talented academic in her own right, left an indelible mark on my writing as she scrutinized each chapter and ensured that I presented my ideas in the simplest and most economical fashion that I was able. Doris Bergen, Robert Crumb, Valerie Hebert, Carolyn Kay, Hugh Paisley, and Robert Teigrob also read portions of my manuscript at various stages of its completion and fundamentally improved this book while helping me to get to the finish line. I hope they each recognize their influence in these pages, and forgive me for any rare instance where, at my own peril, I did not make a recommended change or explore a suggested avenue. I am so thankful to each of them.

I would also like to use this opportunity to thank a number of others who played roles, both large and small, in the completion of this book. Ilse and Karl Koch's daughter, Gisela, could not have been more welcoming or more brave as she confronted immensely difficult questions about her parents that, by her own confession, she had spent much of her lifetime avoiding. I am so sorry that she did not live to see the publication of this book, but hope that her son, Thomas, will find something of value in these pages. I would like to thank Edith Raim, who was both generous and gracious in giving her time to the numerous, frequent, and sometimes complex research questions I posed to her. The assistance and patience of Devin Pendas, Andreas Eichmüller, and former Augsburg district court president Dr. Herbert Veh in helping me to grasp the intricacies and anomalies of the West German legal code and trial system were essential. To the many others who assisted me in myriad ways over the last ten years, I am eternally grateful: Robert Bierschneider, Judy Cohen, Ron Coleman, Tatum Dooley, Lawrence Douglas, Mark Drumbl, Hilary Earl, Max Eisen, Barbara Fredrickson, Eli Gotz, Peter Hayes, Melanie Hines, Stefan Hördler, Mark Jacobson, Katharina von Kellenbach, Andreas Kranebitter, Wendy Lower, Michael Marrus, Jürgen Matthäus, Kathleen McDermott, Ian McLatchie, Solange Mouthaan, Derek Penslar, Steven Remy, Patrick Rieblinger, Albert Rosenberg, Connor Sebestyen, Vincent Slatt, Arthur Smith, Thomas Steck,

Richard Steigmann-Gall, Nicola Vohringer, Nikolaus Wachsmann, Joe White, Rebecca Wittmann, and all of my colleagues at Toronto Metropolitan University.

This book, and the research it was built upon, was made possible by a number of generous grants and fellowships. This project began in earnest when I took up the Laurie and Andy Okun Post-Doctoral Fellowship at the Center for Advanced Holocaust Studies at the United States Holocaust Memorial Museum in Washington, DC. In the years that followed, extended and fruitful periods of archival research in both Germany and the United States were facilitated further by an Insight Development Grant from the Social Sciences and Humanities Research Council of Canada and by generous grants from the Faculty of Arts at Toronto Metropolitan University.

My final words are reserved for my family. To my wonderful wife, Ella, and to my children, Sal and Desi, I love you so much. I could not have done it without you.

Index